# The Last Bastion

# The Last Bastion

CHILD ABUSE AND CHILD NEGLECT IN THE
BROTHERHOOD OF AMERICA'S SCHOOLS

Dianne Prinz Callin PhD

Copyright © 2017 by Dianne Prinz Callin PhD

All rights reserved. No part of this publication may be reproduced, stored in a retrieval system, or transmitted in any form or by any means, electronic, mechanical, photocopying, recording, scanning, or otherwise, except as permitted under section 107 or 108 of the 1976 United States Copyright Act, without either the prior written permission of the publisher or the author. For permission requests, write to the publisher at the address below.

Published by RFK

Limit of liability / disclaimer of warranty: While the publisher and author have used their best efforts in preparing this book, they make no representations or warranties with respect to the accuracy or completeness of the contents of this book and specifically disclaim any implied warranties or merchantability or fitness for a particular purpose. No warranty may be created or extended by sales representatives or written sales materials. The advice and strategies contained herein may not be suitable for your situation. You should consult with a professional where appropriate. Neither the publisher nor the author shall be liable for any loss of profit or any other commercial damages, including but not limited to special, incidental, consequential, or other damages.

ISBN-10: 0998751413
ISBN-13: 9780998751412
Library of Congress Control Number: 2017953572
RFK, HEMET, CA


RFK Publishing

*For my sisters, Patricia and Johni*

# Table of Contents

List of Tables · · · · · · · · · · · · · · · · · · · · · · · · · · · · · · · · · · · · · · · · · · · · · · · · · · · · · · · · xi
Preface · · · · · · · · · · · · · · · · · · · · · · · · · · · · · · · · · · · · · · · · · · · · · · · · · · · · · · · · · · · · · · · · xiii
Introduction America's Schools: The Last Bastion
of Cloaked Abuse · · · · · · · · · · · · · · · · · · · · · · · · · · · · · · · · · · · · · · · · · · · · · · · · · · xvii

| | | |
|---|---|---|
| Chapter 1 | One More Brotherhood · · · · · · · · · · · · · · · · · · · · · · · · · · · · · · · · · · · · · | 1 |
| Chapter 2 | Bullying in Schools · · · · · · · · · · · · · · · · · · · · · · · · · · · · · · · · · · · · · · · · | 7 |
| Chapter 3 | Defining Teacher Bullying · · · · · · · · · · · · · · · · · · · · · · · · · · · · · · · · · · | 11 |
| Chapter 4 | Bullying as Abuse · · · · · · · · · · · · · · · · · · · · · · · · · · · · · · · · · · · · · · · · · | 17 |
| | Perpetrator and Victim · · · · · · · · · · · · · · · · · · · · · · · · · · · · · · · · · | 19 |
| | Teachers are Caregivers · · · · · · · · · · · · · · · · · · · · · · · · · · · · · · · · | 21 |
| Chapter 5 | Laws Relating to the School's Responsibilities toward the Minor · · · · · · · · · · · · · · · · · · · · · · · · · · · · · · · · · · · · · · · · · · · · · · · · · · · · · · · · · · | 23 |
| | The Laws · · · · · · · · · · · · · · · · · · · · · · · · · · · · · · · · · · · · · · · · · · · · · · · | 23 |
| | The Schools' Responsibilities · · · · · · · · · · · · · · · · · · · · · · · · · · · | 26 |
| | Summary · · · · · · · · · · · · · · · · · · · · · · · · · · · · · · · · · · · · · · · · · · · · · · · · | 28 |
| Chapter 6 | Child Abuse · · · · · · · · · · · · · · · · · · · · · · · · · · · · · · · · · · · · · · · · · · · · · · · | 29 |
| | Child Sexual Abuse · · · · · · · · · · · · · · · · · · · · · · · · · · · · · · · · · · · · | 30 |
| | Child Physical Abuse · · · · · · · · · · · · · · · · · · · · · · · · · · · · · · · · · · · | 36 |

|  |  |
|---|---|
| Child Emotional Abuse | 39 |
| Summary | 51 |
| **Chapter 7  Child Neglect** | **52** |
| Child Physical Neglect | 53 |
| Child Educational Neglect | 59 |
| Child Medical Neglect | 76 |
|     Physical Health Neglect | 76 |
|     Mental Health Neglect | 80 |
| Child Emotional Neglect | 86 |
| Summary | 90 |
| **Chapter 8  Scream Rooms** | **93** |
| Restraint and Seclusion | 94 |
| Fifteen Principles | 96 |
| Summary | 106 |
| **Chapter 9  Unravelling Teacher Child Abuse and Child Neglect** | **107** |
| Dissecting Abuse | 108 |
| What We Can Learn | 117 |
| Summary | 118 |
| **Chapter 10  Things to Know about Human Behavior and Communication** | **120** |
| Single Incident, Habitual, and Systematic Child Abuse and Child Neglect | 121 |
|     Single-Incident Child Abuse and Child Neglect | 122 |
|     Habitual Child Abuse and Child Neglect | 123 |
|     Systematic Child Abuse and Child Neglect | 124 |
| Verbal and Nonverbal Communication | 127 |
|     Verbal Communication | 128 |
|     Nonverbal Communication | 128 |

Verbal Active-Aggressive and Passive-Aggressive
Communication······················································· 129
    Verbal Active-Aggressive Communication ········· 130
    Verbal Passive Aggressive Communication ········ 130
Nonverbal Active-Aggressive and Passive-Aggressive
Communication······················································· 131
    Nonverbal Active-Aggressive Communication····· 131
    Nonverbal Passive-Aggressive Communication ···· 132
Complicating the Picture ····································· 133
Summary ······························································ 134

## Chapter 11 Teacher Tactics for Child Abuse and Child Neglect ········ 136
Selected for Punishment······································ 139
Rejecting································································· 141
Labeling································································· 145
Death Threats······················································ 149
Creating Fear······················································ 154
Ridiculing······························································ 160
Grade Manipulating············································ 163
Other Teacher Tactics of Abuse and Neglect ··········· 167
Summary ······························································ 169

## Chapter 12 Teacher Child Abuse and Child Neglect Defenses·········· 171
Ignoring································································ 174
Denial···································································· 174
Arguing Reality···················································· 177
Rewriting History················································ 178
Creating a Fictional Reality································ 180
Making the Student Look Bad ······························· 182
You're Disturbed ················································ 184

    You Overreact ·················································· 185
    Attention Seeking ·············································· 187
    Problem Student ··············································· 189
    You're Part of It ················································ 191
    It's Your Own Fault ············································· 195
    Summary ························································ 197
Chapter 13 Guilt by Avoidance ········································ 200
Chapter 14 The Minions ··············································· 206
    The Child Minions ·············································· 208
        Primary Child Minions ····································· 209
        Child Collateral Minions ··································· 214
        Delayed Collateral Minions ································ 215
        Fostering Minions is Child Abuse and
        Child Neglect ············································· 217
    The Adult Minions ············································· 218
        Adult Administrative Minions ····························· 222
        Adult Support Staff Minions ······························· 227
    Summary ························································ 231
Chapter 15 Retaliation ················································· 233
Chapter 16 Bottom-Up Change ········································ 241

Epilogue The Whispers Never End ····································· 253
Works Cited ··························································· 257

# List of Tables

Table 1. US Illiteracy Statistics · · · · · · · · · · · · · · · · · · · · · · · · · · · · · · · · · · ·62

Table 2. Graduates Completing Requirements
　　　　　for UC/CSU · · · · · · · · · · · · · · · · · · · · · · · · · · · · · · · · · · · · · · · · · ·67

Table 3. Percentage of California Students Scoring
　　　　　Proficient or Advanced · · · · · · · · · · · · · · · · · · · · · · · · · · · · · · · · ·69

Table 4. Percentage of Students Taking SATS and Average
　　　　　Scores by Year · · · · · · · · · · · · · · · · · · · · · · · · · · · · · · · · · · · · · · · · ·71

Table 5. Percentage of Students at or above Proficient · · · · · · · · · · · · · · · ·72

# Preface

Completed thoughts sometimes emerge from our minds as if they were already written—waiting to be recorded and directed. We write a few lines but after writing feel empty. Maybe there is nothing more to say. Then instantly —in the middle of a discussion about nothing, maybe the long shadows of the sun or perhaps the drizzle of rain on the roof, the missing but connecting thoughts appear somewhere in the corner of our sight. We look away until these next lines peek out, gather themselves, and flow onto the paper. Scenes we've had bumping in and out of consciousness since our earliest days begin to connect and twirl around.

Our minds hopscotch. They create. And they avoid. In everything we see, a touch or a taste of another connection appears. Every time we experience even a variation of what we have known forever, a little offshoot appears and touches all that is in its pathway. But short of disease or injury, our minds don't really lose much. The matrix begins at birth, and many will agree it begins to form long before that.

One day, the tiniest act closes a connection and the entire script lights up and sings like a pinball machine, hitting every possible angle and line. Every connection is made, and the picture is as clear as fresh celluloid at the local IMAX theater. Voilà.

I've danced around this book for years. The collection of my own experiences and those experiences of countless others, along with so many variations, has been incubating since early childhood. I was late into the writing of this book when the threads returned me to my early elementary school days. This period in my life was a point of clear consciousness, otherwise filled with childhood normalcies. But, looking back, there was an incident that started this story. Over the years, this one elementary school experience connected everything, like the first brick in a wall, the first shovel of dirt to break ground. It built over decades, feeding on experiences, sights, and sounds.

When everything that we know comes together, it can be so powerful as to usurp our other well-laid-out directions. We must set to work to empty that batch of coagulated information, that first batch. Each of us must decide what to do with the stuff of our own lives. This book comes from a decision to empty out what I know, as I understand it, onto pages of paper.

I walked home from school every day. Often alone. I didn't know anyone who went to my school. Except there was my sister Pat who was two years older than me. She was probably in fourth grade. Pat and I sometimes walked home together, across a state highway and a mile on to our house. Yet, I didn't see her after school that day. I was very young and wasn't sure what to do. But I knew my way home, so I crossed the highway and trudged along the winding streets.

I was pretty much always in my own little space, and a tap on a shoulder startled me. It was an older girl; she had her schoolbooks as I did. In those days, it was piles of books and papers. We carried everything in our arms, long before backpacks. She could see the startled look on my face and said, "Sorry, sorry."

I didn't talk to strangers back then, so she broke into my silence, "Aren't you Patricia's sister? You know, the big girl with the braids?" I guess I stumbled through some affirmative response because she continued. "She's in the office at school. Mrs. Rapp has her in there. Pat told her friend she was going to eat a crayon. So, Mrs. Rapp said she can't leave the school until she eats it. She's making her stay until she eats this red crayon."

Memory fails me now, perhaps because I didn't utter a word. I probably just stood there looking at her, trying to make sense of what she was saying.

Like there was no route to connect the words with anything in my brain. My own home life was pretty unpredictable. But this set of words didn't compute. I remember walking fast and thinking that I hoped my mother was there at home and that she would listen to me and that she might know what to do. But I wasn't sure that any of that would happen.

I was probably four or five, because I started school early and skipped a grade, just as my older sister had done. Pat couldn't have been more than seven years old. There was a thumping in my chest, I was short of breath, and tears kept running out of my eyes so it was very hard to see. I kept my sight pinned to the sidewalk so I wouldn't stumble on the uneven place where tree roots had lifted the cement. I tried to walk faster, but I was always a half-size child. My younger sister, who hadn't yet begun school, had already grown to my size or bigger. It was hard to hurry with short legs. The books kept slipping and the papers would fall out. Who would know what to do about a red crayon? What would happen if she ate it?

That walk from school to home will continue in instant replay, probably forever. I remember the weather, the sun was shining, no rain. No rain was unusual, so it had to be late fall. After hurricane season, or at the end of the season, there was a brief time before the rains began again every afternoon. But I didn't have a sweater, so it couldn't be too late in the year because it got cold early in our part of the South, usually by Halloween. The sun made it harder to go fast that day because it was glistening on the water that was pouring down my face.

I know now that I was scared. My sister was in danger, and I was scared. How someone so young could have a real sense of danger can only be explained by experience or instinct. I had had some experience of danger in my to date small life, but my short legs had never needed to run with fear until that day.

Those memories of my own panic are as vivid as the sun that day. But only now do I understand that my sister was a victim and Mrs. Rapp was an abuser. We were both victims of abuse. Mrs. Rapp was the principal, and she was the first bully, the first abusive adult I had ever known.

The girl who told on the principal never crossed my path again. She had a critical role to play in her own life and as well as in mine. And probably in Pat's life too. But Pat is gone now, and I can't ask her. I sometimes wonder what happened to that assertive little person who had the courage to run after me and tell what was happening. Did she already have some experience with abuse at that school, perhaps at the hands of that same person? Was she just born knowing what to do? I'm sure I'll never know, but not knowing leads to so many other possibilities, so many more connections.

> "The last of the human freedoms…
> to choose one's attitude…
> to choose one's own way."
> —Viktor Frankl (1905–1997)

# INTRODUCTION
# America's Schools: The Last Bastion of Cloaked Abuse

> "The greatest colony of gulls can follow the wrong lead,
> Refuse to be turned, and be lost at sea."
> —D. P. CALLIN

There are organized groups that are so enormous and far-reaching that they create their own rules. These groups become structures with dense overlays so that their core can barely be seen, or even known, by those outside of the organizations. These bastions can mandate and dictate outcomes both inside and outside of their own structures. They are afforded control over their members by virtue of the rules of membership. Not surprisingly, large, organized groups extend their control beyond the group to interface with and influence communities, industries, and governments. The exertion of control and influence by these groups is commensurate with their ability to gather and use resources.

The influence of large, organized groups on their individual members can take almost any shape that is necessary for the furtherance of the organizational agenda. This influence may be political or legal; it may be inside of the community or throughout the region or country. These groups are the bastions.

Not all large organizations that exert power and control over others are bastions. The criteria must include certain key elements for the metamorphosis of a simple organization into a dominant force. Primary to the definitional mandate of a bastion is that the content of the service, which is provided by the organization, be considered essential to the society in which we live. Even though we as individuals may not agree on whether an organization provides an essential service, as a group, we have decided that the service exists and that it must continue to exist for the welfare of all. Then the definition is generally stated in functional terms. That is, if most perceive that the service is essential, then that service is essential to all.

One example of a large organization that is not a bastion is sports franchises. These organizations are so large that they spend millions on sports equipment. Contracts to provide equipment can come with demands from the organization, which shape or alter the behavior of the manufacturer. Issues, such as who the manufacturer advertises with, what it does and doesn't say in press releases, and which stores it has contracts with to handle the sports merchandise all become subject to the sports franchise's interests, whatever they may be. So, the independent manufacturer is controlled by the interests of the sports franchise. We might also say that the fashion industry or the entertainment industry each exert some power over those both inside and outside of its own membership.

But influence from an organization in which nationwide participation is nonessential precludes that organization from becoming a bastion. Many individuals perceive the sports, entertainment, fashion, and other industries as essential to our culture and lifestyle. However, while they may have some positive and some negative influence outside of their memberships, their influence is ever changing and truly nonessential. There is no requirement to participate in or to support these industries or organizations.

The secondary definitional mandate of a bastion is that its influence and power cannot be eliminated, regardless of the circumstance. In expanding the definition of bastion, we have narrowed down the number of its member groups. The bastion organization must provide services for which the needs exist over time, regardless of circumstances. Over multiple generations and over many centuries, the bastion provides services that we believe essential to our survival.

Tertiary to this definition is the final caveat: people must fight to have the services provided. Generally, but not always, the services that are fought hard for are provided by large organizations. Therefore, if there is a total absence of the needed service, people must feel they are willing to fight to create that service. They must believe that they cannot exist without the service. And inherent in any service one is willing to fight for, within the group that ultimately provides the service, there is power and the opportunity for a bastion to be born.

The definition of a large organization that exerts enormous power over others, a bastion organization, becomes thus:

> "A large number of individuals grouped together to provide an essential service that is required by those inside and outside the group, is continuously existing, and is demanded and fought for in its absence."

Some large organizations, including those requiring enormous educational qualifications and other difficult requirements for admission, are strangers to the term *bastion*. Many professions are not designed to award significant power to any individual or group of individuals in ways that affect the lives of many. Consider the roles of architects, archaeologists, accountants, and other professionals whose work action exerts little control over others, notwithstanding the small work units. While their large organizations serve the needs of their membership and meet the needs of their specific clientele, they are nonessential in difficult times and therefore cannot act in concert with the label *bastion*, as they exert little power over others.

The bastion is further delineated by the degree of superiority one human is assumed to possess over another. Powerful professional specialties exist in medicine, law, religion, politics, and other overlooked arenas, such as the pharmaceutical industry and medical insurance companies. These powerful groups are the bastions, and its members are the brotherhoods.

Brotherhoods are self-defining. They define their own goals within some broad societal expectations or parameters. They make decisions about how to best meet those broad external demands while continuing to meet their own internal goals. Brotherhoods set their own rules for success and failure. And even if those outside the group see the brotherhood as a failure and finance this failure, they are powerless to change the direction, output, or outcome of the brotherhood's functioning.

These large organizations have some tiered groups, usually called administrators, who are, of course, made up of their own members. This is intended to keep the brotherhood on track to meet its goals. As with many enormous entities that serve private citizens and receive public money or private contracts, they generally have a board to interface between the public and the brotherhood.

In some nonessential organization, or those organizations that exist to earn money, the board has some power to act, direct, oversee, or control. However, in the true bastion, the board is almost exclusively figurative, relegated to mundane chores such as stamping hiring and firing decisions, handing out awards, and providing exposure for the organizations social needs.

Bastions are self-defending. Their stated goal is to provide an essential service for others; their unstated goal is to accomplish that goal at some minimally acceptable level. Generally, their private goal is to assure their own existence. As a result, their service is provided for the greatest gain of the organization and at the minimal acceptable level to the public. The bastion organization is so large that it can vote in or simply elect to protect itself to any extent, using the money that was allocated for the good of the people to protect the good of the organization. Any assault from the inside or the outside of the organization is met with swift and sometimes unpleasant response.

None of this is perhaps surprising. In poor countries where socialism has been perpetrated on the citizens for their own good, there is nary a socialist dictator without wealth and power beyond measure. The church operates in pretty much the same way. We honor God, and hence we are admonished to support our faith. It's hard to understand the degree of wealth and power of some churches borne on the backs of peasants around the world. Nevertheless, these bastions are so powerful that all the imaginable abuse has been easily covered up, ignored, or denied, under the penalty of God himself, for centuries. Anyone who condemns them is then themselves condemned.

These examples go on; it's a long and common list. The degree to which bastions are dangerously self-protective correlates directly with the risk of loss the organization might succumb to in times of trouble. The risk might be to the organization, the individual, or to the profession. At a hint of scandal or liability the brotherhood close ranks and protects themselves, one another, and the bastion to which they belong at all costs.

This process of self-protection operates in every close, interdependent group. It begins with the family. Behavior goes bad. Shame begins. Fear of being found out ensues. Defenses rally. Family members join forces. A unit is formed where perhaps no unit was visible throughout the entire family history. Without thinking, but always knowing where one's loyalties lie, blood strangers become allies, and everyday human differences disappear. This happens without a glance back or out. Suddenly, we've always been a family. Family comes first. We protect our own. Then a cloak of silence and ignorance envelopes the new but omnipresent unit. We're all on the lookout for any sign of attack, even if that attack is a defense against some part of that unit gone bad.

A rewriting process begins. "It didn't happen that way," "You misunderstand," "You overreacted," "You misinterpreted," or "It was entirely your own fault to begin with." In no time, work, family, and other types of units become masterful at flipping events, rewriting history, and creating an entirely new reality. "This never would have happened if only you..." "You asked for it..." "You were part of it..." These are the common phrases used in the brotherhood to cloak the bastion. The accuser or victim is made to look responsible.

It's instinctively simple to see the human tendency to form brotherhoods in the same way we operate inside the family unit. Brotherhoods can be powerful advocates for equality and fairness. Such was the origin of the worker's unions. They came together to gain the strength needed for the group to assert a force equal to the power unit the workers faced every day. Unions derive far back into American history when Thomas Jefferson defined the legal criterion for having an interest in the governance of the states.

Despite great objection, he fought to expand the right to vote. He rejected the British colonials' authority to limit governance, the right to vote, to only those who were deemed to have an interest by virtue of their land ownership. Those who had an interest were called freeholders. Jefferson began the movement in America that would eventually include a broader base for actual representative government, fair to all. Representative government provided the model for representative workers' unions.

As simple as it is to see the value of the brotherhood, it's equally overwhelming to see the power of a bastion that exists for all the wrong reasons. This happens when brotherhoods move away from their purpose and find themselves in a secret society of hushed voices and closed eyes. Members of the brotherhood not only allow the cover up of wrongdoings, they also go to appalling lengths to quell any discovery of the crimes, even those of the most heinous crimes.

Individuals within a unit are complicit when they take no action after finding that within the brotherhood they are in the company of just ordinary, sad hoods. The world is rife with such hoods. Call them by any name. Call them abusers. Call them bullies. But just as the dysfunctional family gathers around the bad seed, brotherhoods unite in excruciatingly dysfunctional ways strictly for self-preservation regardless of the cost to others.

For the past few decades, we've watched untold numbers of slaughters from sanctified brotherhoods unfold. This is another long, sad tale overdue in its telling. Yet, the uncovering could only happen in its own time. As Americans have become increasingly exposed to other voices from different times and places, the world becomes a safer place to find a voice. The news media, the Internet, social media, and every other form of communication have created an opening.

There is a gathering of glimpses. Then sounds are heard. Feelings are expressed. Gradually, the sounds become words and are joined by other words from other places. A few brave souls risk ruin by speaking loudly after believing that the time is right. These are the real heroes. They risk the wrath of the brotherhood, the members of the bastion, by just saying or perhaps honestly stating that the "Emperor has No Clothes," bad things have happened, and bad things have happened to me. Some speak the first words standing alone. Even brothers and family disavow them. These are the Harriet Tubman's of our world. These are not the great orators surrounded by thousands. Those come later. They enter the slaughter long after the brave few have risked everything.

Over time, empowered by others who came before us, we find our group voice. Dramatically, and with the greatest pain, brotherhoods are crushed under their own silence by the voices of the few. It is a remarkable truth that the very force that has brought many together for good purpose is the same force that destroys. The myth of good will, positive camaraderie, and philanthropic intent are all shattered. The brotherhood is shamed, and we all grieve. There are no heroes, just another bunch of thugs.

Men of God were hiding behind their robes and platitudes. They were touchable by no one but God. They said that they sat at the altar for all of us. So did many priests abusing so many children. Athletes, our strongest role models, are found to be cheating. They were our best heroes; their accomplishments were hard-won. They gave us hope that anyone can be a winner. If they could do it, we could do it. But they were lying. They were users.

We gave our children over to coaches. It was good for them. Our coaches were there for us and for our children. Then our coaches hid in the shower room with our helpless and frightened children. The list is as long as time. We struggle, we grieve, and then we recover some of our faith. We begin to search for new role models. Now, we are warier. We persist in the belief that we will always need our heroes—but where are they?

Along the pathway to today, we've struggled with painful realities such as child abuse, spousal abuse, and sexual harassment in the workplace. These crimes are just as ugly as the crimes of the brotherhood, blinded by its own need for survival. But, because the crimes are most often committed by individuals or small groups, we are more willing to assert ourselves. We are more used to these crimes now. They seem familiar. It's safer, less risky for ourselves if we speak out; there is more opportunity to do good.

We have moved across time and, in some ways, across space. When we were children, we knew what kind of abuse was happening around us. We were neither deaf nor dumb. We were not stupid. But we could not speak. We were not heard. Our parents were afraid. They covered for our fathers, uncles, and grandfathers. They kept their silence and prayed that maybe the priest was really doing what was best for their children. It wouldn't hurt the children. The priests knew things that we could not understand. They acted for God. Our families gathered together with knowledge and an unspoken rule. It was wise to be silent. No one leaves the unit. No one challenges the brotherhood; everyone fears the wraith of the bastion.

In what we would like to see as a new reality, we are beginning to understand that people then, and now, are wrong for sanctifying any human role. There are no cloaks of invisibility. We've beaten the beast. We've faced the horrible truths. Nothing is sacred; we're facing it all now. No more false heroes. Leave that to the movies.

But think again. Is something incomplete? Is there just one last demon? What could possibly be niggling somewhere in the recesses of our poor and humble human brains? Am I confused? Maybe with so much loss of faith, I've just become suspicious. I've learned that I've created the myth of the hero for my own need, for something to believe in. I've learned that believing in the myths has hurt so many for so long. Why is it, though, that I continue to repress a thick, perhaps deceptive, reality? I push back against having to grapple with another failed faith.

# CHAPTER 1
# One More Brotherhood

> "I have only one request, may I never
> use my reason against truth."
> —Hasidic rabbi prayer

Schools in the United States have failed. Not always for the one, but certainly for all. America's schools exist for the education of all, for each and every child. But these bastions of education have become bastions of failure; they are the brotherhoods of cloaked abuse. From the aides to the administrators, from the fields to the classrooms, from the kindergartens to the colleges, American education is fraught with child abuse and child neglect.

To understand the nature of child abuse and child neglect in our schools, we need to review the structure of the school system and understand how it fits into the bastion and the brotherhood model. Teachers constitute one of the largest work groups in the United States. The US National Center for Education Statistics offers some insight into the size of this bastion (United States Department of Education, Fast Facts-Teacher Trends 2016). A projected 3.5 million elementary and secondary school full-time-equivalent (FTE) teachers were engaged in classroom instruction in the fall of 2014, with 3.1 million being FTE public school teachers and 400,000 being FTE private school teachers. These numbers do not include the vast army of support and administrative staff.

This group of professionals exerts political power to such an extent that it can sway elections and push legislation; this ultimately benefits this group over others. In large states, such as California, where educational success is sadly lacking, the union of teachers has failed at changes that might have resulted in significant improvement in student outcome (California Assessment of Student Performance and Progress 2016). Even when failure is well documented with dropout rates and test scores, teachers continue to be compensated at a rate higher than any other professionals with comparable job requirements, convenient work hours, frequent time off, and freedom from accountability. This compensation stretches far into the future, with state taxpayers funding lucrative retirement plans that create huge deficits for the states, new hires funding existing pensions, and little hope for some that these will be sufficient for funding further obligations (Russell and Williams Walsh 2017). Yet, regardless of the schools and their teachers' failure to educate, while still being paid, none of the recent changes has brought the states' test scores to passing.

On August 24, 2016, the California Department of Education released the latest *Smarter Balanced for English Language Arts / Literacy Statewide Numbers*. (California Department of Education 2016). The reports look dismal. But when you read the report, you'll notice it sounds very positive; in fact, it is improved, at least in the way the numbers are reported. For all the 3,188,014 students tested, 20 percent exceeded the standards. About 29 percent fell in the met-standards group. The rest, 52 percent, did not meet the standards. Yes, that means that more than 150 million students in California aren't educated enough to meet standards. The report struggles to spin the test scores by cutting out a percentage of that 52 percent who didn't meet standards and called that group "nearly met standards." I'm not sure what that means. Does it matter to our students' futures that they nearly got accepted into college? In 2016-17, there were over six million students enrolled in over ten thousand schools in California. (California Department of Education 2017). What becomes of their futures?

The number of students who didn't meet the basic standards in the core subjects of reading and math is a big number; that big number comes with a big price tag, somewhere in the range of $53 to $88 billion dollars, depending on who's calculating it. On a per-pupil basis, the Prop 98 spending per student for K–12 education is $10,643 in 2016–2017, a raise from $10,203 in 2015–2016. Nonetheless, that's not the real cost; when all funding sources are considered, per-pupil spending for K–12 is $14,799 in 2016–2017 compared to $14,302 in 2015–2016 (California Department of Education, "2016–2017 Budget Act Letter" 2016).

The price tag for the tax payers for these failures is almost incalculable; however, we can calculate that 49 percent of California's students have met the state-set academic standards. The last time I looked, if your work performance score was 49 percent, you'd be fired.

The permanent demand for education creates a machine with a life of its own. There is no expectation that education will cease at some point in time to eliminate the need for teachers. Many industrial complexes come and go, but education is a given, a fact. The status of teachers, their huge numbers, and their unionized influence on the political and government process affords them not only continuity, but also social and legal power. Teacher unions are one of the most influential brotherhoods in the world.

Think for a moment about the media coverage of the teaching profession. Generally, it's positive. Media coverage has a broad range, including educational press releases and reports on current events, legal issues, new innovations, sports and academic competitions, and more. We like that. We feel reassured that something good is happening. Stories about great accomplishments, influential individuals, and innovative programs are covered in great detail. We want to believe that all is well, change is happening, and we can rest easy.

On the other side of the news, failures are briefly reported and at times with no follow-ups. But the failures, like most current events, are quickly forgotten when some interesting event captures our consciousness.

Despite the annual newspaper reports of failed educational systems and embarrassing city, district, county, and state test scores, the reaction is momentary with little momentum for change. The obscene test scores, the gross failures, the sad numbers of school dropouts, and the overreaching costs are pushed out of consciousness. The power of the education bastion in the United States makes sure that the individual incidents of child abuse and child neglect by teachers only see the light of day when a parent files a lawsuit or when law enforcement is involved. And, even then, only a small percentage of these cases are reported because the public, including the media, don't have access to essential information regarding any disciplinary actions taking place in schools. Giant legal firms, working on unending taxpayers' dollars for the brotherhood, overwhelm most individuals who know their children have been injured and are fighting for justice. Charges are dropped. A deal is cut.

When humans feel hopeless and helpless in the face of enormous power, they file away the emotion. Individuals may despise what they see as the teacher's unearned privileges—short working days, multiple weeks of holiday and months off in the summer, and full benefits and generous retirement—in exchange for their failure to educate and protect their children. But parents and students alike believe that they are impotent to act on their anger and resentment and that the brotherhood of teachers is impossible to be successfully confronted. It's been years since I've told a parent to talk to a teacher about a problem without hearing the same response, "You know that only makes it worse." When we know that there is impotence on a group level, it can only be worse for any single individual. And abuse is known to target single individuals, one child at a time, perpetrated by one teacher at a time, and supported by the last bastion of cloaked abuse.

The members of the teaching profession are no less self-protective than the members of any other brotherhood. The aura that this profession likes to project is one of helpfulness and caring. Group members want to keep it that way. Like other helping professions, such as medicine, law enforcement, and church, the teaching profession espouses an image of a greater purpose. They manage their reputation carefully. When teacher-related problems arise—those that are contrary to their image of inspirational quotes and friendly press releases—they are quickly and quietly dispatched.

If the media covers a teacher-related abuse issue, the brotherhood is quick to act. No one knows how many abusive teachers there are, but the few cases that make it to the news are handled expeditiously. We'll relate some of those cases later in this text. The greater problem is when the abusive teacher or the other school employees involved never make it to the news. An individual teacher is easily surrounded by the group, right or wrong, and protected by their brothers in union.

Over the last thirty years as a clinical psychologist, I have been seeing young people through a range of ages in their struggles to navigate their life issues, including their educational issues. In my experience, in the myriad of cases that involved helping parents and students deal with teacher-student abuse issues, not one case was ever resolved appropriately at the school level. At best, the child is saved from further abuse by having a strong parent or an advocate insist on changing the teacher. That's not always possible in a small school. And some administrators do not want to make a change, often out of fear that there will be a flood of demands. At worst, the child becomes a chronic victim.

When an organization is under repeated attack because of the behavior of one of its members, it forms a sort of cognitive dissonance, motivating members to reduce this confusion as quickly as possible. One efficient means of dealing with their problems when they don't want to face them is through scapegoating. As such, whole organizations, such as the brotherhood of teachers, make a practice of flipping the problem back to the victim. Organizations cannot defend what they believe to be indefensible. To save themselves from a moral dilemma, the brotherhood of teachers and other school personnel tell themselves and others that the student is the problem. The group members pull together and offer up every defense imaginable, such as the student has this problem, the parent is that problem, it's a misunderstanding, and so on. The list of ways to blame someone else is endless.

When the brotherhood of teachers closes ranks, it looks exactly like every other powerful group when it finds itself in trouble. The result is an unnavigable terrain for almost every parent and student. This bastion is one of the most powerful unions in our country. Once this brotherhood of like-minded, self-protective professional's moves into action, it is virtually impossible to find justice.

# CHAPTER 2
# Bullying in Schools

> "You think you can change what's right in
> front of you, but you trick yourself.
> You can't change something that you can't
> see, that isn't what you think you see.
> —D. P. CALLIN

Bullying seems to occur in every part of society worldwide. Bullying, it seems, is one of those unfortunate and characteristic behaviors associated with being a human. However, there people from all walks of life who don't bully. It's likely that, short of true personality disorders, bullying is learned and can be managed, much the same as cheating, lying, and other undesirable behaviors.

School educational programs about bullying are generally focused on bullying in schools among children, what I call child-child bullying. A quick search through the available print material shows the child-child bullying literature outweighing other types of bullying literature by roughly fifty to one. More recently, that child-child focus has expanded to another group, to students who bully teachers: child-teacher bullying. Yes, there's some of that going on too. But, notice that the child is still the bully in this new onslaught of bullying information. Child-teacher bullying episodes make the news. It is surprising to some that these episodes occur, teachers are expected to handle every difficult situation and diffuse problems before they explode. But it's quite understandable that child-teacher bullying makes the news. The news covers events that are unique, not often do we tune in to the evening news to see the day's unremarkable events. Making sure the press gets the stories supports teachers demands for more money, and demonstrates to the public how terrible the students are who they have to deal with. If these adults can't manage to deal with a child who bullies them, how will the children ever survive?

Those of us who don't bully others aren't necessarily immediately aware of the behavior at first sight. This is even truer when the bullying originates from a sanctified profession where bullying is little discussed and is generally unthinkable. Just as in the example of the religious figures who have abused countless children over the hundreds of years, we aren't prepared to address bullying when it comes from a sanctified realm—a brotherhood that is deemed sacred in the relationship between children and adults—education.

Naturally, there are enormous social and legal consequences for parents who are found to repeatedly bully their own children. In a world where the privacy of the family has historically been paramount, society has become increasingly less tolerant of parents bullying. But when parents are faced with the situation of their children being actively bullied or abused by a teacher, they are righteously infuriated by the hopelessness they feel when they are disavowed by a powerful self-protective system. They find their concerns ignored, brushed away, or flipped around to reflect poorly on the student or the parent.

In the last few years, there has been an increasing interest in determining how best to stop public bullying of children. In the 1980s, I worked as a supervisor for the county mental health department. We were looking for mental health intervention strategies funded through designated prevention dollars. I proposed a community-wide child bullying awareness plan with training for local businesses. The plan was vetoed as too controversial.

Now, two or three decades later, there may be some movement. A risk-taking change takes time to percolate. Despite the failure to come through with community-wide awareness programs, progress comes along from unexpected places. With parents feeling powerless, at least in one arena, a small group of individuals, students, and their parents are standing up to the giant.

There have been recent breakthroughs in the high school and the college population who are dealing with teachers who are bullies. In years past, parents and administrators have been reluctant to label any teacher as a bully. Educators excuse teacher bullying at the secondary level, reasoning these teachers are "toughening up our teens and young adults," "preparing them for the real world," or, in some cases, "riding herd on an out-of-control kid."

But as this age group becomes more tech-savvy and learns through social media how others are exposing teacher offences, the problem is sometimes, slowly being addressed by the students themselves. Using peer support, various recording devices, media interest, and parent and legal interventions, it is becoming a little more difficult for educators to escape notice for their abuse of power. Here are two reported examples from schools in different states:

- A fifteen-year-old New Jersey boy complained repeatedly that his teacher was bullying him. His teacher ranted vulgarities, verbally abused him, mocked him, and threatened him. After his complaints were ignored, he used his phone to record the classroom events (Strauss, Eric M 2012). The phone recordings were allowed as evidence in the case.
- A nine-year-old boy went to school with a recording device. His father wanted to see if the boy's complaints were legitimate. The father first followed through with every step of the complaint process required by the school and the district. He was told that there

was no basis for the complaint; then the father played the tape, which clearly captured the horrific abuse (Miva, R. 2012)

When we say that the future lies with the young, a change in education is no exception. We see here that our young are brave enough to tackle the greatest and most powerful of brotherhoods. After years of students wasting their time in failed schools, enduring years of insults and humiliation, and being blamed for the failures of teachers, they have sought ways to face the demon.

We hear appalling stories of child abuse by teachers and other school personnel, of children being denied an education, of discrimination in education, and much more. Most of these stories come to us from other countries. We become sympathetic and want to help those children by righting the wrongs. Celebrities take special interest in working to make schools safe and effective in faraway places, such as Africa and the Middle East. Interestingly, but as we all have come to expect, we hear very little about incidents of abusive and neglectful teachers in the United States, unless the media picks up the story. The media has been a part of the struggle to change the devastating silence of those who have been victimized. Accolades for the media! Without real reporting, not just whitewashed banter, we would be decades behind in these battles against every type of abuse and neglect in our schools. We shouldn't have to depend on the media to do our policing of teacher-child abuse and neglect; but without it, the problem of teachers abusing and neglecting their students would be buried alongside so many other crimes, and the brotherhood would live on.

# CHAPTER 3

# Defining Teacher Bullying

> "[T]he good we secure for ourselves is precarious and uncertain, is floating in mid-air, until it is secured for all of us and incorporated into our common life."
> —JANE ADDAMS (1860–1935)

Defining any type of bullying is an arduous task. But there's a serious fault in applying the term bullying to teachers and other school personnel. What is generally called bullying by teachers is particularly difficult because of the teachers' role in children's lives. Society has mixed and confused expectations for those who are responsible for educating our children. Teachers are caregivers. At every level, they are given authority over students, and that authority can be used for a purpose, good or bad.

There are a multitude of somewhat poorly delineated rules regarding teacher authority. These rules are both federal and state, with each state writing its own version of teacher authority. But regardless of good effort to put some rules on paper, all rules require interpretation, and interpretation is dependent on the traits of individuals and groups interpreting those rules and their relationship to the district in which the rule may apply.

Saying that no teacher "shall demean or injure any child" is only useful post-abuse. It's necessary to have an established body of writing to refer to it in a legal manner. Vaguely written rules are easy to circumvent, manipulate, and reinterpret based on circumstance, no matter how conjured up the circumstance may be.

Teachers bully and intimidate students. When this happens, the charge is often dismissed. There are cases where teachers have been dismissed for failing to "treat the students with dignity and respect." There are some cases where the teacher has been wrist slapped for "failure to act in a manner that maintained the honor and dignity of the teaching profession." At these times, when the school personnel are held accountable, you may think justice is done. But the charges and findings do not directly address the issues by name. Rulings are generally vague. Because of this vagueness, these rulings are unlikely to set a clear precedent for later cases of teacher bullying.

As of this writing, only nineteen states have legislation addressing bullying. None of this legislation directly addresses the problem of teachers as bullies. My own state, California, introduced bill number 2180 in February 2004 and then amended it twice, in March and April of the same year. California legislative information is available at http://www.leginfo.ca.gov/guide.html. This bill, although an advance for child protection in the schools, does not specifically define teachers as among the groups targeted as possible bullies. Bully Police USA is a watchdog organization that advocates for bullied children and reports on state-level antibullying laws (High, Brenda 2010). The organization graded the California law a B and noted that there was neither a definition of bullying or harassment nor anything to address the need for protection against retaliation, reprisal, or false accusation.

Section 35294.21 of the California Education Code was amended to include only one line in a paragraph that vaguely supplies a platform for including teacher bullying: "Assuring each pupil a safe, respectful, accepting, and emotionally nurturing environment" (California Education Code 2005).

While this vague assurance for students could be the beginning for some future laws with teeth, it really doesn't even allude to teachers' behaviors. So, while there seems to be a basis for progress in the rules and laws, maybe there really isn't any, at least from the teacher-child perspective.

Let's look at some current definitions of bullying:

The *Cambridge Dictionary* defines a bully as someone who hurts or frightens someone who is smaller or less powerful, often forcing him or her to do something that he or she does not want to do; overbearing, especially to smaller or weaker people.

Dictionary.com defines it as a blustering, quarrelsome, and overbearing person who habitually badgers and intimidates smaller or weaker people.

The *Collins English Dictionary* defines bullying as the intimidation of weaker people.

The stopbullying.gov reads bullying as an unwanted, aggressive behavior among school children that involves a real or perceived power imbalance.

This definition by stopbullying.gov includes the requirements that bullying must be aggressive; it must include an imbalance of power; and it must be repeated, happening more than once. But what else does this definition include and what does it omit? Notice that only child-child bullying is included. Teacher bullying isn't even mentioned, though teacher-child bullying is an obvious imbalance of power and is certainly aggressive. This is very much a reflection of the focus of our time. Regardless of the fact that many teacher bastions have been called out for child abuse and neglect, and of course, the term *child bullying* has been repeatedly used, this brotherhood defends itself, and the war begins anew.

Bullying in schools isn't limited to school children, as might be inferred by the definitions of bullying. There are plenty of others in the setting: teachers, principals, vice principals, secretaries, cafeteria workers, yard workers, and others. Each of these groups populates the American school system, and each member of each group should be constantly educated about bullying. We've spent the better part of the last decade and enormous amounts of money in inventing, designing, and enacting programs to help children learn about bullying. We teach them to know what bullying looks like when they see it, and the children are repeatedly told they are not supposed to bully. Some of the schools that administer the required schoolwide writing tests use bullying as the topic. Valuable educational time is spent on this subject during the school day. And now the kids know how to address and report bullying, so long that bullying originates from another student.

In a world where adults are free to bully, bullying will never stop between children. In today's schools, the stop-bullying campaigns are useless because they are not evenly applied. Adults, who are the guardians of our children, are role-modeling what we now call bullying for the kids, and those same kids take out their aggression on other kids because they can't fight back when the role-model bully is a teacher.

The stopbullying.com definition would be more direct and powerful if it addressed *all* the bullying that takes place within the confines of the school (or any setting for that matter).

This is how it could read:

*"School bullying is any unwanted aggressive behavior that involves a real power or perceived power imbalance from one (or more) person to another, whether that person(s) is a school employee(s) or student(s)."*

But including adults in the definition of bullying is problematic. In the context of redefining bullying for what it really is in the adult-child, and the teacher-child relationship, it should be stated as follows:

*"Bullying is indistinguishable from child abuse or child neglect when it is committed by school personnel and the victim(s) is an individual student or a group of students, making the occurrence of bullying, child abuse, and child neglect reportable and punishable under state and federal law. Child abuse and child neglect include each of the federally defined categories: physical abuse, psychological abuse, sexual abuse, emotional neglect, medical neglect, educational neglect, and physical neglect."*

Child abuse and child neglect occur when any school personnel abuses or neglects a particular student or a group of students. Singling out even one student can be aggressive, premeditated, power imbalanced, and psychologically and physically dangerous to the student and others around that student.

This essential change in the definition functionally eliminates the term *bullying* from the definition of teacher-child interactions. Much like getting rid of the useless D grade in schools, the elimination of any use of the word *bullying* when applied to an adult in power brings us to a whole new place in thinking about the role of the teacher or the school as the guardian. This new and more correct terminology for abusive and neglectful behaviors puts the common teachers' offences in the category of child abuse and child neglect under the jurisdiction of federal and state laws, where they belong. The proceedings involved in evaluating, charging, and prosecuting child abuse and child neglect laws do not belong in the hands of the public-school system. Psychological abuse, physical abuse, sexual abuse, physical neglect, educational neglect, medical neglect, and emotional neglect of a child should be named as what they really are. They are criminal acts.

It's perplexing that some acts against children are already seen as criminal acts when they occur in the school setting while others are not. Child abuse that is sometimes prosecuted when perpetrated by a teacher or other school employee includes such things as sexual acts and contributing to the delinquency of a minor. Yet, even with this, there are plenty of examples in which you will see that teachers have committed both types of crimes where the result is quite different from what might have happened if they were committed by a neighbor or a relative. Many of the teachers found to be guilty for these types of crimes are simply passed on to other schools, without any accompanying record that states their offences or the reason why they left their last school (Taguchi and Shubailat 2017).

The StopBullying.gov website does elaborate on almost every type of bullying, where and when it happens, and the frequency of bullying. This helpful government website does not specifically address bullying by age or position. Rather, the reader is left to interpret the particulars of who a 'bully' might be. The inference is that all bullying is committed by children—and this is correct. Break the habit of referring to adults who abuse and neglect children as bullies. Teacher and other school personnel 'bullying' of students is child abuse and it is clarified under state and federal child abuse and child neglect definitions. Sadly, we seem quite able to see bullying between school-age kids, but we are almost intentionally blind to the abuse of power that comes from teachers or other school personnel. Each type of teacher-child abuse and teacher-child neglect will be covered in detail in the following chapters

# CHAPTER 4
# Bullying as Abuse

> "A man may sit for hours and talks to
> you about what he thinks.
> But what he really is, you can judge best by what he did..."
> —Isaac Bashevis Singer

When is the bullying of a child really the same as child abuse? A better way to ask the question may be, "Is there ever a case of adult-to-child bullying that is not abusive?" Look at the use of the term *bullying*.

In general, use the term *bullying* when referencing the behavior of people of similar chronological age and mental age and who are also in similar demographic and economic positions. Age is the most obviously measurable term here. Both one's chronological or birth age and one's mental or cognitive age are measurable. The position is static; it's exact and its definition is unequivocal. A position is like a place—fixed and identifiable.

Bullying is distinguished by a power differential. Power is fluid; it can be more or less, greater or smaller. Power is a force or strength. When we say there is power, the word *power* is made to sound like it has a life of its own and directs itself in whichever way it wants. Power can take an action.

When two people are of similar age and position but dissimilar in other ways, we believe that their power is somewhat equal. This is a superficial view, and right away you'll see that there are all kinds of arguments against that. There are always differences between people; there are no two exactly equal people. That's absolutely true. But if we're ever going to ever use the term *bully*, we must agree that two people can be similar in their age and position and then be aware that some type of power imbalance is also present. What makes the interactions between two people bullying, or an unfair fight, is similar age and position with an imbalance in power between the two. For instance, one child may be bigger, stronger, or have more children to back him up in a fight. If the bullying is verbal, one child may be smarter, have a more advanced command of language, or can simply out-talk or yell louder than the other child. Other power differences between children of similar ages and positions may include such things as the bully being the teacher's pet or the willingness of one child to use of vulgarities. However, if the child who is bullying is also the child of one of the teachers, their position is not equal to the position of any other student, and bullying by that child is easily seen as abuse.

The position of power dramatically changes in any relationship as the age and position differences between two people increases. When the perpetrator and victim are in relatively the same position and are close in age but the power structure is uneven, we call the unfair fighting bullying. As the age or status difference increases, the relative power that a perpetrator has over a victim increases. This can be true when the victim is much younger or much older than the perpetrator. The position infers power equity. Power is often equated to age or status. That is, someone older or in a better job or with more money is more powerful that someone who is young with no job or no money. But power differentiation can occur for a plethora of reasons, such as differences in education, physical size, experience, and wisdom.

Bullying anyone who has inadequate defenses is abusive. Children are defenseless when they are bullied by a caregiver. Whether this is parent to child bullying, coach to child bullying, priest to child bullying, or teacher to child bullying, the victim is defenseless because the victim is a child.

Children are the victims of child abuse and child neglect simply because they are young, they have not achieved independence, and cognitively they are not fully developed. Children generally don't have the resources to stand up for themselves to stop abuse. Clearly young people lack the power to have a fair fight with adults. There is no bullying between adults and children, there is only abuse.

Put this into a somewhat different perspective. Consider how most of us feel about the maltreatment of animals. We cringe when people yell at their animals. We want people to be charged and convicted of a crime if they repeatedly demean, frighten, or threaten an animal. Just read the comments following any article related to animal abuse. We know animals are helpless when humans decide to be abusive. And like animals, children have no means of escape. The torment felt by a humiliated and threatened animal is the probably a little different from the torment of abuse felt by a child. But the child suffers the consequences in so many more ways in their complex and extended lives.

The universal reaction to witnessing an adult speaking angrily to a child or roughly handling a child in a marketplace is of disgust, sometimes of horror, but always of anger. When we witness even brief adult-child flairs of anger, we assume that this public behavior on the part of the adult is inappropriate. Our own embarrassment for the child comes from a belief that the parent could have done better. And we assume this inappropriate public behavior of the adult is likely the marker for even worse behavior when he or she is in private. We can only think that an adult who behaves rudely or angrily in public is far more inappropriate in private. Our minds jump over the common idea of bullying and label these behaviors as abusive.

## Perpetrator and Victim

Bullying is different from abuse by the virtue of differences in age, position, and power. What we casually call bullying of a child by a caregiver is actually abuse. These distinctions are essential; they result in legal differences. The language of abuse includes and utilizes more accurate terminology, including the words *perpetrator* and *victim*.

In our educational system, we see many references to bullying. Unfortunately, the words *bully* or *bullying* are umbrella terms that really include any physical act or gesture or any verbally written or electronically communicated expression that:

1. physically harms a student or damages a student's property;
2. places a student in reasonable fear of physical harm or damage to his or her property;
3. substantially disrupts the instructional program or the orderly operations of the school;
4. creates an intimidating and/or hostile educational environment for the student when the bullying is severe, persistent, or pervasive.

The bullying literature in education is predominantly aimed at child-child bullying. There is no definitively written legal protection for the child if he or she is being harassed or bullied by a teacher. And, as you read in the last chapter, this is likely because any harassment or bullying of a child by some teacher or other school personnel is actually abuse. This key point, this absence of written definitions, guidelines, rules, and consequences, creates a canyon-size void and sets up all ages of America's students for child abuse and child neglect. At the same time, this missing link in education, and in rules applying to America's teachers and other school personnel, protects them from being held accountable for their many offenses that injure and sometimes cause the death of our children. As we move into the body of what's really happening in the last bastion, America's schools, we see that it's likely no one responsible adult will come to rescue an abused and neglected child except the parent. And that only happens if the parents are aware of their children's abuse and neglect, their rights, and they are not afraid of the brotherhood that holds all the power.

When any act of child abuse or child neglect is perpetrated by a parent or caregiver, the act or violation is covered under state and federal child abuse and child neglect laws. Parents and caregivers are held to a higher standard of behavior than other adults in society. Every society recognizes the necessity to distinguish competent adults from incompetent adults in their behaviors and responsibilities for children. Parents who are deemed incompetent lose legal control of their own children; their children are then placed in the legal care of the state, which makes decisions about the children's future welfare.

## Teachers are Caregivers

Teachers have been given the role of caregiver *in loco parentis* because of their relationship with, duty to, and responsibility for our children. It is expected that they will fulfill the role of caregiver in every sense of the word.

Teachers are not just any adults. Teachers are believed to be highly qualified to guide, manage, evaluate, and instruct children. They have received specialized training that licenses them to compete for the privilege of being chosen to perform the role of caregiver. In addition to this, they are compensated for fulfilling the specific duties of caregiver. Therefore, there is no substantial argument that they should be exempted from the laws that govern child abuse and child neglect. Nor should caregivers be judged more lightly than parents.

In fact, many teachers and other school personnel have been charged, tried, and convicted of crimes against the students in their care. But as happens in every other brotherhood, the educational organization closes ranks when under fire and strives to protect itself rather than protect those for whose welfare it is responsible. Child abuse and child neglect in our country's schools are out of control. That's not new news.

A startling and terribly sad realization occurred when I began writing this book. In response to every media report that I reviewed about bullying or child abuse and neglect perpetrated by school personnel in this country, uncountable people admitted their own experiences of abuse and neglect at the hands of one or more teachers and other school personnel. There were very few responses to media articles by individuals who could say that he or she never had a teacher bully, neglect, or abuse him or her or someone close to him or her. It appears safe to say that though unreported, or perhaps unrecognized, child abuse and neglect has touched almost every American in some way.

# CHAPTER 5
# Laws Relating to the School's Responsibilities toward the Minor

> "If you do not take an interest in the affairs of government,
> then you are doomed to live under the rule of fools."
> —Plato

The legal rights of educators and responsible parties in the educational system have evolved beginning as far back as the 1700s. The well-established legal term *in loco parentis*, which means "in place of the parent," is still in use today and speaks of the breadth of responsibility given to the schools when the school is in physical control of a child.

## The Laws

In *loco parentis* is really the legal concept that gives schools the power to serve as a guardian of the student. The schools take custody of the child, and the child is no longer in the protection of the parent. The school has all the power of the parent and any other powers given to it by the legal system from which it derives its power.

Schools have a right and a duty through in loco parentis ("In Loco Parentis," *Education Law*) to educate and protect the child. That responsibility extends to the mandate that educational officials report any reasonable suspicion of child abuse or neglect to the proper authorities. This includes suspicion of child abuse or child neglect that they believe may be taking place or has taken place in other settings, including the home (Child Welfare Information Gateway 2016).

When an individual is mandated by law to report reasonable suspicion of child abuse or child neglect, that individual is called a mandated reporter. Educational officials are the mandated reporters. The teacher, the school, and the ancillary personnel are all educational officials. When the minor is in the jurisdiction of the school, these individuals are acting as caregiver *in loco parentis*. By law, the educational officials who suspect child abuse or child neglect are to make an immediate report to the state's child protection agency in the locality where the child is found or resides. All states have laws and statutes that mandate reporting (Child Welfare Information Gateway, 2016: 1).

*Caregiver* (Child Welfare Information Gateway, 2016: 4) is the term used to denote a responsible party in the child abuse and child neglect laws. In the following review of guidelines governing child abuse and neglect, note the language, which includes the caregiver as a responsible party equal to the parent. While laws governing child abuse and child neglect differ from state to state, primarily in their wording, all state laws are either aligned with or can be overridden by federal law.

The federal government's internet publication titled *Child Welfare Information Gateway* (2013) presents an excellent review of the "Definition of Child Abuse and Neglect in Federal Law." The most recent update from July 2016 includes the federal government's guidance to the states by setting a minimum set of "acts or behaviors that define child abuse and neglect." The Federal Child Abuse Prevention and Treatment Act (CAPTA) (42 USCA§5106g), as amended by the CAPTA Reauthorization Act of 2010, defines a *minimum* standard as:

> *"any recent act or failure to act, on the part of a parent or a caretaker, which results in death, serious physical or emotional harm, sexual*

*abuse or exploitation"* or *"An act or failure to act, which presents an imminent risk of serious harm."*

States' individual child abuse and child neglect statutes may differ. Information Gateway, however, provides federal civil definitions that determine the grounds for intervention by state agencies. The civil definitions are readily available and cover separately the following:

- Physical Neglect
- Educational Neglect
- Medical Neglect
- Emotional Neglect
- Sexual Abuse
- Emotional Abuse
- Physical Abuse

In 1985, the US Supreme Court, in a case addressing the issues of fourth amendment rights of students and search and seizure, handed down a ruling indicating that schools and the employees of the school have broad discretionary powers regarding the use of reasonableness, rather than the established standard of evidence. In its decision, the Supreme Court held that schools are not only acting out the role of the parent, but are also serving as the representatives of the state (Tucker 1987).

In 1995, in another fourth amendment case (*School District 47J v. Acton*), the Supreme Court stated that the schools act in loco parentis to the children, and have "such a portion of the power of the parent committed to his charge...as may be necessary to answer the purposes for which he was employed." Therefore, in the context of the public school, the reasonableness inquiry "cannot disregard the schools' custodial and tutelary responsibility for children." Essentially, public schools are recognized as being in a position of control and supervision over minors. Note the definitions of these terms:

- *Tutelary*: Tutelary means that someone is protecting or providing guardianship for another person, or simply someone acting as a guardian.
- *Custodian*: A custodian is someone who is in charge and responsible for a child.

Clearly, the school as an entity and everyone affiliated with that organization has enormous legal power. The legal power given to the schools and school personnel comes with enormous legal responsibility.

## The Schools' Responsibilities

Very little is said about the schools' legal responsibilities beyond education. But the school does, in fact, have other legal responsibilities beyond a typical parent's obligations. First, the school has a responsibility to determine probable or likely events that may be injurious to a child and devise ways to protect that child from those potentially injurious events.

For instance, a parent is not legally obligated to seek out the neighborhood bullies and predict that his or her child may be hurt in some way by any one or all of the bullies. In addition to this, knowing there is a bully in the neighborhood does not legally obligate the parent to report or prevent that bully from harming others.

Conversely, the school is required to be watchful of bullying. They must be aware of bullies in the school. The school has an obligation to correct each and every bully and protect each and every child from harm.

The sense in that responsibility being given to the school is, of course, the reality that the school is the caregiver *in loco parentis* to every child within the jurisdiction of the school. The parent has only the legal obligation for his or her own child and in fact has absolutely no legal authority to discipline or even interact with a child to whom he or she is not a parent, guardian, or caregiver. An individual child in a school is parented by the school, and every child in the school also has the same parent. Just as a parent has to protect one child in the family from his or her sibling's bad behavior, the school has this responsibility with all the children in its jurisdiction.

The second way the school is more legally accountable than the parent is that the school must protect the constitutional and civil rights of each child. Parents are not responsible to anticipate and protect their child from constitutional or civil rights violations. The school must do both—anticipate and protect.

For example, the parent is not required to have separate toilet facilities to accommodate the needs of each child's sexual identification. Nor are the child's parents responsible to have toilet facilities segregated by age. The same holds true for play equipment and participation in various activities. One of the most important elements of civil rights protection is the school's obligation to seek out any child who has disabilities and who may be entitled to special education services. Child Find is a legal requirement under The Individuals with Disabilities Education Act (United States Department of Education "Title 34: Education," IDEA 2017). The school must evaluate any child that it knows or suspects of having a disability from birth to the age of twenty-one. If a need is found, it must then be addressed to assure that the child is able to acquire free appropriate public education (FAPE).

Child Find is not optional; it is a mandate. After all, the only reason the child is in the jurisdiction of the school is because the parent is mandated to provide a means of adequate education, and the school is a highly funded public organization with the single goal to educate children. It makes sense that the schools should be responsible to identify children who need special assistance. Take away the primary and perhaps the only reason that schools exist, namely education, and the child would not have to leave the care of the parent or caregiver of the parents' choice—public schools would not exist.

## Summary

Laws that apply to the school's responsibilities to students are broad and varied, and these laws are heavily intertwined. Schools must provide for the child's educational and safety needs and must protect the child's constitutional and civil rights.

Consider the crossover between civil rights laws, special education laws, and general education laws, in loco parentis, child abuse and neglect laws, and educational neglect statutes. Any violation of a law written to protect a child and meet the child's educational and safety needs violates the child's rights. The violation of constitutional and civil rights occurs when a child is deprived of an education or numerous other civil rights in the care of the educational institution. Violations of education law result in child educational neglect. Child educational neglect is a violation of state laws and most likely a violation of the child's constitutional and civil rights.

As you will read through the next chapters, consider what you now know about the schools' rights and responsibilities. The many laws concerning minors in the United States dictate the behaviors of schools as entities and teachers and other personnel in the school setting when the child is in the custody of the school and the school is the caregiver.

# CHAPTER 6
# Child Abuse

> "Let your heart feel for the affliction
> and distresses of every one..."
> —GEORGE WASHINGTON (1732–1799)

Child abuse is arguably the proper term for what we casually call teacher bullying. It wasn't long into researching and writing that the original title for this book, *Teacher Bullies*, became obsolete. There is very little literature about teachers who are bullies. That's not only because it's a forbidden topic—in the United States there's a long history of keeping quiet about bullying, abuse, and neglect in this countries many bastions and brotherhoods. Realistically, we all know that any adult who bullies a child is abusive. Although rarely called by name, the literature is teeming with references to incidents where children were abused in schools. Even in the most ambitious media reports, incidences of child abuse and child neglect perpetrated by teachers and other school personnel are described, often in detail, but are rarely given a name.

The Child Abuse Prevention and Treatment Act was signed into law by President Richard Nixon on January 31, 1974 (Child Welfare Information Gateway 2017). The purpose of the act was to provide funding for the prevention, identification, and treatment of child abuse and neglect. CAPTA created the National Center on Child Abuse and Neglect (NCCAN) within the Department of Health Education and Welfare (now the Department of Health and Human Services, HHS), and it established a national clearinghouse on child abuse and neglect information. All the fifty states had child abuse reporting laws, but the legal framework for child protection work was often incomplete and unnecessarily complex, and there was a lack of coordination in the child protective process. Federal legislation provided a broad framework and minimal acceptable standards to guide the states and provide the legislative unity and funding to ensure the safety of the nation's children.

These federal child abuse statutes contain three subdivisions, each oriented to a specific set of illegal behaviors: child sexual abuse, child physical abuse, and child psychological abuse. Each of these forms of child abuse is present in America's schools.

## Child Sexual Abuse

Sexual abuse is defined by the Child Abuse Prevention and Treatment Act as:

> "The employment, use, persuasion, enticement, inducement, or coercion of any child to engage in, or assist any other person to engage in, any sexually explicit conduct or simulation of such conduct for the producing a visual depiction of such conduct; or the rape, and in cases of caretaker or inter-familial relationships, statutory rape, molestation, prostitution, or other form of sexual exploitation of children, or incest with children" (Child Welfare Information Gateway 2013).

Sexual abuse perpetrated by teachers is a rampant problem. Teachers in the United States have sexually abused students as young as preschool age. The sheer number of sexual abuse cases in the schools is overwhelming. The cases cited here are simply brief examples. All cases referenced include citations and will lead you to further information and examples. When you begin to research these cases, you will be both horrified and petrified for your own children.

- Kindergarten children: In Ohio, a thirty two year old kindergarten teacher was charged with twenty-three counts of illegal use of a minor in nudity-oriented material and two additional counts for attempts of the same crime; twenty-five in total. He had been filming his kindergarten students in the bathroom. The crimes were accidentally discovered because he had been charged with other crimes and the spy camera pictures of the children were found in a search of his house (Zachariah 2015).
- Elementary children: In California, a sixty-one-year-old teacher was arrested for felony of molestation of twenty-three school children between the ages of seven to ten. He was charged with lewd acts (Gonzalez 2015).
- High school children: In New York, a high school teacher was instructing students on how to seduce instructors. In his physics lab, the students he targeted were given A's on their papers if they cooperated in his manipulations. He was indicted on thirty-six counts, including six criminal sex acts when he took students home and engaged in sex for over a span of four years (Crime Sider Staff 2014).

There is little disagreement regarding what constitutes child sexual abuse. Generally, the existing laws cover child sexual abuse offences when perpetrated by teachers. However, the consequences for perpetrating child sexual abuse are often diminished when teachers are the perpetrators, at times authorities calling sexual abuse "an inappropriate relationship with a minor" and various other creative phrases. But the major exceptions to the prosecution of teachers who sexually abuse minors begin to be argued as the child—under age eighteen—move closer to adulthood. There appears to be an epidemic of young female teachers who have become perpetrators of child sexual abuse of their middle and high school students.

A recent example of sexual behavior in the teaching profession is the newsworthy controversy where a teacher is accused of doing a lap dance as a birthday gift for a fifteen-year-old male student. The *Washington Times* and other print media reported that a Houston middle school teacher had been charged with having an improper relationship with a student (Chasmar 2014). She allegedly gave a boy a lap dance in front of the entire class.

Apparently, the forty-two-year-old female teacher thought this was a good birthday present for the student. According to the police, she rubbed her hands all over his body, got down on her knees and put her head between the boy's legs, all to a song chosen for the special occasion. There's more to the story, but it's just more of the same. Naturally the teacher was charged, but the charge was an improper relationship with a student rather than child sexual abuse.

Dissecting all the issues related to any form of child sexual abuse helps each of us understand the damage this abuse causes the victim. What do you know, and what don't you know? Did the teacher have permission to come into physical contact with the student? Was it sexual in nature? Did the minor feel it was OK to stop the action? Was the student even given time to think about what to do? Continue to ask yourself the question about whether this teacher's behavior falls within the definition of child sexual abuse. Compare this to child sexual abuse in sports and within the priesthood. When is it safe for a young man studying for the priesthood, or a team member, or any young adult to say no to sexual behaviors when these behaviors come from someone in a role of power?

Is sexual contact OK between adults and minors because some people find the lap dance incident amusing? How would a fifteen-year-old boy appropriately reject this teacher's behavior in front of the whole class? Would he be ridiculed if he had refused her birthday gift? Is any single form of sexual behavior between an adult and a minor worse than another, or is it all child sexual abuse?

Consider another student whose sexual orientation might not be clear to him or her. What if his or her religious beliefs or that of his or her family were violated? Would your reaction be the same? Was this teacher's behavior toward his or her student sexually abusive?

If you behave this way toward one of your own teenage children, will that be sexual abuse? What if a neighbor or a babysitter or a relative behaves the same way with your teenage son? Or your daughter? Check the published list of sex offenders in your area and look at their offences. Is anyone listed as a child sexual perpetrator for touching a child? Well, of course, the list is long—sexually touching a minor is a common crime.

Teachers are the caregivers for your children, and they have legal jurisdiction and legal responsibility for your children when they are in school or in a school-related activity. Whether the child is five or fifteen, the definition of child sexual abuse and the laws in every one of the fifty states continues to apply.

The response to the fifteen-year-old boy's birthday present likely included dismissing the teacher's behavior. Because the student turned fifteen on that day, some may believe that he was old enough to say no, and some may say that it wasn't a crime because the young man didn't say no. Others may believe that he was enjoying the attention—how do they know how he felt? But that reasoning misses the point; the behavior was illegal and inappropriate for the teacher. Should we change the law? Will it, therefore, be acceptable and legal for a male teacher to give a lap dance to any of his female students who turns fifteen?

The cases of child sexual abuse in the schools go on and on, with teachers impregnating fourteen-year-olds, using metal rulers to attempt an abortion on a student; piercing students' stomachs in class; raping young students and then killing them; having sex with multiple high school students at once; or having sex with middle school girls and videoing the events, and much, much, more.

Most cases of teacher-child sexual abuse within the school system reviewed for this book were recognized for what they are: teacher-child sexual abuse. But the recognition of child abuse crimes only happens when someone comes forward. So, what about those students who never speak up?

There are about 50,094,000 public school students. The teacher-student sexual abuse numbers are horrific. Thomas Plante, a psychology professor at the Santa Clara University and recognized expert on sexual abuse, estimated that about 5 percent of school teachers and coaches have sexual encounters with their students. What's 5 percent of the 3.5 million teachers in the United States? According to these percentages, about 175,000 teachers and coaches have sexual encounters with their students.

When children are sexually abused, there are two types of abuse involved: sexual abuse and psychological abuse. The psychological damage that can result from a child being sexually used and abused by someone who has power over him or her is significant. This is not an improper relationship with a minor. Every type of child abuse and child neglect brings with it a psychological injury. Child psychological abuse is covered in the next section, but it is a subsection of each type of child abuse and child neglect. Child abuse occurs when children are powerless to act for themselves, to protect themselves, or to access protection from their caregivers. Child psychological abuse begins as soon as the child sexual abuse occurs.

When child abuse and child neglect cases are uncovered, they may take years to prosecute, and there is an enormous toll on the lives of all the victims. Just read about the dreadful sexual abuse cover-ups in our nation's K–12 schools and universities.

If you don't have any children in your life, does this affect you? In just one 2014 case, the Los Angeles Unified School District paid out a $139 million settlement in a sexual abuse case involving eighty-one students. And that was only a part of the cost. Now add in the attorneys, court costs, mediation, discovery, depositions, and the list goes on. If you have children in the schools, you might try to calculate what that money can be used for on behalf of the Los Angeles students. If you're overwhelmed with working to pay the bills, or if your children are in private schools, remember this: These are taxpayer dollars. You're paying for education and then paying again when educators burn up tax dollars to settle criminal suits.

The money doesn't belong to the schools. The tax money you earn at your jobs and businesses pay teachers' salaries, and it pays for very expensive insurance policies to cover lawsuits after what is commonly a $5 million deductible (Stokes 2016). One lawsuit costs $139 million. And each year, schools spend millions buying these policies. Sometimes, the insurance companies don't pay anyway because of some other problem with the policy terms. There are innumerable lawsuits paid out because of some type of child abuse and child neglect in our schools. The schools are liable because they employ, and continue to employ, the perpetrators, even though they have been warned about the teachers' abusive behaviors.

The Los Angeles school district ignored, denied, or purged thousands of child abuse reports (Himes 2014). The administrators were fully responsible for these crimes going on from 1983 through 2009, and they covered for the teacher. Look at your $300 million tax dollars paid out by the Los Angeles school district in just the past four years to settle a wave of child sexual abuse lawsuits alone (Neff 2016). That does not in any way include payouts for other forms of child abuse or child neglect. Los Angeles is only one school district out of the more than thirteen thousand in the United States.

The Los Angeles Unified School District has recently agreed to pay $88 million to settle another teacher sex-abuse lawsuit involving thirty children at two elementary schools (Winton and Blume 2016). In case you think there's something special about Los Angeles schools, you are wrong. This is just an example of one school district, but not unlike what's happening in schools all over the country. Read the accounts.

When schools discover there is a sexual perpetrator in their midst, they do what's become known as "pass the trash" (Taguchi and Shubailat 2017). Schools release the teacher without filing a report with the proper authorities (Reilly 2016). They don't want to go through the trouble of a firing process. The perpetrator moves on to another school, and the sexual abuse begins again with another group of children. Because the schools don't want to be bothered, multitudes of children and their families have suffered unimaginable pain and anguish. Children's lives have been changed forever. Are the professionals who are mandated reporters but have passed the trash charged and prosecuted? Have they lost their jobs? I can't find any records of consequences for those who allowed life-damaging behaviors to go without prosecution. The brotherhood protects the bastion at all costs and no doubt engenders great rewards within the system for saving their districts from having to be bothered with the problem. They let the sexually abused children suffer and set up a new group for abuse.

You pay for all the abuse committed by teachers and other school personnel. Are you concerned about some politician wanting to go to war? You should be equally concerned about what you can do in your own backyard and how your taxes are being abused. When you file your next state and federal income taxes, review how huge chunks of your money are spent. How much can the children of Los Angeles benefit from another $300 million?

We spend a lot of classroom time and lots of money on teaching children to not bully. Yet there are rarely, if ever, child-child bullying cases that can be compared to the teacher-child cases of abuse and neglect. Why don't we teach the children in our schools how to recognize teacher-child abuse and neglect and what to do about it?

## Child Physical Abuse

Child physical abuse has been defined as:

> *"A non-accidental physical injury, ranging from minor bruises to severe injuries, such as breaks, concussions, or death when it is inflicted by a parent, caregiver, or other person responsible for the child. The injuries have occurred as a result of punching, hitting, and beating, kicking, biting, throwing, stabbing, choking, or burning. "Hitting" includes using a hand, stick, strap, or other object. Any other injury that harms the child is also abuse when it is inflicted by a parent, caregiver, or other person who has responsibility for the child. The injury*

*is abuse whether or not the injury was intended"* (Child Welfare Information Gateway 2013).

In Queens, New York, at PS 118 in Saint Albans, a teacher was reported to have tormented and then beaten a ten-year-old student (Nolan and Siemaszko 2015). The male teacher was caught due to an audio recording that was secretly made by a classmate on January 23, 2015. Reports show that the child was begging the teacher to stop assaulting him as the sounds of hitting were recorded. The boy was accused of cheating. A female assistant in the classroom had to pull the male teacher off the student. But the teacher continued to berate and curse even after he was pulled off the student.

Another incident was caught on security cameras. A West Feliciana Parish teacher in Louisiana was videoed kicking, slapping, and berating a first grader (Wallace 2017). The teacher also made the child wait until last in the lunch line and then took part of his lunch for herself. A witness said that the same young child was crying in the hallway as the teacher had him up against the wall. She had a stick. Witnesses said that the teacher was yelling at one student in a loud and degrading manner because the boy was not walking like he was supposed to.

In another case of physical abuse in Chesapeake, Virginia, a ten-year-old boy's hand was crushed in a heavy metal door as the teacher slammed the door to the "scream room" (Robinson 2011). The school staff turned the fan on to drown out his screams. Take a moment to read this report as it details the obvious psychological abuse that accompanies the physical abuse. Note that this case also demonstrates medical neglect. This case is covered in more detail in chapter 8.

In Oakland, California, a security guard was caught on camera repeatedly punching a wheelchair-bound student in the head (Warren 2014). After punching the student who suffers from cerebral palsy, he dumped him on the floor where he was later found. Other students, who defended the security guard, said that the guard's actions were justified because the boy spat at him.

The San FranciscoSFGate.com reported that a family was contemplating a lawsuit against a fifty-eight-year-old teacher in Fremont, California (Lee 2014). A nine-year-old boy and other witnesses said that the teacher slapped him twice. The teacher reportedly thought the boy was mocking him for putting a decimal point in the wrong place.

In Houston, Texas, a teacher was accused of choking a student in the classroom. The Houston Independent School District reported that the history teacher was removed from the classroom and the student was given aide (Barajas 2016). The criminal complaint indicated that the teacher wrapped a shirt around an eleven-year-old student's neck and choked him until he passed out. The teacher reported that he was playing.

A high school principal was accused of shouting expletives at a fourteen-year-old in Pittsburgh, Pennsylvania. The principal and a resource officer beating up the fourteen-year-old boy was also recorded (Price 2017). The school resource officer beat the boy, knocking out one of his teeth and bruising him. Then the boy was allegedly taken out of the range of the camera's capture and Tasered several times.

I'm not surprised when child abuse happens in other countries, and I don't think I'm alone in that realization. We may be appalled, talk about other countries as being uncivilized, compare ourselves favorably to other countries, and feel superior. But every type of child abuse that is committed in other countries is also committed in the United States. Americans go on child-saving missions around the world and often publicize their foreign adoptions and having saved children from some unimaginable wrong. But unimaginable wrongs happen in America. There are hundreds of thousands of children in foster care in the United States. Children here are as needy as children are who live far away. A child is a child, and one's pain cannot be weighed against the pain of another.

In our schools, children are being abused and neglected every day, just as they are in their homes and towns around the world. It does seem criminal that we throw an incalculable amount of hard-earned tax money at the schools and yet are incapable of educating anyone who is not easy to educate. Children, especially those with special needs, are the poor refugees of the United States. They are an inconvenience. They are some of the victims of teacher-child physical abuse, but no one is exempted. Every age, race, size, and shape is represented in reports from the press.

The cases of child physical abuses described here are used to illustrate that there is, indeed, a problem are only a smattering of what is really happening in our schools. These examples and thousands more like them are easily found from an Internet search. Teacher-child physical abuse is alive and well in schools all around America.

## Child Emotional Abuse

Emotional abuse, which is also called child psychological abuse, is perhaps the most devastating kind of abuse a child can experience. Emotional abuse is almost always present when other types of maltreatment are identified. Take away the other kinds of abuse, and child emotional abuse can be difficult to diagnose and very hard to prove. Unfortunately, some concrete or specific evidence of harm or mental injury must be acutely present before child welfare is able to intervene.

Child emotional abuse is:

> "...a pattern of behavior that impairs a child's emotional development or sense of self-worth." Gateway goes on to indicate that "emotional abuse may include constant criticism, threats, or rejection, as well as withholding love, support, or guidance" (Child Welfare Information Gateway. 2013).

Psychological abuse has lifelong negative effects; it seems to imprint in ways that are difficult to reverse or even mediate. Child psychological abuse is really the toughest kind of abuse to overcome. But think about any case of abuse you know about from your own history. Perhaps you have a friend or family member who has been a victim of abuse. Surely there's some story of abuse you've become familiar with from the media. What you'll see in most abuse cases is that when the abuse is visible, the victim has a fighting chance of garnering support to stop the abuser or to find justice. Whether that abuse is physical or sexual or it comes in some form of abandonment or neglect, it's visible to the onlooker. There are marks or scars. The child goes without food, clothing, education, or medical care. The abuse is visible, so we know it has happened. But child emotional abuse is not always readily visible. What we know is what the child says. What we see is its effect on the child's moods, their interests, their affects, their behaviors, and their performance.

In the school setting, child emotional abuse takes many forms, including those listed in Gateway's definition of emotional abuse, such as constant criticism, threats, or rejection and withholding love, support, or guidance. The child emotional abuse component is apparent in all the examples presented in the previous sections on child physical abuse. Following physical abuse and sometimes lasting a lifetime, children feel bad, confused, hurt, angry, helpless, useless, thrown away, minimized, like trash, and any or all of a hundred other negative emotions a human can feel.

Emotional abuse is sometimes a less obvious outcome in cases of child sexual abuse. The only people I've heard say that child sexual abuse was emotionally good for a child were the perpetrators who often talk about how good it made the child feel and how much the child liked being touched sexually. Long into life, people enter therapy to deal with the long-term effects of child sexual abuse. For many people, sexual abuse has defined them, limited their self-esteem, and caused them to live with unrelenting shame and fear that someone could find out they are, or were, damaged.

The long-term effects of child emotional abuse have been investigated for years. In the Hart and Brassard abstract from a 1987 *American Psychologist* journal article, the researchers clearly indicated that child psychological maltreatment is potentially more harmful than other forms of child abuse and neglect and that it "poses a serious mental health threat" (Hart and Brassard, 1987).

Children are expected to move into adulthood and have fully productive lives. But the psychological abuse of children is long-lasting. It has devastating consequences. In an American Academy of Pediatrics' report published online on July 30, 2002, and reaffirmed and updated in the August 2012 print issue of *Pediatrics*, the contributors reported that constantly belittling, threatening, or ignoring children can be as damaging to their mental health as physical or sexual abuse (Hibbard, Barlow, and MacMillan 2012, 372–8). Research shows that the effects of psychological abuse and neglect can be profound and long-lasting, ranging from problems with brain development and a failure to grow properly to problems with behavior and relating to other difficulties. The extensive 2012 clinical report perhaps covers this topic better than any other single report and it is online, available to guest readers.

In an interview with Consumer Health Day, Jennifer Goodwin wrote about the problems of psychological abuse of young people. She quoted Alec Miller, PhD, chief of child and adolescent psychology at Montefiore Medical Center in New York City, who reported that "psychological abuse is so insidious, and is not as easily recognized by the victim or other family members" (Goodwin, 2012).

Goodwin continued, quoting Dr. Harriet MacMillan, a professor in the departments of psychiatry, behavioral neurosciences, and pediatrics at McMaster University in Ontario, Canada. McMillan, who coauthored multiple journal articles for the Academy of Pediatrics, reported that exposure to other types of maltreatment are linked to very negative outcomes in mental health, along with cognitive impairments and impaired social development. She emphasizes that "psychological maltreatment is just as harmful as other types of maltreatment"

We don't have far to look to find examples of child emotional abuse in America's schools. Gateway's list of behaviors that are emotionally abusive, which includes constant criticism, threats, or rejection as well as withholding love, support, or guidance, brings us back to what many call bullying by teachers. But bullying happens when the playing field is near equal; when teachers behave in these ways it is emotional abuse.

On the list of emotionally abusive behaviors is withholding love. Perhaps no one expects teachers to love our children, certainly not in the way parents love their children. But teachers who love children are probably far less likely to emotionally abuse them, far less likely to withhold approval, and more likely to provide support and guidance. Yet if you're seriously involved in any aspect of education, you know that there are teachers who don't like children.

Emotional abuse is a broad issue. When a teacher gets in the face of a student and screams, who will evaluate the outcome for the child? When a teacher cannot control his or her emotions or is guilty of berating or humiliating a child, who is witness to this abuse? Maybe the child is frightened. If a child comes from a family where psychological abuse is not present, the child can be shocked and confused when a teacher humiliates him or her for forgetting a book.

If children who bully were held accountable as adults, they would be prosecuted for abuse. But when teachers commit child psychological abuse, they don't report to the principal's office. They don't get suspended from school.

Child welfare authorities have the power to remove children from their own parents. Adults are prosecuted for psychologically abusive behavior toward children. They are sent to anger-management classes and parenting classes. They are sentenced to jail.

Teachers are the caregivers of our children when the children are at school. They are responsible for the psychological safety and psychological well-being of students. Does this mean that teachers are responsible for the nurturance of every child in every way? No, that task is best left to the people who have a lifetime obligation to the child, to the parents who love and are bonded to the child. However, as with every licensed professional, there is an obligation to do no harm.

Teachers are tasked with the responsibility of imparting knowledge to every one of the children in their care. There should be no exceptions. It is impossible to expect a child or student of any age to learn from someone who is emotionally abusive toward him or her.

Teachers don't have the right to select which children are worthy of an education. The simple act of selection is an act of child psychological abuse of the child who has been ignored or neglected. Teachers are not entitled to decide who they will and won't teach. They are paid for a specified number of hours of work. They have negotiated for these work hours, and they are quick to ensure they are not required to work outside these hours. They are highly paid because they are supposed to be highly competent and trained to accommodate their teaching to meet the needs of every child without discrimination and without inflicting child emotional abuse.

The child is not in the classroom to accommodate the personal or professional needs of the teacher. I have heard more than one teacher or administrator silently agree that some children simply can't or won't be taught. They have already decided that they will single out a student for different treatment. So, they teach to their favorites. There are several studies that indicate teachers pick out children who they find attractive, attentive, and well-behaved. Is that understandable? Does it make sense that the teacher can make choices as to who he or she will educate? Is that discrimination a form of child psychological abuse that will last a lifetime for the child who has been rejected?

So, what is the standard of behavior we assume, no, require, from those who carry the responsibility for the educational future of our children? Is the teachers' behavior emotionally abusive when they yell at the children in their care? Is the teacher emotionally abusive when the child is sent to some form of detention for forgetting a book? What about ignoring a child's questions or requests for materials or instructions for a missed assignment? How about humiliating a child who squirms too much in his or her seat? Is it the squirming child or the one who can't remember the page number or their book? Which child is to be demeaned? Which student needs to be humiliated? Who should be taunted by the teacher? Or worse, does the teacher allow other students to do their bidding? Does the teacher allow other students to taunt their classmate, the one who has the greasy hair, maybe the forgetful student, or the student who is slow to answer? When are any of these behaviors acceptable? Never, of course. So, what do we call caregiving when it becomes ugly and punitive? And how is this anything other than child emotional abuse?

There are lots of examples of blatant emotional abuse in the school system. In some of these cases, parents and sometimes other students have gone through the normal routes to stop a teacher's emotional abuse. Yahoo Health reported the story of a child whose teacher was emotionally abusive to the students in his classroom. The father was smart enough to follow the rules and then have his son carry a recorder with him to class. He then went to the school and reported the problems to administration, but the teacher denied the allegation. The school asked for time to investigate.

It's hard to tell what investigate means when you're investigating yourself. But after the investigation was complete, the father received a letter stating that there was not sufficient evidence that there was verbal abuse. Now remember, the abuse occurred in a classroom where others were present. It was only then that the father played the recording for the school board. The teacher was heard yelling vulgar and frightening threats (Miva 2012).

Children are often at school with their teacher for more hours than they are with their parents. What would you do with a parent who behaves like this abusive teacher, toward his or her children? Threatening or causing children to be chronically fearful, managing them by intimidation, or other abusive behaviors are all prohibited under the child psychological abuse laws. Teachers are trained how to manage diverse children in a classroom. They tout their higher education. They say they are better trained than most parents.

In a group of recorded incidents, students caught teachers on camera (Strauss 2012). Watch the video of Julio being bullied by his teacher. No one believed him when he complained of being bullied. So, he recorded some of the incidents on his cell phone, such threats as "I will kick your [vulgarity] from here to kingdom come until I'm eighty years old." The tirade was prolonged, threatening, and abusive. The teacher was put on administrative leave only after the video was aired.

When a person of any age is threatened with physical harm, he or she is fearful. It isn't called bullying. This threat is sometimes called a terrorist threat. Other times, it constitutes at the least emotional abuse.

There are hundreds of articles to be found on this type of child emotional abuse. Hundreds of reports gratefully come to light through the press. However, the iceberg theory would hold that there are actually thousands more. We only know of about 10 percent or less.

The numbers of people of every age who have commented on these cases are absolutely overwhelming. For every report in the print or electronic media, there are people of all ages, educational levels, cultures, ethnicities, and locales who respond with their own stories. Sometimes there are ten comments per article, sometimes hundreds. Fascinatingly, there are a few people who chime in with their great experiences but use their positive experiences to deny others reality of child psychological abuse in the schools. Their stance seems to be "It didn't happen to me, so it didn't happen to you."

Some of the comments following media reports of teacher-child abuse are heartbreaking. But one thing they generally have in common is anger over being abused by teachers and the school system, even decades after the events. The results of teacher-child emotional abuse are far-reaching and in themselves delineate the breadth and width of the problem.

And there are other kinds of child emotional abuse in America's schools. A six-year-old child was forced to eat lunch alone behind a cardboard divider in the cafeteria because he was one minute late for school (Warren 2015). How ludicrous is it to punish a child who has no control over his parent's timeliness? Guess who handed out this punishment. The principal. Warren reported that the young child's isolation, sitting away from the other children, included a cup with a D for detention. The Oregon child's parents say that their child felt humiliated by the public shaming. How long will the child remember that shaming? How will children who have been publicly shamed think of their educational opportunities in the future? What did the six-year-old learn from being late-shamed?

The *Inquisitr* reported that an autistic fifth grader received awards from teachers at the term's end (Baldas and Zaniewski.2015). The teachers created the awards. They ranged from "most likely to succeed" to "drama king." They let the kids vote for the recipients. At the end of the year, at the field day ceremony, this eleven-year-old child was given awards with titles he didn't understand such as "most gullible" and "drama king." His mother had not been notified in advance. She said that the teachers gave the other kids an approval to be mean. The school's motto is "Teach the mind and touch the heart." A better motto to live by, which would solve some of the abuse in schools, would be, "Touch the heart to teach the mind."

Writing for the Huffington Post, Rebecca Klein reported that parents of an elementary school boy said their son was ordered to lick his desk clean after he doodled on the surface (Klein 2015). The school said the matter would be handled confidentially, and the teacher was still teaching, not missing a single day. Why is the teacher still in the classroom? This may be the result of secret employment contracts that bind the school to nondisclosure; when complaints are brought against the teacher, the complaints and the results of the school's investigation are sealed; the person bringing the complaint is not allowed to see the result. The agreement is written into the teacher's contract—it serves the purpose of protecting everyone in the brotherhood, the teacher, the principal, and the administration. These are publicly funded jobs; all information regarding the behavior on the job of those who are paid with public money should be available to the public unless the job is highly classified. The public has a right to know the consequences when a public employee is guilty of child abuse. We know the likely consequences if a senator or a congressman is guilty of something as ordinary as name-calling; why don't we know what happens with a teacher? How in the world did this fifth grade teacher even get a job—any kind of job? And how in the world did the American public school system get to be a secret organization with secret rules and secret consequences?

In another form of overt psychological abuse, a school replaced a blind child's cane with a foam pool noodle (Stampler 2014). In a media article, it was reported that the eight-year-old child's cane was taken away as punishment for bad behavior on the bus. This obviously put the child in danger and so certainly should qualify for child endangerment. But it was a visible sign to others that the boy was being punished. The humiliating act, which was ongoing for two weeks, could be seen by everyone except, of course, by the blind student. The mother said, "That's his eyes." Most of us would be horrified if our child's glasses were taken away; how about their eyes? Well, the responsible administration at this school didn't seem to be able to think about that logically. What are the odds that other decisions are made in the same way at this Kansas school? What is the likelihood that people who lack acumen regarding psychological and safety consequences might not have the ability to teach other, more complex topics?

In three recent cases of psychological abuse, each extremely humiliating, the undertones are all sexual. In each of these cases there are potential civil rights violations. But they are also frightening and embarrassing to the children involved. When an authority figure, the school acting as guardian, harms our children, who can intervene?

Joel Arak reported for CBS News that at Rancho Bernardo High School in California, an assistant principal lifted girls' skirts in front of parents and boys to check if the girls were wearing thongs! She told girls who were wearing thongs to go home and change because thongs and dancing might cause sexual assaults. A search shows no readily available research that connects wearing thongs and sexual assault, although some may exist. Rape and sexual assault is a tragic and life-changing trauma for the victims, male or female. Creating a spectacle before a school dance can certainly be another kind of trauma.

Then there is the obvious problem with publicly displaying girls' underwear, on demand, to anyone present. Some of the attractive, unfettered young females may have thought that this was amusing. I didn't find that anyone said one way or another. But if only one young woman was embarrassed, humiliated, or fearful, that's child emotional abuse. Even without those reactions from the students, this was likely a civil rights violation. Perhaps one of the girls was shy, or her religion forbade her body being exposed, or her underwear was unattractive, or in tatters, or she was experiencing a menstrual cycle. How long would it be before she could forgive or trust again? How does that one, or many, feel about the violation of her privacy at the hands of an educational institution? Was this child emotional abuse?

In the next case, the Supreme Court ruled that a girl's civil rights were violated. School personnel strip-searched an eighth-grade girl because they got a tip from another student who said she had gotten some medication from her. Because the school thought she might have prescribed ibuprofen hidden somewhere on or in her body, she was told to strip down to her underwear. The court said that the tip—which no one validated—was not "an indication of danger." Yes, her civil rights were violated, but the girl was also severely humiliated. She spent the years between the ages of thirteen and nineteen fighting for her rights. Finally, the Supreme Court reached a decision on her fight and upheld her fourth amendment rights. If this was your daughter, would you consider this child abuse?

A widely broadcasted incident showed about two dozen young children who were forced to pull down their pants (Wheeler 2015). It's doubtful whether if even their parents have ever made such a demand. Now, school authority figures had all the children exposed there, with uncovered private parts and underwear. Why? Feces were found on the gym floor. Parents and students alike were angry. But did they find any feces in anyone's underwear? If they did, how would they know whether that child left feces on the gym floor? Would there be a DNA test to determine who it belonged to? Have an inquisition? Some young children don't wipe well.

Would that child be interrogated? And if the school discovered the culprit, what would they do? How many young children pulled down their underwear—exposed their pubic areas—in front of other children and teachers and were not emotionally abused?

A common problem with young children is functional encopresis. This is a condition where the child, out of fear of defecation, withholds fecal matter in the bowel. But at times when the child is very relaxed, say playing or napping, the body involuntarily ejects the feces. It's a humiliating problem, but one that can be fixed by a visit to a trained professional. Surely, the school has a trained counselor who knew about this and was consulted. Surely, all these well-educated people understand that humiliation would make this problem oh so much worse. The child who is found out by people outside the family would be seriously traumatized. This kind of emotionally abusive event could have a lifelong impact. The lack of education of the school staff is only outweighed by their overall lack of judgment.

Research in child emotional and psychological abuse and neglect affirms the instinctive belief that constantly belittling, threatening, or ignoring children can be as damaging to their mental health as physical or sexual abuse. Every type of abuse does psychological damage when physical abuse, sexual abuse, or any other form of abuse is added to the emotional abuse. Psychological abuse arises from victimization of any type, and the victim has many forms of abuse to live with. I've talked to the parents of children who were victims of emotional abuse; many have said, "Thank goodness it wasn't physical (or sexual)..." But the victims react differently. Children often say things like, "I wish he would have just hit me," or "I wish he had beaten on me like my friend's dad does..."

A sheriff and his deputies in Georgia held all nine hundred students at a school and conducted a search (Balko 2017). There was no suspicion, no evidence, and no specific precipitating event that day. The constitutional rights of every student were violated. Students complained that they were touched inappropriately, even groped. The school administration was definitely on board with that plan. They were looking for drugs. The sheriff had just done a thorough drug search one month earlier. Nothing was found. He apparently believed he didn't do a good job, so he did it again. Nothing was found during either search. Was there any emotional abuse involved when the students were groped by a sheriff?

An eight-year-old student in an Othello, Washington school was told to unclog the toilet with his bare hands (Moran 2015). The boy reported the clogged toilet to the teacher, and he was ordered to clean it out. The janitor wasn't called. The teacher was reprimanded. The parents were horrified. The child had flushed the toilet several times and it didn't go down. The parents transferred their son to another school. Do you think this is a rare or unusual behavior for a teacher? Think again.

A prekindergarten student was forced by his teacher to clean a toilet with his bare hands (Korn 2015). The four-year-old was humiliated. The teacher had admitted what she did, said the child had clogged the toilet before with too much paper, and that she wanted to teach the child a lesson. The Florida child was humiliated and thought everyone was watching him. If there were others around, they probably would have been watching. How would they have felt? Is school now a safe, loving, and supportive environment for four-year-olds?

Child abuse around the country is rampant; we see examples of it every day in the media. Some groups, such as ChildSafe and Childhelp, are moving forces in the prevention of child abuse of every kind. We have myriad campaigns, talks, workshop, books, and articles on the subject practically every day. We say that there is no safe place for child abuse in this country. We all know about child abuse. Supposedly.

Thousands of children who are molested by religious men and women have suffered imponderable years from the emotional abuse of being victimized by people with power over them. Not many people will take the word of a child over a priest or a coach when the child says or shows signs that he or she is being emotionally abused. This is no different when the abuser is a powerful authority, responsible for the education of our children and supported by a powerful bastion with access to the taxpayers' dollars. Many parents feel helpless. Some have been victims of child emotional abuse in schools when they were young. People say, "There's nothing I can do about it," or "Everyone knows you can't win." The brotherhood is too powerful.

## Summary

When children are abused in any way, they are also emotionally abused. Yes, all forms of abuse are painful, and physical wounds may take a long time to heal, but the accompanying emotional wounds are traumatizing. When child emotional abuse occurs without a co-occurring abuse, the damage may be multiplied because of the questioning responses to that abuse. Child emotional abuse traumas persist and create havoc throughout the child's life.

Teachers have a responsibility to the state, the community, the district, the school, the students, and to themselves. Earning an impressive living often means hard work. In any factory in America, every widget that passes through the hands of an assembly line worker is required to meet the standards of excellence. Everyone, with no exception, must meet the highest standard so that there is no chance the widget might fail when put out into the world to perform its task. At the very least, teachers should be held to the same standard as any factory worker. Every child who goes through years of production, shaping of their lives, for hour upon hour, at the hands of a caregiver/teacher/school should be treated with the same high standard that any factory worker is required to treat any single widget. Child emotional abuse can last forever.

# CHAPTER 7
# Child Neglect

> "The worth of our educational institutions can be measured in the numbers of children it has failed. The worth of each teacher can be measured in the life of each child they have neglected".
> —D. P. CALLIN

Child neglect is a highly relevant topic in any discussion of teacher-child interaction in America's school environment. Neglect of students is a substantial phenomenon in a broadly failing educational system. Child neglect is:

> *"...a wrongdoing by absence of a response to a child's critical needs"* (Child Welfare Information Gateway 2013).

There are numerous ways that we are all neglectful. But we must do what we are called on to do, what is possible for us, what we see in our pathway that is correct and necessary, and what we have agreed and committed ourselves to do as the caregivers of the world's children. Any less than what is possible is unacceptable. Our personal interest and well-being is necessarily subjugated to the needs of those we have promised to protect. As parents and guardians of America's children, our actions in the world are the portraits of our characters.

Gateway's *Definitions of Child Abuse and Neglect* breaks child neglect down into four categories: physical neglect, educational neglect, medical neglect, and emotional neglect. These four types of child neglect, with examples, are covered in this chapter.

## Child Physical Neglect

Child physical neglect is:

> *"...failure to provide the necessary food, shelter, or supervision. Providing physical care is the basic function required of every parent, caregiver, or other human responsible for the life of any child"* (Child Welfare Information Gateway 2013).

Food rarely came up as an issue when I was in school. The public schools that I attended and the public schools that my older children attended had real cafeterias. Fresh, nutritious, and delicious meals were served every day. The cafeteria ladies came in early and made giant batches of amazing fresh biscuits from the dough they had left to rise overnight. They cooked huge beef roasts or freshly delivered chicken in mouthwatering gravies with potatoes peeled and mashed that very morning. The vegetables were fresh and well-seasoned, the salads crisp, and the freshly baked deserts were amazing. No one in our school was obese, no one was hungry, no one was refused lunch, and everyone ate, with or without money. Surely food was an issue in some homes, but food didn't appear to be an issue in our public schools.

This may not be the case any longer. In the recent news, there have been multiple cases of food deprivation because kids' parents hadn't put money into their lunch accounts. Apparently, if a parent isn't up to date with payments for children's lunches, those children are not allowed to eat a regular school lunch. In a rash of highly publicized cases in New Jersey, Utah, Massachusetts, Kentucky, and other states, children got their lunches and, at checkout, those lunches were taken away and thrown in the trash. Ironically, some of the students were on free lunch programs. But who cares—the schools had decided to make a point about children and money, and so they often indiscriminately food-shamed the students. The publicity may be new, but this has been going on for years. A study of Minnesota public schools survey showed that 94 percent of districts didn't give kids their regular meal because of money issues (Hawkins 2014).

A cafeteria worker in yet another state thought maybe a child didn't have money for lunch, so she took the lunch from the child and threw it out without asking. The child was given some minimal snack, but the real lunch went into the garbage as the child reached the end of the line (Peart and Tanvier 2015).

This is quite a contrast to the next example, where the teacher forced a student to take her uneaten lunch out of the trash and eat it in front of the classroom. A teacher of a third grade girl forced the child to retrieve her uneaten banana from the trash and finish it for lunch. Will Lerner of *Odd News* was told by the parent, "It is the most bizarre thing I could ever think of doing to a child" (Lerner 2014).

So, in this case, the food that was provided from home was retrieved from the trash, unwashed, and exposed to odor-eating contaminants, perhaps also items such as used tissue or glue. Rather than failure to provide food, food that the child had not chosen to eat and was unclean was forced onto the child. Is this abuse? Is either food deprivation or forced feeding a form of child physical abuse? Is not feeding the child a type of child physical neglect? Well, apparently, these were hardly the worst offences. One teacher had been disciplined in the past. But on this occasion, she reportedly fished a sandwich out of the trash and forced a girl to eat it in front of the class to teach her a lesson. The school where the teacher committed these acts defended the teacher's behavior.

This has to be the ultimate double message for a school to give a child. It's OK for an adult to throw away an entire meal when he or she chooses to, but the school doesn't think that it's OK for a student to throw away his or her lunch from home. Why? Because the teacher says so, and we'll defend his or her right to neglect and abuse no matter what it costs the child and the community. These are classic examples of teachers as role models who follow the following adage: "Do as I say, not as I do."

If the school is the caregiver, how can the school justify the withholding of food from a child under any circumstances? Yet there are multiple accounts of students who have been held in scream rooms (chapter 8) and who have gone without food. And they have gone without water. So, it appears that the caregiver can isolate the child, make him or her forgo food and water, deprive the child of bathroom facilities, take away or throw away his or her lunch, and make the child eat out of the trash as examples of how to be a great teacher, role model, and caregiver.

In elementary school, one of my sons had a friend from a low-income family. In fact, he had two friends who rarely had lunch. Maybe they didn't qualify for the free lunch program. Maybe their families were too embarrassed to apply. Perhaps their families just didn't care whether their children had lunch. Why they didn't have lunch doesn't matter; when lunch time arrives and kids see other kids eating, kids get hungry.

It was about two months before I caught on to the fix my son had come up with for his friends being hungry. He had figured out that he could get all the food he could fit on his plate, including more from the salad bar. That's changed now. In high school, the students get a slice of pizza and some sides. My son wasn't much of an eater himself in elementary school. But he learned what his friends liked, and he made sure that he had those food items on his plate. One of these children loved olives, so my son got an extra-large helping from the salad bar. These kids ate with their hands. One sat on either side of him and ate fast because they were all afraid that they would be caught.

When I figured out that my own son wasn't really eating but was paying for lunch every day, he explained what was happening. From then on, I gave him money to carry in his backpack. He could offer to buy their lunches if he chose to. There were probably many other ways to handle this; I just chose this method so that the problem would never venture beyond the kids. By the way, no one ever noticed them sharing one lunch. I wonder, now, if the adults were too busy looking for the kids in the lunch lines whose lunch they could throw away.

How should the kids' behaviors be described? Whose behavior should we be concerned with here? What should we call this solution my son came up with? There's the option of fraud, or maybe theft. That's tough, because the law doesn't really care much about someone who steals a small amount of food because kids are hungry. In fact, the free-lunch program, free-breakfast program, and other free-meal programs all provide free food to hungry kids and sometimes to their families. My son just found a new way to have a free-lunch program. Some people would like to redirect this brief example of how one child handled child physical neglect and talk about the legality of what was happening. Have at it. Withholding lunch, hungry kids at school, lunch-shaming—what's that all about? What do kids have to do with that?

Let's tell hungry kids who are in the care of America's school employees exactly what it is. Call it failure to provide food, because there were hungry kids who no one noticed. Or maybe you'd like to call it the failure to supervise because no one noticed what was going on.

Child physical neglect includes the lack of appropriate supervision. Ask any child you know where the physical education (PE) teacher is during playground time. Ask students where to find a teacher, a yard supervisor, a PE teacher, or anyone else. Is anyone watching when the kids get bullied? Where is the supervision when sexual talk gets thrown around or when sexual gestures are made by the bullies in the schoolyard? Where are the teachers? Where are the supervisors when the cursing and vulgarity is completely out of control and yet not one caregiver notices or cares? Where are the teachers when racial slurs, bullying, vulgarity and threats occur on the playing field or courts during high school sports? The teachers and other school personnel can't hear what's going on between the kids because they're listening to what's going on with their cell phones. Caregivers are in small gatherings with their peers talking about their next vacation or complaining about why they don't get paid more—to do what? Yes, that's right, talk on their cell phones and hang out with the other adults. Ask around and talk to the children you know about where the caregivers are and who is watching when something goes wrong. Don't forget to ask the middle and high school students about who is monitoring the locker rooms when these young adults are changing in or out of their PE clothes. Ask the kids you know about supervision in other places at school. How many cases of child-child bullying are there in any school on any given day? There are too many to count.

Some parents might wonder if schools spend valuable class time teaching the kids about bullying because it exonerates them from responsibility when something goes wrong. Teacher bullying is spoken of when the teacher cries "Bully!" about some angry or aggressive student who confronts him or her. Where is the caregiver's supervision that provides for the safety of our children when they are being bullied?

A twelve-year-old autistic child was brutally attacked by a boy twice his size (Beyer 2015). The media reported that the young boy was beaten unconscious, had his jaw broken, and his skull was fractured. The damage to one of his ears is likely to be permanent. The parents had reported the attacker to the school in the past because of other incidents. This incident happened in the cafeteria's lunch line in a bully-free zone. The school is in Missouri. Nothing had been done about the earlier incidents, despite multiple episodes of intimidation and a registered letter to the school principal.

Another media report disclosed cases in Oregon and in Washington, where students were intimidated and beaten up by gangs of older students. Asking the schools for help didn't result in any changes, so the students were injured. The cases are sad, but they comprise only two of many incidents across the country.

In Missouri, an honors student was one of four on a hit list (Thomas 2015). The mother had warned the principal that her daughter was threatened, but the warnings were ignored. The sixteen-year-old was attacked by twenty students. The attack was filmed and posted online. The families of the threatened girls had said they were going to move their daughters to another school for their safety. Even with warning, the school failed to provide physical safety. The mother asked for physical safety, and her daughter got physical neglect.

In Florida, a teacher stood by, watched, and filmed as one student kicked a classmate and hit that student in the face and on the body ("Florida Teacher Suspended after Filming Kindergartner Beating Other Students" 2015). She was filming because she wanted evidence of the boy's aggressive behavior. But she forgot to protect the children in her care. She also showed the video to other students, violating student confidentiality. Then she used her foot to push the student into the hall and leave him there with no supervision. This was a kindergarten class. She forgot that she was being handsomely paid to be the guardian of all the children in her care. She allowed the student to be assaulted and then she did the same. Physical neglect is a crime. Physical assault is a crime. In this case, the accessory to child physical abuse came with the package.

A survey titled "Student-Reported Overt and Relational Aggression and Victimization in Grades 3–8," prepared for the Institute of Education Sciences (IES) with the US Department of Education, showed some startling findings (Nishioka, et al., 9). For overt victimization, 12–61 percent of girls and 17–60 percent of boys reported being victimized, at least once, during the last thirty days, and 2–10 percent of girls and 3–14 percent of boys reported being victimized, once or more than once, a week. While the report—which used responses from over fifty thousand students—is amazing and worth taking the time to read, the relevance to child physical neglect is pointedly obvious. Where were the caregivers when all this bullying was going on? Where were the teachers, the aides, the supervisors, the administrators? Where were the adults responsible for our children's welfare?

Child physical neglect comes in many forms. Failure to provide food, clothing, shelter, and safety are all forms of physical neglect. We hand our children to the care of the schools and teachers and trust that our children matter to them. We agree to pay them to be the caregivers. If any caregiver had allowed the events that you just read about to happen, they would be guilty of a crime. Recently, for example, parents came under the watchful eye of Child Protective Services, because they allowed their children to walk to the neighborhood park unattended.

Unlike Child Protective Services, wherein public-school personnel are warned that a child is in danger, the caregivers in charge sometimes choose not to intervene. The reported rate of children being bullied at schools indicates that caregivers, teachers, and other school personnel haven't stopped bullying in schools. "It's the parents' fault" and other excuses are heard too frequently to be taken seriously. Caregivers must provide the necessary food, shelter, and appropriate supervision. It really isn't an option based on how many e-mails you have to return that day, or how tired you are of providing supervision, or how you'd rather play a game on your phone or talk to your teacher peer group. Our schools and teachers as caregivers are guilty of child physical neglect every day.

## Child Educational Neglect

The second type of child neglect is child educational neglect. The United States' law requires parents, guardians, and caregivers to provide an education for the minors in their care. The failure to educate in the United States seems a bombshell waiting to explode. The criterion for educational neglect is:

> *"...failure to educate a child or attend to special education needs"* (Child Welfare Information Gateway 2013).

Compulsory education is a law all fifty states, with the last state law requiring mandatory education passed in 1917.

There are somewhere between twenty four and thirty six states that individually include child educational neglect statutes as part of their state regulations. Kudos for those states. The purpose of drawing attention to the federal statutes for this text is not to establish the federal government agencies as some higher power as some judge and jury for determining failure of schools. Rather, the definitions of child abuse and child neglect serve as recognized definitions, along with others, to form a framework for discussion regarding abject failure in American public school education.

Parents send children to school to meet their educational needs. Children spend a substantial number of their productive waking hours in some type of school system. There are serious consequences for parents who fail to provide for an appropriate compulsory education for their children. Taxpayers pay billions of dollars which constitute public money that is specifically spent for all children to be educated. As a society, we agreed on public money being routed to the grand systems of education found in our country. Schools and politicians continually talk about, meet for, and seek electoral votes based on their personal educational platforms. Politicians chronically tout their promises to turn school failures into successes. So, they throw money at the educational system, but this barely addresses the problems that lead to increasing deterioration and the failure of education in America.

Attempting to force their school to provide the necessary classes for college entrance, six students in a high school enlisted the aid of an attorney. In an *Education Week* report, the students in an Oakland, California, school filed a motion asking a judge to force state education officials to intervene in their educational issues. They asked that the system be forced to offer the classes they needed to graduate and prepare for college. The students argued that they were enrolled in classes where the students ran errands or sat around and did nothing. In an excellent review of the suit, from its' origin through 2015, Vergara versus California, *California Lawyer* published an article that supplies much information on the background of the suit (Davis 2015).

How in the world did we get to the point where students have to sue to get an education? Endless money is thrown down the education waterslide. The United States' rating in the world of education has sunken miserably and steadily over many years.

The Organization for Economic Cooperation and Development (OECD) in the *Program for International Student Assessment* (PISA) for 2015 gives us more data on the performance of US students (Education GPS, OCED 2017). More than half a million fifteen-year-olds took part in the OECD's latest global education survey, known as PISA. Every three years, the *Program for International Student Assessment* ranks about sixty participating countries on their fifteen-year-old students' educational performance in reading, math, and science. The United States is ranked somewhere around thirty-sixth in the world, though there are some new statistics that show a drop in this year's school performance. In 2015, the main focus of the PISA survey was science, an increasingly important part of our economic and social lives, but the repeating focus is on reading and mathematics. There's additional information presented in the OCED report by country. For instance, the youth expected to graduate from upper secondary during their lifetimes in the United States is 81.9 percent; the OCED average is 85.4 percent. This reflects the 20 percent dropout rate mentioned in this section on educational neglect.

Aside from the roughly 20 percent school dropout rate in the United States, consider the number of students with a K–12 education who after spending thirteen years in our education system cannot read and write at even the basic level. Does it really take thirteen years of education, one hundred and eighty days a year, and seven or more hours a day to teach a child to read? That doesn't include work that must be completed after school hours.

Compare this to the adult literacy programs working with non-English speaking and illiterate adults that succeed in helping people to learn to read. It doesn't take years. It doesn't take five days a week. No testing is required. These programs are successful. The staff is primarily volunteer based. Many of the volunteer teachers have only a high school education.

According to the National Institute of Literacy, in 2013, 19 percent of high school graduates could not read (Fitzgerald 2014). This doesn't mean that they are not proficient; it means exactly what it says—on top of the roughly 20 percent dropout rate, another 19 percent of high school students who graduate are illiterate. Check out this table on literacy in the United States.

Table 1. US Illiteracy Statistics

| | |
|---|---|
| Percent of US adults who can't read | 14% |
| Percent of US adults who read below a 5$^{th}$ grade level | 21% |
| Percent of prison inmates who can't read | 63% |
| Percent of high school graduates who can't read | 19% |

US Illiteracy Statistics

Only 20 percent, did you say? That's only one-fifth of the adult population that can't read, one out of five adults. Not as bad as I thought. No, wait a minute. That's 20 percent of the US high school *graduated* population. A full 20 percent of the population *drops out* of our high schools every year. But wait—what about the people who are here and never *go* to our high schools? They are not counted in either the dropouts or the graduates who are illiterate. It's likely that if someone wasn't taught to read in the thirteen years of school, he or she won't learn later unless the person is willing to attend an adult literacy program or learn on his or her own, maybe with help from family and friends.

Corey Fitzgerald, writing for the Science of Learning Blog, said that high school dropout rates "are staggering" (Fitzgerald 2014). He noted that one in three kids drop out of high school—that's more than 1.2 million students just in California. That's even more than the figures (Table 1) used in the last statistics. How many dropouts can't read, adding to the 19 percent who have graduated from high school and still can't read? In a 2013 *Huffington Post* article, Marilyn Crum said that the illiteracy rate in the United States hasn't changed in ten years (Crum 2013). But this year, just to top it off, the US Department of Education has reported that the illiteracy rates really haven't changed for twenty years (National Assessment of Adult Literacy 2015).

If you or I had the goal of teaching our own kids to read and do basic math, could we do it in thirteen years? What have these teachers and students been doing for thirteen years if they hadn't been teaching reading and math? When teachers are paid to educate our kids for thirteen years and a large proportion can't read, are the teachers responsible for perpetrating some kind of fraudulent behavior? Child educational neglect is a crime.

There is some aspect of fraud here, a crime in which the perpetrator is guilty of deceit, trickery, shoddy practice, breach of confidence, or breach of contract perpetrated for profit or to gain some unfair or dishonest advantage. If you can't read, you can't get most jobs. However, getting a job is probably more productive than sitting around for thirteen years and never learning to read or do basic math, provided you could get a job instead. Today's employment market for the unskilled, illiterate worker is practically nonexistent. With so many corporations taking their plants and unskilled labor jobs to other, more business-friendly countries, unskilled and illiterate Americans have few work choices.

What are these teachers doing when they aren't teaching? Well, in the 185-day work year, there are also sick days and personal time-off days. There are minimum days, and there are play days. There are many, many testing days, and there are movie days. Then there is release time. Add in the continuing education hours. How about assemblies? And my all-time favorite is time used for cell phones and other personal activities during the work hours when the teachers are actually in the classroom.

Some of the time not spent in teaching is allocated to texting, messaging, or playing games on cell phones. Teachers are behind their desks playing games with their cell phone on their laps, which makes them appear to be looking between their legs. This has resulted in a whole new string of middle school joking in poor taste. These teachers assign lots of work, or put the kids in front of the computer, or have them copy off the board and spend the hour on his or her cell phone.

The PE teachers are huddled off the playing field either gabbing or on their phones. Kids are angry because they need help. Kids are angry because their adult role models/teachers/caregivers can just play on their phone. But the kids get in trouble if they have a phone in use during school hours. Maybe they're being bullied. The teacher is too busy with a cell phone to notice, take the time, or fend off problems. Plus, little to no learning is happening. Why in heaven's name are teachers allowed to have cell phones out during work hours? That is preposterous. What happened in education 20 years ago when there were no cell phones?

It's criminal to perpetrate this kind of educational hoax on so many kids. A hundred years ago, kids learned to read and write, do math, and learned history with nothing but a cold, one-room schoolhouse and a slate—if they were lucky. And they did learn. They learned all the basics in education in a very few years. They could read and write. They could add and subtract. They learned a lot. There aren't many statistics from these years to compare. And not everyone went to school. However, if you have relatives who did go to school several generations ago, take a look at their penmanship. Ask them to read to you. Have them help your elementary level children with addition and subtraction. Many of the older generations in my family didn't speak English as their first language. They only went to school until the fifth grade because they had to work to support the family. There were no social programs to pay for food or for shoes. But when they went to work, they succeeded because they were literate and had accrued skills that enabled their success.

Teachers have lots of reasons when they explain educational failure. The reason I most often hear is that teachers fail because they don't get paid enough. This is a scary argument. It infers that teachers know how to teach and would succeed in their jobs but only if they get more money. That smacks of extortion! I hear that argument as "You pay me, and you can't afford for me to quit, so if you pay me more, I'll actually do what I'm paid to do."

The National Assessment of Educational Progress (NAEP) reports US schools test scores for reading and math for fourth, eighth, and twelfth grades. The categories are advanced, proficient, basic, and below basic. Basic and below basic are euphemisms for failure. Not all grades are tested every year. The latest reported scores are from 2013 and 2015. For reading, the grades fourth and eighth were reported in 2015. For grade eight reading, 25 percent of all students in the United States did not score at the most basic level; they scored below basic. For grade four reading, 32 percent of all students were in the below-basic category, for they couldn't read. The latest twelfth grade test scores reported are for 2013. Reading at the twelfth grade level wasn't happening for 27 percent of all students in the United States. These numbers are in line with every other reported assessment of the state of US education.

In math, the numbers are equally dismal and some are worse than in reading. In 2015, the fourth and eighth grades were tested. For the fourth grade, 19 percent of US students did not have any basic math skills. At the eighth grade level, a full 30 percent of students tested are below basic. When math was assessed in 2013, NAEP reported that a full 36 percent of all students in the United States could not do the most basic math.

Are teachers, who are our children's caregivers, guilty of child educational neglect because they fail their mandate to educate? This doesn't have to happen. Every small problem, obsolete idea, or dogmatic behavior that is ingrained in education in America needs to change. There's no room for more stupidity, abuse, and neglect!

Here's a preposterous example of failure thinking in US education. When a child is having trouble keeping up or grasping letters, sounds, or numbers, what do you think happens? Here's an example.

A child was seeing me in therapy; he wasn't keeping up in school, and he wasn't ready for the first grade. He had been in kindergarten all year, but he just wasn't prepared for first grade work. Several times, he brought his workbooks to his therapy sessions. He struggled with slow progress. His mother worked with him, his babysitter worked with him, and his older brother worked with him. He just wasn't ready. He was sad. He said he was in the low group at school and he knew it. What a neat young man! He was animated, expressive, and sometimes talked too much as kindergarteners are likely to do. His mother and I discussed what to do for the next year. He was small for his age. He was five. He would turn six for the first grade beginning in that fall. We strongly agreed that he should repeat kindergarten. There was no sense in him struggling each year just to keep up when another year of growth and development would make all the difference. He might get frustrated by always being in the low group. He might learn to not like school. So, holding him in kindergarten was the plan.

The teacher said no. He could be held back only after the first grade. The principal said no. He would catch up eventually. The school district said they didn't get involved; it was up to the principal. Well, there was no help. Mother, who worked hard and had a regularly changing schedule, didn't have any extra money. Each year, it was harder to provide as her salary never kept up with the cost of living. She borrowed the money. She put him in a private school's kindergarten. He grew up a little, learned his letters and numbers, he could count pretty well, and then entered first grade on an equal footing with the other first graders. He never needed to wait to fail the first grade. He really didn't have to be humiliated that he was left behind and his big first grade friends were now ahead of him. He just needed more time.

Who failed here? Why is it so critical for the child to go into a grade for which he or she isn't prepared? We aren't paying for a one-size-fits-all system. Our students learn less, perform worse, and struggle to succeed in life at an ever-increasing rate. When a family works hard to help their child succeed, but the child is obviously not going to benefit academically or psychologically from being thrown into an arena for which that child is unprepared, who pays the price?

*Ed-Data* provided the charts below. To look at the scores for the United States, go to the *Ed-Data* web page and check out your own home state. We'll use my home state as an example to show you what to look for. Table 2 shows how many students graduated from high school in California with the courses needed to enter the university or state college system.

Table 2. Graduates Completing Requirements for UC/CSU

| Graduates with UC/CSU Required Courses by Race/Ethnicity State of California, 2012–13 | | |
|---|---|---|
| Race/Ethnicity | Graduates with UC/CSU Required Courses | Percentage of Graduates in Each Ethnic Group |
| American Indian or Alaska Native | 787 | 26.2% |
| Asian | 28,367 | 67.7% |
| Native Hawaiian or Pacific Islander | 899 | 34.8% |
| Filipino | 7,176 | 54.4% |
| Hispanic or Latino | 57,966 | 29.1% |
| Black or African American | 7,900 | 29.2% |
| White | 59,119 | 47.1% |
| Two or More Races | 3,710 | 46.8% |
| None Reported | 597 | 30.2% |
| Total | 166,521 | 39.4% |

Graduates Completing Requirements for UC/CSU

For the year 2012–13, as shown, the total statewide percentage of students graduating from high school with the courses they need to enter a four-year college or university is 39.4 percent.

By the way, the other 60.6 percent have very few choices (examples follow), since they don't have the classes needed to attend college:

1. Do nothing. They have no job training and hence aren't qualified to do anything. Some districts have begun to add a few skills training classes but don't have traditional trade schools. The idea is that every child should go to college. Too bad about not knowing how to read!
2. Go in the military. I believe this is a good idea for many young people, especially those who haven't been trained in any trade and could have an opportunity to learn basic math and reading skills. Unfortunately, the military is being downsized and the opportunities are limited. Plus, to enter today's military there are educational tests to pass.
3. Go to a community college. Yes, an enormous amount of money from the community college budget has to be spent evaluating and teaching eighteen- and nineteen-year-olds how to read, add, and subtract in remedial classes because thirteen years at school isn't enough. So, now they have to spend a year learning these skills before they are community college-ready.
4. Pray for a job. Jobs are in high demand and harder to get than one may believe. It's a buyer's market. But the salary won't support you, and getting a second part-time job is nearly impossible because of the scheduling conflicts.

The rest of the options are what we all know too well. Go on welfare, have your aging parents support you forever, or go it on your own. The outcomes are predictable, yet politicians are wondering what to do to improve the youth unemployment rate.

Table 3 depicts the percentage of students who scored proficient or advanced proficient, by subject, across California (California Department of Education, *EdSource and the Fiscal Crisis & Management Assistance Team* 2015).

Table 3. Percentage of California Students Scoring Proficient or Advanced

| STAR - Percent of Students Scoring at Proficient or Advanced State of California, 2012–13 ||
| --- | --- |
| Subject | Percent |
| English-Language Arts | 55% |
| Mathematics | 50% |
| Science | 59% |
| History-Social Science | 49% |

Percentage of California Students Scoring Proficient or Advanced

These figures reflect scores for students who were *in* school *and* took the test. It doesn't count the 20 percent of students who dropped out of school. The subject-matter proficient rating percentages ranges from 49 to 59 percent. If you ran an auto factory and only 49–59 percent of your workers were proficient or above in their jobs, would the car run? Could you stay in business? How about running a medical school? If 49 to 59 percent of your student applicants came to you from a California school, would you let them in? Do you think that only 49 to 59 percent of your students being proficient in your medical school, or veterinary school, food handling school, or even driving school would allow you to stay in business?

Not last and definitely not the least, of the students who remain in school, 39 percent take the SAT (Scholastic Aptitude Test) for entrance into a four-year college or university. So, what are we saying is the percentage of students who are actually planning to go to a four-year college or university? This looks like the same 39 percent who actually took the required classes to qualify for entry into a state college or university.

So, after 20 percent drop out, of the remaining students who graduate, 39 percent may plan a four-year college career. It's doubtful if that number is correct because the high school now arranges for the students to take the SATs, so the students may be captive test-takers. But wait! The total possible score for the SATs, which is used for college admissions, is 2,400 (since 2005–6). Notice the average SAT score for high school graduates is 1,492 in California. I did go to school in the olden days, when there were real blackboards and chalk. In math class, we learned that these numbers tell us that the average high school graduate scores about 62 percent on the SATs. This is about average for the United States as a whole, and I think we should have learned that a 62 percent is a failing grade. There's no way that students with a score like that can compete. There's a good reason why our universities—which are supported by our tax dollars, collected from those mothers and fathers who had to borrow money to put their child in a private kindergarten so he wouldn't fail—are now filled with foreign and out-of-state students. Aren't we glad we pay our taxes? We support teachers who fail our children, and we support universities and colleges that most of our children will never attend.

Table 4. Percentage of Students Taking SATS and Average Scores by year

| | \multicolumn{3}{c}{SATS Average Scores National 1999, 2007, 2015} | | |
|---|---|---|---|
| | 1999 | 2007 | 2015 |
| Percent of seniors tested | | | 39% |
| Critical Reading | 505 | 502 | 495 |
| Math | 514 | 515 | 511 |
| Writing | (no test scores) | 494 | 484 |
| Total Average Scores | | 1,511 | 1,490 |

Percentage of Students Taking SATs and Average Scores by Year

The *Nation's Report Card* is the only ongoing assessment of what US students know and can do in different subjects. This table summarizes the percentage of students at or above proficient in the entire country for the testing done at grades four, eight, and twelve. Not all subjects are tested every year. The data is the most current comparative score chart compiled in 2016, following the 2015 testing.

Table 5. Percentage of Students at or Above Proficient

| Subject | Grade 4 | Grade 8 | Grade 12 |
|---|---|---|---|
| Civics | 27% 2010 | 23% 2014 | 24% 2010 |
| Economics | — | — | 42% 2012 |
| Geography | 21% 2010 | 27% 2014 | 20% 2010 |
| Mathematics | 40% 2015 | 33% 2015 | 25% 2015 |
| Reading | 36% 2015 | 34% 2015 | 37% 2015 |
| Science | 38% 2015 | 34% 2015 | 22% 2015 |
| Technology and Engineering Literacy | — | 43% 2014 | — |
| U.S. History | 20% 2010 | 18% 2014 | 12% 2010 |
| Writing | — | 27% 2011 | 27% 2011 |

Percentage of Students at or Above Proficient

To find the percentage of students who are *not* proficient in each subject, subtract each score from 100 percent. The results are both startling and dismal. United States History is taught in elementary, middle, and high school. By twelfth grade testing, 88 percent of students are not proficient. Math is taught every year for thirteen years. At the end of those many years, 75 percent of students are not proficient. There is no accountability for the educational failures, for substandard teaching, or educational neglect.

To confirm all that we already know about one more brotherhood but feel powerless to change, look at 24/7 Wall St.'s (247wallst.com) list of America's best and worst schools (Frohlich, Stebbins, Sauter, and Comen, 2015). Check out you own state; the lists are available online. States are given grades, scores, and ranks in pupil-spending, high school graduation rates, and eighth grade proficiency in math or reading. Scores ranged from B to D. There were no A's. The country as a whole was given a C grade.

The average American worker is on the job 2,080 hours a year—that's 260 eight-hour days. Aren't the teachers who are being paid for part-time work, about 185 days a year, supposed to be qualified to teach young people? No? Aren't these teachers the people who are with these children in the classrooms for thirteen years? For sure, we know that there is a percentage of high-performing students who will succeed even if the teacher just throws work at them and they learn on their own. These are in large part the students who are proficient or advanced in math and English. Educational neglect is rampant. Maybe some teachers only teach the students they like, or the students who look or behave in a certain way, or the students who don't ask questions and always have a pencil.

Teachers in the United States are generally paid a straight salary based on experience and education level. Nothing else is factored in, such as the number of hours in the classroom, student performance, and so on. There are endless sources of a teacher's salary calculations. It would be helpful to have a calculation of how much each teacher would make around the world, based on how much the student has learned. Another interesting calculation would be based on the hours the teacher is actually in the classroom, actually with the students, correlated with how much they make whether or not they are present.

One of the most important points of this section on educational neglect has to do with money and jobs. It's fine that we pay our teachers lots of money for less hours of work than the United States average number of hours worked. We pay them because they tell us, and we believe. that they are highly educated and trained for the task at hand. They want more money, because they are so very well qualified. Their years of education should pay off for the taxpayers. Their training and expertise is supposed to qualify them to teach every child in their classroom. They are not paid to address a few children and dismiss the rest. They are supposedly trained to teach all our children. They are not paid to teach or address *only* the kids who could learn on their own if they had to.

Teachers tell us that their salaries should be increased because they work so hard. There are thousands of jobs in which people work hard. Those workers usually accomplish the tasks for which they are hired. If teachers are working that hard that they should be paid more, then they should show some results. They are failing; they have been failing for twenty or more years. There is no improvement. Rather than a pay increase, they should probably try another line of work.

Teachers' grades are the students' test scores. There has been lots of discussion in the last few years about how to evaluate teachers. We've all heard screaming from some groups who believe that it isn't fair to the teacher if his or her performance is based on the students' performance. They continually tout extenuating circumstances; basically, it's OK to fail at the core of their chosen work because it's not their fault. It's the children's fault. It's the parents' fault, it's their language's fault, or it's their race's fault. It is never the fault of the teacher that they fail!

Then what is fair to the student? If the student doesn't test well, the student is penalized by the limited choices a poor education reaps. If the student doesn't learn to read and write, add and subtract, and pass their tests, their economic future is virtually unsalvageable. If the teacher's performance doesn't matter, why should the student's performance matter? If the illiterate student wants to go to Yale or UCLA, he or she should get to go. Why? Because performance doesn't matter! The students have as many extenuating circumstances as the teachers. All that matters is that no one should have to be evaluated based on whether or not he or she has done his or her job. Tell that to a private business owner, a corporation manager, or any worker in China or India. Guess what happens when you really are responsible for your own work and you tell the boss, "I don't want an evaluation! You shouldn't be able to fire me if I don't do my job. It's not my fault. It's the extenuating circumstances. It's the customer's fault."

Teachers' grades should be based on the percentage of students who are prepared for college or are fully trained to do a meaningful job after thirteen years of public education. Teachers' grades should be based on the percentage of students' outcomes: outcomes that include students who have not been trained, those who have dropped out, and those who have failed to learn to read and write. And frankly, if teachers are not capable of doing this job with their own passing grades, they need to be fired.

Parents go to work to pay the taxes that pay the teachers who are supposed to be teaching their children. Parents work a full workday. If you count grading papers and doing lesson plans, the teacher might work as many hours per day, but definitely not as many days per year. The students are in school the same number of hours their teachers are in school, maybe even more as the teachers are gone so many days during the year and there are substitutes in the classroom. Then the children come home and do more work. They didn't do enough in school, so they have to do it at home. Why? Why isn't the child doing enough work at school? Why are the parents teaching them at home? Children have a longer workday than most adults. Children stay in school from early morning to until mid- to late afternoon. Why in the world should children work more hours than an adult? And they still can't read and do math! Why does a child have homework, sometimes for hours, each evening and weekend projects and test preparations? Every night your child has homework, ask him or her to describe the hours he or she spends in school. Have your child talk about what he or she actually accomplished during the school day in each class. Compare that hour for hour to the take-home assignments. Where is the work getting done? What has your child learned in school that day that now he or she has to learn more after school? The adults get to watch television and relax.

Parents get nasty letters if their children are not in school. They are legally responsible for their children to be in the seat every day when the bell rings. But where's the teacher? The estimate for a teacher's *paid* absence ranges from ten days a year to 10 percent of the school year days! So, who is teaching the students? Anyway, that's far above the absence rate that is acceptable for the student.

Child educational neglect has to be the most expensive, painful, and useless outcome of all the endeavors every attempted in the United States. There is something pathetic about self-righteous complaints from educators who are all members of the brotherhood, who accept no blame for one of America's most costly and historic failures. Teachers are our children's caregivers. Parents are mandated to deliver their children into the hands of these professionals. Do our children return to us better off than they were when they left home? Are their needs met? Are they well educated? Are they safe and well treated? Is it possible that parents, who go to difficult jobs twelve months a year to pay these educators and send their children to these many destinations, should be the responsible party (besides the student) for illiteracy in the sixth grade? So, who is guilty of the crime of child educational neglect?

## Child Medical Neglect

This third section of child neglect, as defined by CAPTA, is child medical neglect. Its appearance in the school setting seems less prominent than other abuse and neglect issues. But that makes me suspicious. The section of CAPTA defines medical neglect as a failure to provide for a child who requires:

> "...medical or mental health treatment be provided that medical or mental health treatment by parents, guardians, or other caregivers" (Child Welfare Information Gateway 2013).

Failure of the responsible parent, guardian, or caregiver to provide for these needs is considered child medical neglect and is grounds for intervention by state child protective authorities. Are your students' physical and mental health medical needs cared for in their schools of attendance while they are under the jurisdiction of school as caregiver?

## Physical Health Neglect

Schools offer many types of health services to students. They check for vaccinations, they often do vision and hearing checks, they assess the child's weight and height, how many push-ups the child can do, or how far he or she can run. Schools have been pretty good about dealing with education about sex, tobacco, drugs, and alcohol. Now schools are working on issues of sexual preference, watching out for the mental health of those students who may have issues with their preferences. That's because the schools are mandated to look out for their children's physical health and mental health, both of which are equally important to a child's medical wellbeing.

Medical neglect of physical health is less common when there is an obvious physical injury. But when physical health is ignored by the schools, the results can be devastating. According to the Centers for Disease Control, about 45 percent of playground-related injuries are severe—fractures, internal injuries, concussions, dislocations, and amputations (United States, Centers for Disease Control and Prevention. "Playground Injuries: Fact Sheet." 2012). About 75 percent of nonfatal injuries related to playground equipment occur on public playgrounds. Most occur at schools and daycare centers. Injuries do occur at schools. Injuries are generally accidental. Some are not. If your student is injured at school, does the school provide the access to medical health intervention?

Most information on physical injury in the schools is anecdotal. Why is it that we learn about physical injury in the schools through the word of mouth? Because many school injuries aren't reported or litigated. My friend's son was a high school football player. He was hit on the head during football practice. He lost consciousness. His coach was standing over him when he regained consciousness and told him to get back on the field. No one was called. His parents weren't notified. I spoke to his mother at length over the next few months. Days after the injury, when he complained of a continuous headache and blurred vision, his mother took him to his physician. He had a serious concussion.

When my daughter was in kindergarten, she liked to swing on the hard metal climbing bars at recess. One day, she swung directly into the bars and whacked her head in the center of the frontal lobe area. When we picked her up after school, she had an enormous lump on her forehead and serious bruising. No one called. No one thought it was important. It was the first of three serious head injuries. All three were, in some way, related to school activity.

The stories can go on to fill the rest of the book. But don't miss the point. Do America's schools attend to their students' medical needs? Perhaps sometimes. Do America's schools ignore their students' medical needs and hope that they go away? Yes.

Let's not look at all the injuries that occur at school. Forget the small concerns like bruises and scrapes, pokes, slaps, and falls. Look at only one medical issue—the head injuries. Why would a teacher or a coach ignore a serious and recognizable head injury that results in the loss of consciousness or severe swelling and bruising? Go to the office for a scrape. But ignore a concussion? Willing to take a guess? The most likely scenario is self- and organizational protection: the brotherhood, the bastion, the entire system. Nondisclosure is the simplest and quickest way to avoid a consequence. Serious injury can mean money and bad press. Yes, so can a neglect lawsuit, but odds are that the system will skate around such litigation. The risk of not reporting at the expense of the child's health and welfare is more beneficial to the school system, the bastion, than reporting every serious injury.

There are many other kinds of medical physical neglect that occur in the schools. Schools are notorious for rewarding students who are in their seats every day. If they are frequently absent but reported and excused for illness, it does not avoid a threatening letter from the school or district. These are lengthy, confrontational, accusatory, and demanding letters.

What's the problem with absence quotas? Not all students have the same physical health concerns. Many have recurrent physician appointments that cannot be scheduled in non-school hours. There are also dental appointments, physical therapy, allergists, vision, and hearing problems. But mostly, children get sick. And this is the rub. If a child is ill, the child should stay at home. No parent wants his or her child to become ill just because some other child might come to school so they don't ruin their perfect attendance record. Children, students of all ages, don't want to sit next to a student who is coughing, blowing his or her nose, and can't keep his or her eyes open. Schools are not looking after the physical health needs of the students if children who are ill are encouraged to attend and make other kids sick. Pressing attendance in this way is medical neglect; this is why there are cases of whole classrooms of students become ill.

We all know that schools are under pressure to keep the seats filled; seat count is the basis for funding. Too bad teachers aren't paid by the number of days they're actually in the classroom doing something useful. That's not fair to say to the teachers who are present and who are teaching, but those are not the teachers who should be penalized; they're already doing what they have agreed to do. It's equally unfair to the students if their learning is derailed by teacher absences. It also sets up a double standard that students are well aware of: "The teacher gets paid by the taxpayers and isn't here…" or "That money is tied to whether I'm in my seat, so why isn't the teacher in her seat?" Parents see this as a one-way street; teachers get money based on their children's attendance and then they don't have to show up. OK, the system is a train wreck, but does that mean my child has to become ill because a parent is threatened if his or her sick child stays home?

Physical neglect is multifaceted. Gateway provides a reference guide for suspected child maltreatment. The signs for possible neglect are listed in chapter 2. The first sign reads, "Seem inadequately dressed for the weather (e.g., wearing shorts and sandals in freezing weather.)"

In June 2015, a mother was arrested for taking a tough love approach with her son, who repeatedly missed his curfew (Crain 2015). She made him sleep outside on the patio with a blanket and a pillow. It happened in May. Many kids love sleeping outside. But this boy didn't like it. The boy called the police, and the mother was jailed for the deprivation of a minor. Her other children were placed with the grandmother. Yet think about the case where the students who had on the wrong type of jacket were told to go home, without a coat, in the freezing weather (Zander 2015). What will child protective services do if the parent has caused that child to be cold—or go to the park with a sibling without a parent—or sleep on the back patio with a blanket and pillow? There will be consequences. But if the school has children walk home without proper clothing in freezing weather, there is no punishment.

There is only one of the above-mentioned incidents that is specifically covered in the child abuse and neglect laws: "inadequately dressed for the weather." The word *abuse* implies a voluntary action, directed, which could harm a child. The word *neglect* implies no action, something that should have been done and wasn't. The case in which the students were compelled to walk home without their coats was intentional, not neglectful. We're calling this child medical neglect, but it's really both abuse and neglect. The article addressed the school behavior as passive aggressive, a term that is defined and discussed later in the book. The children's coats were at the school. The school kept the students' coats and made them walk home without any protection from the weather. The act knowingly could have resulted in medical harm in the form of exposure to the freezing weather. What should we call this? Are the teachers and the school guilty of child medical neglect and child abuse?

Unfortunately, the medical neglect stories that make it to the news are all about control. With unreported physical injury, the bastion is looking out for itself and wants to control its liability. Taking away twenty students' coats without notice because they are of the wrong color is about maintaining control through random punishment. Rewarding student for not missing one day of school in thirteen years, even when they're sick, is about trying to control revenue streams. Medical neglect is a crime.

## Mental Health Neglect

Consider the presence of mental health issues in the school setting. Let's start with serious mental health problems, mental illnesses that might be obvious to a student, the student's peer group, or the school personnel. If the problems are behaviorally obvious, as with schizophrenia or other psychotic disorders, the child is likely to have been identified outside the school and receiving care. But there are exceptions.

At times, serious mental illness is misdiagnosed and misunderstood by everyone in the child's area of influence (Anderson and Kavitha 2016). The child may be labeled as one with a behavior problem without ever having an evaluation. In these cases, the student is already doomed to the failure track. The school personnel, as the caregiver, have failed to seek, find, identify, and provide for the student's needs. Absent discovery and intervention of a student's mental health problems, students are frequently found to:

- Drop out
- Be expelled
- Go to a continuation school
- Sit in a desk, do nothing, and get passed on
- Be shuttled out of the school so that the problem of education reverts to the parent to homeschool

If the obvious mental health need is not already being cared for, the school is responsible for making referrals and quickly providing the appropriate resources and placement.

Many mental health issues, such as depression and anxiety, are not so easily seen and therefore are less likely to be identified. Students can be so severely depressed that they commit suicide. Everyone seems surprised, but suicide is a leading cause of death for children and adolescents. Yet the peers and the school personnel say, "If he or she had just told someone… asked for help…if I had only known…"

Every state is mandated under the IDEA laws to Child Find. This mandate requires all school districts to identify, locate, and evaluate all children with disabilities, regardless of the severity of their disabilities. This includes all children who are *suspected* of having a disability, including children who receive passing grades and are advancing from grade to grade. These laws are briefly reviewed here as they apply to medical neglect, but they were covered more thoroughly in chapter 5, including the section titled "The Schools' Responsibilities."

"*Disability* is a very broad term; the definition often eludes mental health professionals when the disabled person is an adult, and it is even more difficult to discern when the disability belongs to a child. But in the language and laws relevant to education, disability at its minimum includes children up to the age of twenty-four who have learning, physical, and mental disabilities and even those who have not been labeled. It includes children who need an appropriate modification of educational material and accommodations so that they can access FAPE. Accommodations that don't alter the material but provide for specific situational/environmental/equipment changes are covered separately under section 504 of the Americans with Disabilities Act, a federal law. Child Find is very broad, and like many other obligations assigned to caregivers, Child Find means that someone or everyone in the educational setting is supposed to be looking.

There are some minimal resources put into place by school districts. Some schools consider that they provide sufficient care by making a referral to a county mental health program. Some schools use school counselors to talk out the problem. Either of these interventions is appropriate, but neither is adequate in most cases. Strangely, a student in a public-school system for the majority of his or her productive waking hours for nine to ten months of the year for thirteen years can be totally invisible. The obvious signs of such common childhood mental health issues as depression and anxiety go unnoticed. Yes, thirteen years and no one notices anything.

The Centers for Disease Control's Youth Risk Behavior Surveillance System (YRBSS) monitors six types of health-risk behaviors that contribute to the leading causes of death and disability among youth (Centers for Disease Control and Prevention, "Youth Risk Behavior Surveillance System 2016). The Jason Foundation's Parent Resource Program reported in a summary of the CDC's report that youth suicide is an epidemic that results in one hundred deaths a week ("Youth Suicide Facts & Stats" The Jason Foundation 2015). The Jason Foundation indicates that their 2013 data puts attempted suicides at one in every thirteen youths. Both organizations widely publish information about youth suicide. Where do the youth spend the majority of their waking, productive, professionally supervised hours? In America's schools. It is in these schools that responsible caregivers are mandated as part of their employment to be constantly vigilant with their students, to watch for and evaluate the students' mental health status.

The school is by law the caregiver during the students' hours of attendance. The educational institution and employees act *in loco parentis* in many ways. The school's right to discipline, compel, search, and perform other parental duties is granted in order to keep each and every student safe and support an orderly process that is conducive to learning. Yet there is some imbalance in the mix. While the school's rights and needs are supported by the law, the students' medical and mental health needs may go unnoticed. Child Find is generally ineffective when mental health issues are the topic. The majority of America's youth who commit suicide are attending a public school, yet they were not helped by child find.

The Centers for Disease Control offers some insight into the number of children in the United States who are in need of mental health care (United States, Centers for Disease Control and Prevention, "Children's Mental Health" 2017). The estimate is that one in every five children—20 percent of the population of children—sitting in a classroom somewhere in America are in need of mental health care. What better place to be? The educational professionals have years of training in all child-related areas needed to identify problems. Their education, which is related to developmental stages, needs, and issues of childhood and adolescence, far exceeds that of any non-teacher parent. Yet, 80 percent of the youth with mental health needs go untreated.

Clearly, one half of the medical health needs of children are physical health and the other half is mental health. There is an evaluation for push-ups. There's an evaluation for hearing and for vision. Unfortunately, when the school is the cause of mental health problems for children, there may be no help. There is no evaluation for teachers' mental health. And there is certainly not an evaluation for teachers' impact on the students' mental health.

Child medical neglect concerns widen when a member of the brotherhood is the source of the students' mental health problems. An enormous, unaddressed mental health/medical neglect problem exists in the bastion. When a problem requiring mental health intervention has been caused by the school or by one or more of its employees, what procedures are in place to facilitate a responsible intervention for the student? Who is notified at the school level that a student has developed a mental health problem, such as anxiety or depression, as a result of a school employee's behavior?

This complicated situation arises every day in America's schools. When teachers and other school personnel are guilty of child abuse and child neglect, how often does the caregiver organization, the bastion or its members, and the brotherhood follow through with an appropriate referral for care for the victim—the student? There is a long list of questions that arise when the school is in charge of the care of the student in need. When a child's mental health problem is caused by a teacher who is neglecting or abusing the student, the conflict of interest between the student's needs and the bastion's needs is enormous.

Even the questions that need to be asked are circular and overlapping. But they are geared to eke out answers that might otherwise be evasive if they are not asked in myriad ways. Here are some of the formatted questions, all of which address the same point. How can the perpetrator and his or her supporters also be the caregiver? Put in another way, if a teacher commits a crime but his or her family, friends, coworkers, and bosses won't hold him or her accountable, is the teacher trustworthy to provide care for the victim of the crime he or she committed?

Until schools are removed from the conflicted and multilayered roles of the judge and the jury, the prosecutor and the defense attorney, policeman and the caregiver, they can never be objective enough to be responsible for their students. It's because they wear all the possible hats and are so self-policing that they cannot be responsible for child medical or mental health neglect.

In the event you need to participate in accessing help for a student victim of teacher abuse that results in a mental health problem, here are a few preliminary questions you'll want to ask:

- What efforts, under Child Find, have been made to determine whether the student has a mental health problem?
- What happens to the teacher when the mental health problem is serious and teacher-related?
- Will the student receive care within the school, where the problem arose?
- Who will follow the student's progress with mental health care?
- Who will be responsible for resolving the issue that caused the mental health problem in the first place?
- Will the child receive a referral to an outside mental health practitioner?
- Will the child be sent to the school psychologist or the school counselor?
- If so, is he or she qualified to manage mental health problems that have been caused by one of his or her colleagues?
- What are the guarantees that the victim will not be treated in the same way as the perpetrator treated him or her?
- Will the chosen mental health professional help the victim to recover without minimizing the problem?
- Who will bring forward a student issue that has been found to be caused by a teacher or other school personnel?
- How will the school work to uncover the source of the child's problem if the problem is the teacher?

It's valuable to reiterate the obvious. Until the schools are removed from the conflicted and multilayered roles they play, they can never be objective enough to be responsible for their students.

There's a long, worldwide history of child abuse and neglect of every kind being hushed, minimized, spun, ignored, denied, and rebranded. Child victims are punished for their disclosures. There is little written about the obligation of the school as caregiver to provide mental health care. Does the school's behavior qualify as child medical neglect when there is a failure to act? Is the school guilty of child neglect when the problem goes on and on without resolution, and the student becomes more angry and resentful of having to attend school? Or maybe the student becomes anxious or fearful? Perhaps the student becomes depressed. Have you ever seen a child sit quietly in the classroom and not do any work, fade into the background, and become invisible? Who in the educational bastion is brave enough to be a hero when he or she knows that a teacher is at fault?

## Child Emotional Neglect

The final category covered under the laws related to child neglect is emotional neglect. This is perhaps the most pervasive and the most damaging of the child injuries covered under the child neglect laws. You might think that educational neglect is more injurious because of the school's failure to fulfill its most basic mission, the reason it exists, and the school's responsibility to educate. Yet there is widespread, tangible, and measurable evidence of the schools' failure to educate. We all know that our schools have failed; the whole world knows our schools have failed. What makes child emotional neglect along with child emotional abuse so deadly is the fact that it is often invisible. But it nevertheless victimizes the individual student and creates serious damage that will likely never be answered for nor remediated.

Child emotional neglect addresses the:

*"...inattention to a child's emotional needs, failure to provide psychological care, or permitting the child to use alcohol or other drugs"* (Child Welfare Information Gateway 2013).

It's difficult to track the events that result in child emotional neglect. Again, neglect is passive. Neglect literally means one does nothing. But that's not the same nothing you or I may do on a Sunday when we sit in the yard and look at the sky.

Emotional neglect is a complicated concept. The term infers that something has already happened to a child and/or is now happening that requires action, but there is instead inattention to the child's emotional needs. The something that has happened or has already happened may be specific. Child sexual abuse or child physical abuse is specific. Child educational neglect is specific. Child medical and physical neglect are specific. If nothing is done to help the victim of these crimes, the problems are cumulative. There is the original crime and then there is inattention to a child's emotional needs, a form of child emotional neglect that serves as another problem added to the first specific event.

One more form of child neglect is specific; this is related to the use of alcohol or drugs. Not attending to children's use of addictive substances, allowing children to use alcohol or other drugs, ignoring whether children are using these substances, or not being watchful over children to ensure they are not using drugs or alcohol is covered under the child emotional neglect laws. This subsection of emotional neglect would be best made into a category of its own. The problems are universal, not controlled, and are very specific. And like all other types of child neglect and child abuse, every form of abuse and neglect results in child emotional abuse and child emotional neglect.

Our world is inundated with every type of illegal and legal drug that we've been able to create. The lives of countless young people from every demographic dimension have been ruined by early addiction. There's big money in addiction.

Sixty years ago, parents should have been concerned about alcohol, but it wasn't as common to bring alcohol to school then as it is now. There was plenty of available alcohol, and there were very loose or nonexistent drinking age limitations. There wasn't much novelty in the use of alcohol, and novelty and the thrill of doing something dangerous or illicit is a big draw for young people.

Schools are responsible for keeping drugs and alcohol off the campus. This is a big job, and at times I think the school personnel get substance use policing fatigue, just as parents do. Make no mistake about this; there are lots of cases of teachers contributing to the students' use of drugs and alcohol. There are cases for you to read where students are the dealers for the teachers and cases where teachers are the source of students' drugs. They aren't cited here, but they are easy to research. Allowing minors to access drugs and alcohol is a crime. Encouraging them to use drugs and alcohol or drinking and drugging with minors are serious crimes. These crimes are neglectful of the minor's emotional and psychological well-being. They also impinge on physical health and can easily cross over to sexual abuse and physical abuse.

But most child emotional neglect, like child psychological abuse, is nonspecific. That is, teachers create and then ignore problems for students that then require psychological care. The results of physical, medical, and educational neglect are devastating, but the sheer numbers of students who are injured due to a teacher's behavior is impossible to calculate. The active abuse and the passive ignoring of the emotional needs of a child are not describable in the way that any specific abuse or neglect is looked at or seen.

The number of students who are injured due to a teacher's behavior is impossible to calculate. If no one can calculate the injuries to students at the hands of teachers and other school personnel, it becomes impossible to expect that even the smallest percentage of injured students ever receive the care required to repair the damage, so child emotional neglect is endemic. A teacher-induced need for students to require psychological care is insidious and dangerous. The long-term effects are permanent. Whether a child grows into a success or his or her growth and development are stymied, the adults who have influenced that child's life are always part of the equation—sometimes a large part of the equation, and sometimes the foundation upon which the equation is built. There are innumerable factors that come to play in the life of any human, and a child, a youth, or a college student's relationship with every teacher is part of that equation.

As with every human relationship, certain qualities are essential for the two to work together during the time they spend in each other's company. There's a list of the essential characteristics that make a relationship work and maybe even make it work well; the list isn't long. This list has been rewritten over decades of both extrapolation and research, and the list of necessary qualities is no different from what any schoolchild can tell you when asked—no research necessary. This part was pretty easy to write; it's all the stuff kids say from kindergarten to college when they're being open about what they want from their teachers:

*Unconditional acceptance*: "Everyone wants to matter and be accepted no matter who they are. I can accept who you are and every one of my teachers are even though they are all different from one another, and I want that from you. You and I are different—there are no two people alike, and I don't want to be with people who throw away other people because they are different. I don't want you to throw me away without *giving you* a chance to show you that you can accept me."

*Genuineness*: "I want to know that you are who you say you are, and I want you to stay being that person so I know who I'm with and who to expect every time I come in your room, even if one of us is tired or unhappy. If you stay who you say you are, you can see me the way I am. I don't want to have to be someone else every time I come in your room. I want to know who you are so I can give you a chance to know me."

*Kindness*: "Even when there is something you don't like, you don't have to hurt me when you tell me. I want you to smile when you see me because

I'm human, and it matters that you don't make faces at me, or say rude things to me, or use a hard tone with me, or ignore me when I have a genuine question. I want you to be kind to me when I'm wrong or a mess or forgetful. I'm kind to you no matter what you do because I know that you're just a regular person."

*Honesty*: "Honesty is the same as trustworthiness. I want to trust you to do what's right; I want to trust that you want to do this job and that you care about what happens between us. I want to know that you're not just saying you love to teach. It's a hard job, and we'll all be unhappy if you don't want to be here, and that means you too."

*Fairness*: "I want the same rules as everyone else. I want the same grades as anyone else who did the same quality of work. I want my opinions to be fairly considered even if they aren't the same as yours, even if I don't write the same way you do, draw the way you do, or talk the way you do. Even if you can't like me or care about me, you can still be fair."

We take something and we leave something each time we interact with another person. Our relationships are all that we have, and they define who we are without exception. It isn't good enough to have some good relationships and convince ourselves that's all that we need, that the others don't mean anything to us. That could be true that some relationships don't mean anything to us, but they tell a lot about us.

Child emotional neglect has its own aura, its own peculiar part in our ongoing lives, that can't be erased. We want to believe that no one knows of our neglect of the children in our care, but the child knows and so do we even if we deny it, and that's two people too many. And teachers should know that what you put out comes back to you when you least expect it, for better or for worse.

## Summary

America's schools are guilty of child emotional neglect. America's schools, teachers, and coaches are guilty of physical neglect, medical neglect, and the most ironic of neglects—child educational neglect. So, who is supposed to provide the emotional care needed for the children whose needs have been both created and neglected by this bastion and the members of the brotherhood?

Schools have budgets for meeting the emotional needs of the students. How often do the children bring problems that have been created within the school to those professionals? How often are they referred for help? Neglect is a humiliating experience for a child. To be neglected is to know that you are not worth the time you use or the space you occupy in the world. Neglect is devaluing: "Our needs aren't worthy of attention; I'm invisible."

Do your own search to see what's happening in schools around the country. Ask around. Poll your families and neighbors. Ask the students. Ask them about what they did when they had a problem at school and when that problem was caused by the school. Who did they talk to when they were lunch-shamed? Who helped them when they were injured on the playing field? Who helped them when they were injured and then neglected by some teacher or other school personnel? How does it feel to spend useless hours in school, be emotionally neglected, and then come home with mounds of busy work that is now self-taught but should have happened in the school? Who will help when the student feels like a failure and is afraid for his or her future because of massive educational neglect? What should have happened?

The second half of this book covers all the ways that teachers and other employees in the educational system emotionally and psychologically injure our children, the methods they use, how they defend themselves, and how others participate in these crimes against children. The primary focus of chapter 9 through chapter 14 is the active and passive behaviors of teachers and other educational staff who psychologically and emotionally injure students. From ignoring to death threats, from denial to flipping the blame, the entire scope of psychological and emotional behaviors that debilitate so many students in America's schools are named, defined, and explained.

Child neglect by the teacher or other school personnel working under the protection of the bastion has to be addressed if we are to ever regain control of our educational system. No system can survive if it fails to address the needs of the people it serves. Worse, no bastion should continue unchallenged when our children's educational, physical, medical, and emotional needs are in the hands of those who injure and those needs are silenced.

# CHAPTER 8
# Scream Rooms

> "Why are America's schools putting students in solitary confinement? Since when did our schools become prisons? Already America violates international standards in our prisons. Internationally, it is considered that solitary confinement is a form of torture. Yet, here they are going a step beyond the prisons. This method is being used to punish school children, school children as young as kindergarten. We are raising a generation of young people to become used to solitary confinement. What does that say for the future?"
> —November 2012, KATU News

Scream rooms present such a special circumstance that they are impossible to classify under any single child abuse and child neglect law. "Scream room" is the term used most commonly to describe restraint and seclusion rooms in America's schools. The discussion on the use of scream rooms is quiet and deadly. I use the word *deadly* for a very good reason. Restraint and seclusion of minors relates to many of the concerns already covered in the section on child abuse and neglect. And children have died in scream rooms in America's schools.

## Restraint and Seclusion

Restraint and seclusion have all the elements of physical abuse, physical neglect, medical neglect, emotional abuse, emotional neglect, and educational neglect. Did I miss anything? Surely, I exaggerated. Review a few cases and the recommendation for laws covering restraint and seclusion in the United States. Then check the state by state status of schools near where you live to see if they even have specific guidelines.

Today, schools across the country use scream rooms. When children have emotional needs, such as when they are distraught or in a mental health crisis, schools from Massachusetts to Texas to Arizona and beyond put the children into an isolated room until they are no longer disruptive.

Elizabeth Erwin reported their use for CBS5 on February 23, 2012, in her article titled "Valley Schools Put Students in Padded 'Scream Rooms'" (Erwin 2012). The mother of a seven-year-old second grader said her son has been put into a five-by-five-foot padded box, which is kept in an empty classroom. She went to the school and took pictures. Her son said he had been kept there all day and not even let out to go to the bathroom.

And that's just one of the hundreds of examples. In Middletown, Connecticut, parents said their kids were being locked in closets. WVIT's Lauren Petty reported that parents had complained that their children were not learning because of the (negative) school environment. She said that teachers and staff put the children, including those with special needs, in what parents called the scream rooms (Petty 2012). There were reports of blood on the walls and urine on the floors. One parent said that the students were actually locked in the boxes.

Some parents believed the time-out rooms, as they are called by the school districts, are comfortable—maybe stocked with beanbag chairs or a few books—to resemble "a sort of Zen like atmosphere" to help kids to calm down (Kalthoff 2015). But in a North Texas elementary school, Bridget Villegas said her son Edwin was manhandled into a concrete room that looked like a jail. Edwin's mother said he is a special needs child but hadn't had problems in his previous school.

In prisons, locked cells separated from other inmates are called isolation cells. Isolation cells are mostly reserved for prisoners who have been tried by a jury of peers and sentenced to jail time. They receive due course decision-making on the part of the appropriately trained professionals using strict guidelines before they are housed in isolation. Isolation cells have toilet facilities, and the prisoners have water available to them. They are fed at regular intervals.

In locked psychiatric facilities for the severely mentally ill, there are isolation rooms for patients who are a danger to themselves or others. Patients who have been fully evaluated and committed by experts in the field are briefly placed in an isolation room until the crisis passes. There are strict laws regarding the conditions under which those patients are secured. There are two-way windows, and the patients must be observed; in many states, the law requires that observations be recorded every fifteen minutes. In some states, they must be observed continuously. Mentally ill patients have rights. They have a right to the least restrictive environment, use of a toilet, water as needed, and so on. Most importantly, they have a right to due process under the law.

If a classroom teacher or an aide is free to make isolation decisions, how are these decisions monitored? There is no evidence that students who are put into isolation rooms are cared for in any way. There is no evidence to support how the child's emotional needs are met in a situation that can clearly precipitate a behavioral or an emotional crisis or exacerbate on ongoing crisis.

The Autism National Committee, in 2013 and again in 2016, published a summary of state-by-state seclusion and restraint laws (Butler 2016). This document is eye-opening. Many states obligate their staff to protect only the rights of students with disabilities. Other states cover the use of restraint and seclusion under general laws relating to children. Some improvements have been made over time in the laws and statutes, but they may not translate into action within individual schools.

For example, although the door to a seclusion room can't be legally or actually locked with a formal lock, it can be functionally locked by being blocked, even with heavy furniture or other heavy equipment. In addition to this, permissible mechanical restraint includes duct tape, binding, and tying the child to the furniture. States do not generally require continuous supervision of children who are restrained.

Teachers and schools are the guardians and caregivers of our children in our absence. They are the people who yell, berate, bully, and humiliate. They are the people who put our children into isolation cells without due process. Where are the guidelines?

## Fifteen Principles

The United States Department of Education published a Restraint and Seclusion: Resource Document (US Department of Education. "Summary of Seclusion and Restraint Statutes, Regulations, Policies and Guidance, by State and Territories." 2013). The document contains extremely useful information, including state-by-state policies and, most importantly, the fifteen principles that the Department of Education put forth in regard to seclusion and restraint. The entire document is available for anyone to download at: www.ed.gov/policy/restraintseclusion. The document was endorsed by Arne Duncan, the former secretary of education, on May 15, 2012. It is reprinted here to clarify what are principals, not laws. I've italicized the words should consider to emphasize that these are not mandates, merely suggestions.

> "The Department, in collaboration with SAMHSA, has identified 15 principles that we believe States, local school districts, preschool, elementary, and secondary schools, parents, and other stakeholders *should consider* [italics added] as the framework for when States, localities, and districts develop and implement policies and procedures, which should be in writing related to restraint and seclusion to ensure that any use of restraint or seclusion in schools does not occur, except when there is a threat of imminent danger of serious

physical harm to the student or others, and occurs in a manner that protects the safety of all children and adults at school."

The following was included as a footnote to the principles:

"This Resource Document addresses the restraint or seclusion of any student regardless of whether the student has a disability. Federal laws, including the IDEA, the Americans with Disabilities Act of 1990, as amended, and Section 504 of the Rehabilitation Act of 1973, as amended, must be followed in any instance in which a student with a disability is restrained or secluded, or where such action is contemplated. This Resource Document does not, however, address the legal requirements contained in those laws.

"The Department (of Education) recognizes that States, localities, and districts may choose to exceed the framework set by the 15 principles by providing additional protections from restraint and seclusion.

"Every effort should be made to prevent the need for the use of restraint and for the use of seclusion.

Here are the fifteen principles that schools *should consider*.

1. Every effort should be made to prevent the need for the use of restraint and for the use of seclusion.
2. Schools should never use mechanical restraints to restrict a child's freedom of movement, and schools should never use a drug or medication to control behavior or restrict freedom of movement (except as authorized by a licensed physician or other qualified health professional)
3. Physical restraint or seclusion should not be used except in situations where the child's behavior poses imminent danger of serious physical harm to self or others and other interventions are

ineffective and should be discontinued as soon as imminent danger of serious physical harm to self or others has dissipated.
4. Policies restricting the use of restraint and seclusion should apply to all children, not just children with disabilities.
5. Any behavioral intervention must be consistent with the child's rights to be treated with dignity and to be free from abuse.
6. Restraint or seclusion should never be used as punishment or discipline (e.g., placing in seclusion for out-of-seat behavior), as a means of coercion or retaliation, or as a convenience.
7. Restraint or seclusion should never be used in a manner that restricts a child's breathing or harms the child.
8. The use of restraint or seclusion, particularly when there is repeated use for an individual child, multiple uses within the same classroom, or multiple uses by the same individual, should trigger a review and, if appropriate, revision of strategies currently in place to address dangerous behavior; if positive behavioral strategies are not in place, staff should consider developing them.
9. Behavioral strategies to address dangerous behavior that results in the use of restraint or seclusion should address the underlying cause or purpose of the dangerous behavior.
10. Teachers and other personnel should be trained regularly on the appropriate use of effective alternatives to physical restraint and seclusion, such as positive behavioral interventions and supports and, only for cases involving imminent danger of serious physical harm, on the safe use of physical restraint and seclusion.
11. Every instance in which restraint or seclusion is used should be carefully and continuously and visually monitored to ensure the appropriateness of its use and safety of the child, other children, teachers, and other personnel.
12. Parents should be informed of the policies on restraint and seclusion at their child's school or other educational setting, as well as applicable Federal, State, or local laws.

13. Parents should be notified as soon as possible following each instance in which restraint or seclusion is used with their child.
14. Policies regarding the use of restraint and seclusion should be reviewed regularly and updated as appropriate.
15. Policies regarding the use of restraint and seclusion should provide that each incident involving the use of restraint or seclusion should be documented in writing and provide for the collection of specific data that would enable teachers, staff, and other personnel to understand and implement the preceding principles.

The guidelines were distributed in a letter to each of the fifty states and their prospective school districts. The entire document, including seclusion and restraints statutes, regulations, policies and guidance by state and territories can be found at: www.ed.gov/policy/restraintseclusion.

The U.S. Department of Education document further stated as follows:

"In cases where a student has a history of dangerous behavior for, which restraint or seclusion was considered or used, a school should have a plan for: (1) teaching and supporting more appropriate behavior; and (2) determining positive methods to prevent behavioral escalations that have previously resulted in the use of restraint or seclusion.

Unfortunately, a plan doesn't seem to be in place. It has been years since the document was produced and distributed. It would be important for anyone with children in both private and public school to ask for a written copy of the district's seclusion and restraint policy. This gives you valuable information for any difficult situations that might arise while a child is at school. Knowing the seclusion and restraint policy gives parents an idea of how problems are handled by that particular district. Districts can develop their own plan separate from the states. When there are student behavior problems, many schools don't appear to use a uniform policy.

There has been a recent trend to follow a three-step intervention with students who are having issues in the classroom. This involves talking to the student and the student writing some school and self-directed responses to his or her behavior. However, this doesn't stop the teacher from embarrassing the student, which might include name calling, yelling, threatening, harassment, and employing some character assassination. Then, if that doesn't work, the student can be placed in what has been named the opportunity class by some school districts. This 'opportunity' is often an age and subject mixed class, often with one teacher who monitors work which has been assigned in that room. One of the middle school boys who suffers autism and is seen in my practice tests at the tenth to twelfth grade level. His mother brought copies of the first grade work he was given: there was no attempt to continue education at an appropriate level, and therefore no opportunity'. Finally, some schools use sitting all day in the office, again with nothing to do, no educational material. And suspension is a popular tool. Despite these many common options, restraint and seclusion continues to occur in the United States.

There are vast differences from state to state. Some states that say they have statutes and regulations addressing seclusion and restraint. Some states have statutes but no policies and guidance. This is the case for California, while other states, such as Colorado, have extremely detailed policies and guidance, making any restraint and/or seclusion of a child highly regulated. The United States Department of Education makes available a "Summary of Seclusion and Restraint Statutes, Regulations, Policies and Guidance, by State and Territories," this is available at: https://www2.ed.gov/policy/seclusion/seclusion-state-summary.html.

According to the US Department of Education, "School should be a safe and healthy environment in which America's children can learn, develop, and participate in instructional programs that promote high levels of academic achievement." This is a worthy pronouncement. But the US Department of Education, as well as the many states, counties, and school districts around the country, have with few exceptions failed.

Hearings before the House of Representatives were revealing. The testimony before the Committee on Education and Labor before the House of Representatives can be found at http://www.gao.gov/new.items/d09719t.pdf. The account was published by the US Government Accountability Office (GAO). It covers selective cases of child death and child abuse with the use of seclusion and restraint at public and private schools and treatment centers. The testimony indicates:

"...GAO found no federal laws restricting the use of seclusion and restraints in public and private schools and widely divergent laws at the state level. Although GAO could not determine whether allegations were widespread, GAO did find hundreds of cases of alleged abuse and death related to the use of these methods on school children during the past two decades. Examples of these cases include a seven-year-old purportedly dying after being held face down for hours by school staff, five-year-olds allegedly being tied to chairs with bungee cords and duct tape by their teacher and suffering broken arms and bloody noses, and a thirteen-year-old reportedly hanging himself in a seclusion room after prolonged confinement. Although GAO continues to receive new allegations from parents and advocacy groups, GAO could not find a single website, federal agency, or other entity that collects information on the use of these methods or the extent of their alleged abuse.

In addition, the GAO found that the cases reviewed were similar in several ways:

- they involved children with disabilities who were restrained and secluded, often in cases where they were not physically aggressive and their parents did not give consent;
- involved restraints, which can block air to the lungs and be deadly;
- involved teachers and staff who were often not trained in the use of seclusions and restraints;
- involved teachers and staff from at least five of the ten cases continue to be employed in education.

The findings are horrifying but not at all surprising. These are our children's caregiver-educators. When you fail at your primary goal of education and nothing happens, why do anything correctly? Why would any parent whose child attends a failing school or a school where the students all talk about the teachers' bad behaviors believe the school is going to do *anything* appropriately?

In chapter five, titled Laws Regulating Schools Responsibilities to Students, we covered the in loco parentis court rulings. Several states have incorporated in loco parentis into their laws and codes. Then educators have the right to discipline students to the same degree that parents may legally discipline their children.

But do parents have the right to seclude their child by force in a box? What would happen if your teenage son or daughter was out of control and you use the minimum force needed to restrain them for their safety or for the safety of someone else? Let's say it was for your own safety—how would that work? What do you think would happen if you wrangled or otherwise dragged your ten-year-old autistic child into a large box and restrained him or her in some way so that he or she cannot hurt you?

In most states, teachers, vice principals, principals, or other certificated employees of school boards operating under state law are allowed to use the same legal degree of physical control over children as the parent. They have immunity from criminal prosecution and penalties when they use physical control. Do you have immunity? Almost all the states have the same school rights to discipline students and have been given immunity from criminal charges.

Let's say you've restrained your thirteen-year-old daughter because she becomes hysterical when you say she can't go out on a date, won't do her homework, or refuses to do her chores. She won't budge. Every time you try to get her up off the floor in her room, she starts yelling and kicking all over again. Can you restrain her and isolate her? Maybe, but I don't think it's a good idea. If you do, imagine what happens on Monday at school when she tells her friends that you held her down on the floor, they tell the teacher, the teacher calls the office, and then your daughter tells her story to the school's vice principal.

It's likely that you'll be visited by law enforcement and your county's child protection agency. There are frequent cases of children being removed from their homes even before a thorough investigation is done. Then how long does it take to get the child back into the home? And how much damage has been done? Just imagine what could happen if light bruising occurred on the arms or shoulders where the out-of-control teen was held down.

But if your eleven-year-old son has a temper tantrum at school, refuses to leave the floor, refuses to do his work, and screams when someone tries to move him, will he be restrained and carted away? If he continues to yell in the office, he will likely be secluded in some manner. Yes, probably. If this happens with some frequency, the school will of course develop a plan that assures safety and guarantees your child's FAPE, regardless of his mental health needs, right? No, unlikely.

So, how is it that the law allows the school to have rights beyond the parents' rights? Well, the case law is pretty clear. The school has exactly the same rights. The school does not have more rights. But schools use corporal punish, seclusion, and restraint. And the school is exempted from the incurred penalties or liabilities when they exercise these rights. Are you exempted when you exercise these rights? So, who do you believe has more rights? Have the US Department of Education's fifteen principles had an effect on the schools' behaviors?

Some states have banned isolation booths (Dungca 2013). But schools have gotten around the bans by calling them isolation rooms ("Oregon Archives" 2014). An April 2014 post reported that the Oregon schools easily bypassed the state ban. Voilà! Change the name of what was called the isolation booth to isolation room and the practice goes on unchanged, regardless of the change in the law.

The results of the use of restraint and seclusion are pretty easy to guess. Children are frightened. They don't know what will happen to them. They are traumatized. They have nightmares. Children wet themselves. There are many reports of children being forgotten in the box. At times, they are yelled at; at other times, they are ignored. There doesn't seem to be any time limit in isolation.

In 2014, many school districts still had no guidelines. That hasn't changed. In 2012, school administrators in Washington actually said that the "therapeutic booth" is "beneficial" (Zhao 2012). Who do they benefit? Certainly not the child. Where's the research? In 2014, one child had been twenty-one times to the isolation room. What has he learned? Certainly, no education is happening in there. He's not learning history or math or how to behave. His mother said he is growing more resistant.

Other children have been locked up even more frequently. They spend from a short time up to all day in isolation. Children are locked in, restrained, not fed, and not allowed to use the bathroom, wet and soil themselves, and get scratched and bruised while being dragged into isolation. Children as young as five years are isolated. They are scared. In one year, more than sixty-six thousand instances of restraint and isolation were recorded. These are only the recorded incidents. Although the states are required to report every use of seclusion and restraint, some are not reported and some states simply turn over no data. With the great success rate of America's schools' accountability, do you wonder how many thousands more are not recorded? The children are not supervised. Many of the rooms are premanufactured and are about four-by-four feet.

There is no limit to the documentation that restraint and seclusion of children, or in the words of Dr. Keith Ablow, is "psychological sadism"; there are thousands of articles and complaints (Ablow 2014). But is this the tip of the iceberg? How many parents or children have not reported their school's use of restraint and seclusion? What if the parent is illiterate and doesn't understand? We already know that illiteracy is a terrible problem in the United States. A significant percentage of our population, including high school graduates, cannot read and write. Maybe neither the child nor the parent speaks English. Perhaps they are here illegally and are afraid to report the abuse by the school. And then there are parents who just don't care. Or the school has convinced the parents that there is nothing else they can do with the child, and it is best for everyone. Who exactly is everyone? Is what we know about seclusion and restraint in our schools all there is to know, or is this the tip of the iceberg?

Does anyone ask the student about claustrophobia or whether he or she needs water after he or she has lost control and have been dragged to the padded cells? There is absolutely no law about how often an isolated child must be viewed. There is no due process, and there is no recourse. Does your child's school have an isolation box? How about a written restraint policy? Is it detailed? Use the links provided above and check out the policies and procedures related to seclusion and restraint around the country. How does your state stack up?

Who is qualified at your neighborhood school to restrain a child? Who is qualified to decide if it's safe a child to be isolated? Who's in charge? Unlike jail and mental institutions, there are no guaranteed rights. There are no legal proceedings. Unlike criminal jails, there are no term limits in our schools' jails. However, it would be inconvenient for the school staff to lock up a student overnight. If school hours were longer, would you like to guess whether scream rooms would also be occupied for longer times? How do we protect them against those personnel who just like to abuse children and actually cause escalation of behavioral meltdowns when the child can no longer cope with that teacher? Who is the school's watchdog? Is this the same watchdog who disregards most teachers' complaints? Is the fox watching the hen house? Who evaluates each school's use of restraint and isolation, or do the schools just get to say that they have a particularly bad group of students? Maybe they blame the families or their cultures.

How much money do we spend each year in the name of behavioral interventions that are not interventions at all, but rather are barbaric deprivations of the constitutional rights of every American—especially children? When will schools be held responsible to educate our children and keep them safe?

## Summary

Seclusion and restraint is happening right here, right now, in the American school system. Is this bullying, or is it worse than any abuse you've seen in your life? Our last bastions, our great brotherhoods of educators have been given unending rights because they know what they're doing and there's no one who is powerful enough to stand up to them. These are professionals, right? They educate, right? Civilization has not advanced much when scream rooms are our solution to students' problems.

## CHAPTER 9
# Unravelling Teacher Child Abuse and Child Neglect

> "To speak the truth...won't necessarily lead anywhere, but it might."
> —Vaclav Havel

Reading about teacher child abuse and teacher child neglect tells us how real this problem is in our society. Yet, when we were injured as children and when our children are now subjected to injury or abuse by a teacher, we're not always sure of what we're seeing. To help with that, we're going to dissect an incident of abuse by a teacher. I'm using an example again from my own experience. It's best to use real material because all the details are accurate and the outcome is known. There are thousands of cases that have been publicly reported, but we don't have every detail of the events. More importantly, others need to see that no one is unaffected by child abuse and child neglect in America's schools. If someone thinks he or she is exempted, it only means that person isn't looking around.

Preschool is a good place for young children to learn social skills. The children's role models shift from the parents to the teachers and the aides in the preschool environment. The children are usually between two and five years old. Many children in this age group have had little exposure to the outside world. They are innocent and naive. All the rules are new. The simple procedures they learn, such as standing in line, are first-time experiences. We want to trust that our precious children are trained, guided, or instructed with patience and kindness as they experience and explore a new world away from home.

The educational environment in the United States demands that our children have a high degree of knowledge about and compliance to the institutions' rules. So, all the little people go off to preschool to practice for the big world of elementary school. As carefully as they can, parents select a safe and family friendly setting for their munchkin's first venture into the big world without the constant protection of family. Parents hope that they have made the right choice. They hope that the teacher is well qualified and experienced. Parents hope that the teacher will care about their children as much as they do. Small children assume that everyone loves them. They trust that their parents wouldn't have them do anything that would injure them.

The next vignette is as accurately narrated as memory will allow. The purpose in reviewing the events is to follow, in detail, an incident of child abuse and child neglect from the beginning to the end. The goal is to help parents track the steps involved in following the evolution of an event, to watch it unfold, and to understand how doggedly determined professionals can be in demanding control over a child (not their own); it also seeks to show how scary it is to see criminal acts unfold, how willing a professional is to risk his or her license and livelihood based on an unsupported, illegal, and immoral behavior. Because he or she feels like doing it.

## Dissecting Abuse

I'm always surprised at how people want to hang on to their own unsubstantiated beliefs and defend their indefensible behaviors. Unabashed, brazen statements meant to rationalize stupidity can surprise the listener. Sometimes, divining a response to mumbo jumbo can take time. This incident is an example of a complex child abuse event. In a fairly bizarre incident, when one of my sons was young, he was traumatized by the poorly considered and dangerously criminal behavior of one of his favorite teachers. Here's the background.

On a monthly calendar, a snack day was assigned to each parent for the preschool class. The snack menu was very specific and posted in advance on the calendar. On this particular Wednesday, the snack was crackers and cheese. But the parent who was responsible for the snack that day didn't bring her child to school, nor did she bring the snack. My four-year-old went to school as usual. He was always happy to see the other children, even though he was very shy.

Because there was no snack, someone at the school was sent to the nearby store with instructions to purchase food items; this somehow wound up to include some form of breakfast sausages. Our own children didn't eat breakfast sausage. We didn't want them to get a massive dose of chemicals and preservatives. We didn't want them to have the high salt content, nor did we want them to eat that much pepper. Equally, we didn't want our children to eat the fat. Other families may have made other choices. Some probably found nothing wrong with this food for their children. But being a sweet four-year-old in our family includes doing what your parents have taught you to do. This includes not eating anything that isn't particularly healthy, especially foods that are understood to be full of chemicals. Last time I looked, this is something of a free country. Parents get to choose for their young children.

Generally, children know what choices their parents have made for them. On this particular preschool day, the unplanned sausages were served for morning snack along with some other item. My son ate the other item but said, "No, thank you," to the sausage. That was the beginning of the worst day in his preschool life. Whatever trust he had in others to treat him kindly was dashed. This four-year-old child was given the sausage, despite his polite decline. It was put on his little paper plate. He was told he had to eat it. He again said, "No, thank you." Then the unthinkable happened.

The teacher told him, in front of the class, that she had a one-bite rule and that everyone had to try what was provided. There was to be no exception. We had never heard of this rule. If we had, we would have formally addressed the issue and denied the school the right to feed my child whatever they wanted.

What followed was the "or else" that ended in his not ever wanting to go back to school. The teacher humiliated a four-year-old in front of the entire classroom. His teacher made his eating the sausage the priority of her morning. He was called out in front of the class and reprimanded for refusing the sausage. She went to his seat and told him repeatedly that he had to take a bite. She held the sausage in front of his face while she made him stand in front of her. The other children were encouraged to tell him to eat the sausage. They were all brought into the "or else" by the teacher. She made them her little minions, and they were directed to do her bidding.

My son later said that they were "all against me." He thought that they were his friends, but after the incident, he never wanted to see them again. He thought that the teacher was nice, and he had trusted her. But now he was afraid of her.

He continued to shake his head when he was repeatedly told to eat the sausage. The teacher became more aggressive and began to belittle him. She stood in front of his class and his newly made friends and told him that he was acting like a baby. Then she told the class that he was going to the baby class where he belonged if he didn't eat the sausage. Again, he said nothing. He said later that he was too scared to talk. He repeated the reason feebly to me as well: "Mom, you know we don't eat sausage!"

Her failure to get him to eat the sausage on demand obviously infuriated her. She proceeded to have the aide take him by the arm and march him at a fast pace to the classroom where the two- and three-year-olds were sitting at their tables. Then this aide announced to the entire two to three-year-old group, and their teacher, that my son was going to stay in their room until he learned to eat what he had been told to eat.

I can only imagine what went through the little minds of the small children who were abruptly interrupted with this grand announcement. What did that mean? How can you go backward in school for not eating a sausage? That must be a really bad thing! This boy must have done something really bad. The best I can come up with is that this dramatic event—in the lives of the small people in the classroom as well as for my son—engendered fear and mass confusion.

The aide left him there. He started to cry. The teacher for the younger children completely ignored him. She didn't question the decision, she didn't offer comfort, apparently she also didn't inform any other adult. No one called me. He sat there for the rest of the school day. He didn't talk to anyone.

When we picked him up after school, he was very quiet. But that wasn't unusual. He was a particularly quiet child, shy and reserved. It wasn't until we were alone, at bedtime, that he slowly started to ask questions. He wanted to know if it was OK to say no. Then he wanted to know if he had to go back to the baby classroom tomorrow. Then he started to cry and said that he was afraid that I was never going to be able to find him because he was not in his class. I had no idea what he was talking about. Then he found the words to say what had happened that day and where he had been. He was afraid, and he held on to me as if someone was going to hurt him again. I was so stunned by what he told me had happened that day; I simply couldn't assimilate. We just sat glued together for a very long time.

At this point, what are you thinking about the sausage incident? Here are some responses that I have heard:

- He should have just eaten the sausage;
- His mother was overprotective, and it was her fault;
- The teacher must had had another reason to behave that way;
- The child must have been a problem kid for the teacher to do what she did;

- The teacher was crazy;
- The teacher was bizarre;
- The teacher had a problem; and
- The teacher committed several criminal acts.

Thankfully, I had gotten to know the parents of some of the other children. I called one of the mothers the very next day and calmly asked her if she would check something with her son. I wanted her to ask him if anything different had happened with my son earlier the previous day. She did so gladly, and later that evening, she called back. Her son described the events and then said he hadn't seen my son since and that some of the children in his class were whispering and afraid. The mother was appalled by what her son told her and wanted to know if there was anything she could do. I thanked her and said I'd take care of the incident.

It took several days to work through what had happened before I called the teacher to hear what she had to say. She didn't ask about my son. She demanded to know where he was. When I asked her about what had happened, she became adamant that her one-bite rule had to be followed. She sounded stunned when I said my son did not want to return to school and that I was unsure of what I would do next. I scheduled a meeting with the administration.

The meeting took place the next afternoon. Apparently, word had gotten around the K–8 school, via the children, that something was wrong. But not everyone knew what had really happened and so immediately there was an assumption by the children—who hadn't witnessed the events—that that boy had done something wrong. It's very likely that even the little people who were witnesses to the events and those who were made to participate were still confused by what they saw. How could they think that a teacher might do something wrong? It must be that the child did something really bad thing. As always, many people believed that teachers could never be the culprit.

I began the meeting by clearly saying I didn't want to be interrupted, that I had not yet made a decision about any further action, and that I would leave that topic depending on the outcome of the meeting. I related the events as they had been told to me. I asked for confirmation by the aide, the classroom teacher of the baby class, and my son's classroom teacher. No one wanted to speak. I explained that unless this was dealt with, I would include all the families of the children who were involved. There would be a public disclosure of this event. I would retain legal representation. Other parents could discuss the incident at home and make their own decisions about their children's place in the school. After all, the teacher had already involved all the children of the two classes and the others through rumor.

This is the gist of the incident that, when dissected, includes the following:

1. The menu for morning break didn't have to change. All the parents knew what their children were going to eat, and there was no reason that the person who went to the market couldn't get the expected food items. Sausage was not then, nor had it ever been, considered for the morning snack menu. It appeared that sausage was chosen because the shopper wanted to eat sausage.
2. Children were always free to bring their own morning snack. They never had to participate in the available snack. My son had planned to eat the cheese and crackers and so did not bring a snack. But he was in no danger of starving in the two-hour period. Eating a snack was not mandatory.
3. There was no one-bite policy. Despite her protestations that she had always had a one-bite policy, no parent had ever heard of this policy and it did not appear anywhere in writing.
4. The teacher had previously been warned by the administrator that she was not the parent of the children, that she could not act as their parent, and that she could not override the parent. There had been previous incidents involving her.

We covered other topics at my insistence. It did seem that the seriousness of the incidents, and the number of adults involved, indicated that this group of teachers had no training in child management, nor did it seem they were educated in child abuse and child neglect laws.

These are the topics we covered:

- Force-feeding children is abusive. Force-feeding is defined, in part, by the threat of serious consequences if the child does not eat what is handed to him or her. It can have long-term health consequences, such as bulimia and anorexia. Force-feeding can easily result in an association between food and fear.
- There is absolutely no evidence that making a child eat some of everything has any positive effect on his or her life. Children who are selective in their food choices do not die of malnutrition, do not live limited lives, and they do not fail to experience other wonderful opportunities as adults.
- Public humiliation of a four-year-old child is child psychological abuse. Child psychological abuse results in long-term problems. Public humiliation results in the victim being embarrassed and afraid. Public humiliation is straight out of the medieval pillory, when people were put in head and hand locks in the public square to be publicly humiliated to teach them a lesson.
- Threatening and demeaning children is child psychological abuse. Reread the federal definition provided in the section of child psychological abuse. Threatening to move a child to a setting in which he or she does not belong causes the child great fear. Actually going so far as to move the child causes more fear. The child has no idea what might come next. Children have no cognitive ability to comprehend why they are being threatened, why this is happening to them, and why they have one rule at home and a different rule at school. When a parent says don't eat sausage because it is bad for you and has no nutritional value, children are terrified when another adult punishes them for not eating something that they know as bad.

- Minions are created when children are involuntarily dragged into the abusive behavior of an adult. Psychological manipulation of innocent children is child abuse. Innocent children have to make a quick choice about who they are going to support when a teacher becomes an abuser. The resulting forced choice causes children who are bystanders to feel guilty and bad about themselves. Children know when something wrong is happening. Children know when other children are being abused. They know they are taking part in the same wrong thing the adult is doing. Yet they are forced to abandon their support for their abused friend because they themselves now feel afraid, confused, and uncertain about the consequences for them if they don't go along with the teacher.
- We call little people children because they require patient guidance at the hands of real adults. If these small people could make wise and logical decision and if they could stand up for themselves and take care of themselves, we would call them adults, and parents and teachers would not be required as guardians. Guardians are responsible for protecting children because they cannot protect themselves. Children must be kept safe in school; they are defenseless against powerful figures that are set up to be role models but instead humiliate them on a whim.

At the end of the meeting I asked the question, "What should the outcome be?" Rather than attempt a responsible answer, only one person in the room spoke, and that was in the form of a question. I was asked by the adult who had committed child psychological abuse, "What are you going to do?"

What I would have liked to say was, "Are you kidding me?" I continued to see that this group of professionals did not understand their responsibilities. They sounded anxious that they were there to be punished and were unable to move into the necessary adult role. The question they asked was all about them and not the child. The first question should have been, "What can we do to make this right?" Here are some examples of the questions which open a dialog and put the responsibility back on the perpetrator. Choose any of them or all. Which one would you start with?

- What should happen next?
- How do you see this problem being resolved?
- How will you change the outcome for the student?
- How will you change the outcome for yourself?
- How will you develop and demonstrate concern for your students?
- What will you do to help the student witnesses?
- What have you learned from the problems you created?

What should you, as the reader, take away from this example, this dissection of teacher-child psychological abuse? A critical lesson here is that a parent should never accept the defenses of some teacher or other school personnel. There are some things to learn about responses before we go on to identifying types of teacher abuse tactics and the teacher defense tactics in chapters 11, 12, and 13. Here are the lessons:

1. Take as much time, days if needed, to care for your child who has been shocked, confused, and frightened.
2. Use as much time as you need to gather information.
3. Take the time to calm yourself so that you are able to evaluate the possible outcomes, both good and bad.
4. Examine every part of this complex example of teacher-child psychological abuse; this is critical to the outcome.
5. Make a list, write out the events, make good notes, and record the entire incident in some useful way.
6. Gather information from outside sources if they are available.
7. Edit what you know when you get new information.

8. Consult with outside professionals if possible. Counselors and attorneys are good choices.
9. Anticipate denial and retaliation as you formulate a plan of action.

## What We Can Learn

The teachers and staff involved in the sausage incident needed training. It was obvious that no one in the room had the experience of being held accountable; even if they had, they certainly hadn't learned anything positive from the experience. The administration did not take a lead role—actually, no role at all! It appeared that administration had moved through the ranks on some pathway that didn't include leadership experience. The administration also had no control over the teacher's behavior. No one was in charge. The meeting continued, dragging out the issues, and dragging the adults through a damage assessment of all the students before finally getting to the question of what was next. A lack of education complicated the problem.

Where were these teachers when they were supposed to be in classes for child behavior and child psychology? Where were they when they were supposed to be studying stages of child development? If they took the classes, if they passed the classes, and if they stayed awake during the classes, they had definitely not learned how to apply the material. Or perhaps the classes were as inadequate as many of the classes we see today, from kindergarten through twelfth grade. The classroom teacher responsible for the abhorrent incident had been crying through parts of the meeting. Her first and only suggestion was that she would stand with my son in front of the class the next day—if I would let him return—and make a public apology, explaining how wrong she was. I had a flash vision of her standing in front of the class, bawling her eyes out and clinging to my four-year-old, begging for forgiveness. Don't forget that this teacher had already been warned about her overbearing and parental behaviors with the students, and obviously nothing had changed.

In response, we discussed the potential problem of enabling a small child to have an experience of power and control over an adult who is a role model and caregiver. There were reasons that we were careful about when we wanted to make amends. We agreed on two things. First, she would privately apologize with an uninvolved board member present. This would provide some structure for the teacher and some degree of weightiness, as a warning about her future behaviors. Second, she would calmly explain to the class that there is no one-bite rule and that she made a mistake for which she was responsible. If any of the children wanted to talk about what had happened, they were told that there was a special person who would be in the office all week to talk to them alone. They were encouraged to tell their parents what had happened, including the fact that there was no one-bite rule. A note was to be sent home assuring parents that there was no one-bite rule and that it was an error on the part of the teacher.

The sausage incident wasn't the first and it wasn't the last at this school. It's only a sample of what goes on in today's educational environment, how to address this kind of problem, and see that it's possible to stand your ground and procure a result.

## Summary

There are two lessons to be learned here before you begin to better understand the bastion that supports teacher abuse. First, by the time you've thought these steps through, you will come to see that there are no excuses, no defenses, and nothing OK about child abuse. If you stand your ground with what you know, stick to the facts and don't deviate, you won't be controlled by the anger, the self-righteousness, or the position of the perpetrator.

The second lesson taken from this example is to never accept an explanation or rationalization for anything that is absolutely wrong. Explaining why a child had to be injured is absurd. Remember, there is no right excuse;

any excuse is just a delaying action meant to deflect the perpetrator's accountability.

The next chapters cover everything necessary to identify the types of psychological and emotional child abuse and child neglect in schools. In addition to this, there is significant material regarding what to anticipate from the perpetrator once confronted. Taken together, dissecting child abuse and child neglect in the school won't be so fear inducing. When the next negative problem occurs, reread these chapters. Dissect the event to prepare your responses. Don't give up and don't allow someone who is in a position of power over your children put you on the defensive. Fight using the tools you have to stop child abuse and neglect.

# CHAPTER 10

# Things to Know about Human Behavior and Communication

> "No problem can be solved from the same
> level of consciousness that created it."
> —ALBERT EINSTEIN

Teachers who abuse and neglect children have been around forever. They are protected from consequences by their position and because they have an enormous bastion to whitewash all complaints. Parents and students have no recourse unless they have a thorough working knowledge of how teacher-child abuse works. Once everyone can see and understand what goes on when a teacher abuses or neglects, there is some chance of documenting, labeling, and calling out the perpetrator.

Chapters 9 through 12 are particularly important because most types of emotional and psychological teacher-child abuse and teacher-child neglect are described here in ways that every schoolchild can understand. Children are the victims, and they need to know how to identify what they are seeing. Each type of child abuse and child neglect is given a name. It's easier for students to talk about teacher neglect and child abuse if they have the word to use to express what they are experiencing as the problems occur.

Students know how they feel, and they know when something is wrong. But teachers are still seen as the all-powerful by young people. In many cases, they are stunned by maltreatment. Young people from average families only suffer the wrath of their parents if there is an extraordinary event. Most average families discuss issues. Sometimes a reasonable and just consequence is applied. In the classroom, a reasonable and just consequence might include a reduced grade for turning in a paper past its due date, a call home when a student talks too much, or a poor grade if work is incomplete.

But when a young person faces consequences that are not reasonable and just, he or she becomes angry and confused. In addition to this, unlike in their own homes with parents or guardians, kids have no means to combat the offending teacher. The students' only possible defense begins by understanding what's happening, knowing what they're looking at, and having a name to label the abuse and the neglect.

In the following section, major profiles of teacher-child abuse and child neglect are fully described. This covers a lot of ground. Even so, there's a good chance you can add a few profiles that aren't on this list.

## Single Incident, Habitual, and Systematic Child Abuse and Child Neglect

Incidents of child abuse and child neglect can happen and they can happen only once. Any person can make an error in judgment that results in injury, but it is nonintentional. That's a single incident; it has never happened before and it doesn't have to repeat itself. If the incident is repeated, happening over and over again with little change, child abuse and child neglect becomes habitual. The perpetrator's behavior is part of his or her habitual pattern. Habitual child abuse and child neglect that is preplanned, targeted, and carried through is systematic. When a perpetrator repeats abuse and neglect of the children in his or her care, we say his or her problems are systemic; that is, the perpetrator's crimes are a part of his or her system. The abuse and neglect is a significant part of who he or she is as a person.

## Single-Incident Child Abuse and Child Neglect

In chapter 9, the section titled "Dissecting Abuse," the behavior of the preschool teacher who accepted the abused child into her classroom was likely guilty of single-incident abuse (the sausage incident). Her allowing the child to sit and cry for the remainder of the day is an excellent example of a classic teacher-perpetrated child psychological abuse. But the accusation of abuse and neglect was dumped on her by the offending teacher, who not only wanted to control the student, but also took control of the teacher who received the child with no announcement. This may have been the only time that this receiving teacher in the sausage incident behaved in this very dysfunctional way. Because I didn't hear of other times from the administrator or from one of the other parents, that doesn't mean it didn't happen a second time or it didn't happen repeatedly. And some type of abusive behavior could have been aimed at another child in another year. However, it is equally possible that this was a single-incident abuse, and the receiving teacher was an adult victim and not an intentional perpetrator. A single incident refers to the frequency of the teacher being abusive or neglectful in the past—whether or not this is an isolated incident.

For the benefit of doubt, let's say a teacher has some awful home problems that are temporarily and seriously affecting his or her behavior and judgement. The personal problem gets cleared up, the offending professional educator realizes the enormous problem he or she has created with one student or many students, and he or she immediately sets about correcting his or her own behavior in a mature and responsible way.

Not likely, though. Actually, many people would deny and ignore complaints rather than face the responsibility of owning up to their own huge missteps. But following the offence, in the event of the offender becoming aware and remorseful and taking a corrective action in an educational context, the abuse is now given the name of single-incident abuse.

## Habitual Child Abuse and Child Neglect

The very nature of human functioning is, in part, dictated by its resistance to change. We resist change because we are *required* to habituate. To habituate is to get used to something, often a behavior, a substance of some type, or a psychological way of conducting ourselves. We are built to habituate. We habituate to almost everything. The way we swing our arms and the way we blink our eyes are all habitual. There's a long list of negatives we can readily recite, such as habituation to drugs, tobacco, gambling, credit cards, and carbohydrates. The list of habituations is too long to imagine.

Most of us know about negative habituations and may even have one or two of these ourselves. But we don't think too much of our habituations in comparison to positive things. We do things without thinking, such as getting up without an alarm clock, brushing our teeth, and washing ourselves. Or we habituate ourselves to sleeping late. We habituate ourselves to dance steps, to how we hold a pencil, to even the accent that distinguishes our culture or origin, and to the emphasis we are placing on certain words while speaking. And there are millions of other habituations.

Look, for example, at driving a car. Once you've driven for some time, you have been habituated to driving. Grab the keys, unlock, slide in, put foot on brake, start engine, look over the left or maybe the right shoulder while buckling the seatbelt, check the mirrors, take the foot off the brake and slowly move it onto accelerator, back up, turn the wheel, and so on it goes. Is your personal pattern a little different? Of course it is. Because everyone has their own pattern to which they have uniquely habituated. But what would happen if we hadn't been habituated to that pattern? Well, we would then have to reteach ourselves to drive a vehicle every time we have to operate that particular piece of machinery. Our patterns of repeated behaviors or habituated behaviors are unique to each of us, and once established, they are enormously difficult to change.

Don't believe that? Try driving a standard shift rental car in London for the first time. Sit on the right side of the car, shift with the left hand, clutch with the left foot, drive on the left side of the road, and then enter and exit the roundabouts in morning traffic. Or try renaming the signal light colors. Call red "go," green "slow down," and yellow "stop." Yes, we're still driving, but the change is extremely difficult, and no one voluntarily puts themselves through these changes unless they have no options. Try moving your office two blocks from your old office. Ever turned the wrong way while heading home after you have moved to a new house? That's because we all habituate to whatever behavior we have chronically repeated.

So, this is it with humans. We don't easily change. We resist change. Even with determination and even when it's in our best interests, we might not stop cursing or being sarcastic, abrupt, or nonresponsive. We are habituated to even ourselves. We are habituated to our own thoughts. Association tests evaluate which of your thoughts most commonly follow the previous thought: black/white, up/down, good/bad, and so on. Our repetitive expressions, the way we walk, and our hand movements are all habitual. Hence, so are the labels that we apply to the people around us. We call people cheerful, curmudgeons, sullen, kind, and other names because of a group of repeated behaviors or habituations we observe in the individual.

So, what's the chance that a dysfunctional person is going to repeat a dysfunctional behavior? Almost 100 percent. What is the chance of an abusive, neglectful teacher repeating these behaviors, whether or not you are there to see them? Almost 100 percent. So, let's say that a teacher humiliates you in front of the class. Even if it is a single incident for you, the chance that it is a single incident or it is the only time the teacher has behaved in that way is almost zero.

Teacher-child abuse and child neglect are habitual. Teachers become known to the students by their horrible behaviors. Whether they are lazy and neglectful or mean and abusive, they have decided that these habits suit them, and it is unlikely that they will change with future students.

## **Systematic Child Abuse and Child Neglect**
Most teachers who abuse and neglect are habituated to these behaviors and, as with the habitual credit card spender, they may get a great rush

from their behavior. But over time, the behaviors may become increasingly intense and more frequent. And as with the sarcastic or rude person, the credit card addicts or the alcoholic, they know they really can't and don't want to stop these behaviors. Their repeated behaviors are habitual, predictable, and ugly and they become systemic. The person who systematically abuses and neglects a child is not going to change just because someone gave him or her a talking to or wrote a negative review. That abuse and neglect has become systemic, a part of the person, and the behavior is habituated and systematic. And that person might be your child's teacher.

Systematic child abuse and child neglect is different from habitual abuse. Yes, it's habitual, but it is also preplanned and targeted. Much teacher-child abuse and child neglect really appears to be systematic and/or systemic. Systematic and/or systemic dysfunctional behaviors are ongoing and dangerous. Ongoing unacceptable behaviors repeat themselves in a multitude of ways. We have said that child abuse and child neglect are likely to be repeated because repeated behaviors, good and bad, are best understood as one aspect of common human functioning.

Systematic means following a set method or pattern. Systematic behaviors, thoughts, feelings, attitudes, prejudices, and so on have a method, a plan, or a pattern. The individual habituates to behaviors, and child abuse and child neglect are almost always habitual, a problem that envelops the perpetrator. When an individual begins to use these habituated behaviors in a string of planned actions, then child abuse and child neglect becomes systematic.

There was a local teacher who had his class line up every day for the bell. This was also the teacher who showed up to the class about fifteen minutes late every day. How could that happen? This teacher habitually and psychologically abused and academically neglected his students. No one held him accountable. But his habitual problem of habitually avoiding his job had facilitated an entire *systematic* behavior pattern of child abuse and child neglect. This is how it played out for the teacher and for the students.

First, this teacher varied the exact number of minutes he was going to be avoidant or late—usually within a five-minute range. When he arrived, he would catch one of the students somewhat out of the lineup. By the way, the specific behavior of catching (or inventing) a bad behavior that is meant to divert attention away from your own bad behavior and toward a victim is called *deflection*. We'll go over this again in chapters 11 and 12, where we will talk about patterns of abuse and patterns of defense.

This teacher didn't have any information about what was happening with the students in the time-lapse between when the bell rang and when he finally showed up because he wasn't there. But probably on his way to the classroom lineup, he would create some scene that included the use of anger. He probably had a collection of accusations that he had practiced over years. I only say this because his patterns were described by many different people in different ways, but all the descriptions confirmed the underlying patterns. When he arrived on the scene, he would look and act angry that the students were not in a perfect, quiet line. Remember now, these are young people who were on time. They were standing around, waiting for him for about fifteen minutes, knowing that he was late and knowing that they would have to rush through the remainder of the allotted class time. The ritual of standing in a straight line at the sound of a bell without moving around, without talking, or without getting restless while waiting for someone who chooses to be late every day doesn't belong in an educational setting; there's no education in this scenario. This behavior would be part of a military training boot camp.

So, this teacher put on his angry act and handed out consequences on a daily basis. Sometimes the consequence included making someone look bad, shaming, calling out a student for the look on his or her face, or for talking when the teacher was walking up the line. Sometimes it was worse; he would take away a ball and not return it, make up some offence that didn't exist, and so on. Sometimes he used it as an opportunity to psychologically abuse a student he didn't like. He would then proceed to use a made-up, pretended, and self-righteous anger to manage the students for the remainder of the class period. He would act as if the students' morning lineup behavior was his reason to be in a bad mood all day.

He fully escaped any recourse for his own bad behavior. The kids were silent and often fearful of participating in his class. That is, except for the few minions. This problem of minions is covered in chapter 14.

The late teacher had first habituated himself to various abusive and neglectful behaviors. Here, he was putting together these habituations into a string of intentionally harmful actions. He had developed a system. This wasn't just repeated or frequent abuse and neglect; it was systematic. It was planned and intentional. In this situation, the teacher was committing child psychological abuse and child educational neglect. This teacher's systemic dysfunction was acted out as systematic child abuse and child neglect for years.

Of course, there are thousands of vile, horrible reports of systematic child abuse by teachers. Many of them are forms of sexual abuse or physical abuse, and they all contain some measure of psychological abuse. Systematic child educational neglect is commonplace. Any teacher who hands out work and uses the classroom for more fun activities while the students do the meaningful learning on their own at home is guilty of systematic child educational neglect. The example of the angry excuse-maker who refused to come to class on time isn't dramatic; it is commonplace! We can learn about dramatic abuse from the media. We need to look into common abuse and neglect that happens every day to understand why America's schools are failing.

## Verbal and Nonverbal Communication

There are lots of types of communication. When we think of communication, we usually think of words. Words are commonly a part of communication, but they are a limited part of communication. People regularly say things like, "We need to communicate." What they often mean is that they want to use words. But most communication is not through words.

## Verbal Communication

Verbal messages are pretty easy to observe. Obviously, that's because you can hear them. We use verbal language to convey things such as information or opinion. Words are necessary in almost every part of our lives. In fact, we generally think in words; it makes one wonder how people gathered their own thoughts and conveyed messages in times before language arrived. But the part of any message that delivers the most meaning is really the nonverbal message. The words we use become influential or are given meaning because of the nonverbal messages we send along with those words.

## Nonverbal Communication

Nonverbal communication accounts for a large part of any message that passes between people. There are myriad books available on popular psychology and communication; there are book markets that address communication. But simply put, most of the messages that we send or receive are sent through some other means than the words we say. Other than messages that contain specific information, messages are primarily transmitted through facial expression. The eyes convey the majority of the message. The mouth, the forehead, and the face as a whole deliver messages that are easily readable. Body posture and posturing are other forms of nonverbal communication. And finally the tone, the speed, and the inflection of the message say almost everything else.

We can turn a group of identical words from a statement to a question by changing the inflection on the end of the sentence. We can turn an observation into a command by changing the inflection, the tone, and the volume. Try saying "I love you" using different tones, inflection, volume, and speed of delivery. The meaning of the words is altered with every delivery. Now, add to it many different facial expressions. Say the words with raised eyebrows, puckered lips, frowns, a very straight face, a smile or laugh. Finally, say the words "I love you" with your head in various positions. The meaning of the words "I love you" continues to change.

It's sadly amusing that teachers can use nonverbal messages that are as obvious as any used by their teenage students but believe that their students somehow don't know what they are doing. Making faces, rolling eyes, grunting, making negative sounds, or acting horrified or inconvenienced are all ways that teachers ridicule students using nonverbal messages.

We need nonverbal language to express feelings and attitudes that words simply can't convey. Words are a poor representation of the complex process of thinking in our brains. There are many words in the English language—between one and two million. And the average adult may know twenty to thirty thousand of those words, but he or she really only use a couple of thousands. So, we know about 2 percent of the words in the English language, but we use far less. Describing our complex thoughts and emotions is highly inefficient if we use only words. Nonverbal language expresses more thoughts and feelings than words express. We may use more verbal language than nonverbal language in some of the scientific and mathematical exchange of information. But even then, we rely on nonverbal language to add emphasis and clarity. In fact, it's practically impossible to talk without nonverbal language.

By now you see how obvious it is that a part or all of every message is nonverbal. So, abuse and neglect aren't always heard, and they are often seen only by the intended victim. In fact, the perpetrator of nonverbal abuse may work hard to assure that only the victim receives the message.

## Verbal Active-Aggressive and Passive-Aggressive Communication

Verbal active-aggressive communication and verbal passive-aggressive communication are two very different kinds of communication. In both types of verbal communication, as the name tells you, words are used to convey a thought. The title also tells you that this isn't your usual communication with your best friend; both forms of communication are aggressive.

## Verbal Active-Aggressive Communication

Verbal active-aggressive communication is thought of as shouting or yelling, but it can also be very quiet. Quietly making aggressive comments can be pretty intimidating. Threats of abuse are frequently whispered. Whether done noisily or quietly, active-aggressive communication is direct and clear. It's heard and it's seen by all, accompanied as it is by facial and body appearances. Because the communication is aggressive, it has been delivered to include some degree of threat.

## Verbal Passive Aggressive Communication

There's so much written about verbal passive-aggressive communication that it's hard to know where to start. The passive-aggressive communication isn't hard to spot. Let's say your phone is ringing, and someone thinks you didn't notice; they pause to let you know that there's a call. You respond with, "You want to answer the phone?" The question contains some simple straightforward, easy to understand words. But the question "You want to answer the phone?" if asked in a tight or tense voice or with a negative facial expression, is actually very aggressive. It might mean that you should mind your own business, buzz off, or a number of other aggressive thoughts.

In the classroom, teachers are frequently verbally passive-aggressive. A teacher recently said to a student whose 504 accommodation required instructions for assignments in writing, "Oh, yes! You have to have yours in writing." The teacher made that comment so others could hear; it was seriously aggressive, meant to embarrass the student, and conveyed an ugly annoyance for having been so imposed on to have to provide written instructions for projects or complex assignments. In a truthful communication, the teacher would have said that she didn't want to give out written instructions, but because that was not her decision to make, the result was an angry passive-aggressive communication.

Another classroom example is not giving information that is necessary and then saying, "I thought everyone would have known." This behavior can have serious consequences for a whole room of students. If this applies to some work that has already been done and now needs to be redone, is marked down, or late after being corrected, the teacher has effectively displayed his or her dislike of his or her position by using passive-aggressive behavior and punishing everyone for his or her own misery.

One extremely verbal passive-aggressive teacher behavior is giving out assignments or reciting notes before the bell rings so that anyone in class who isn't sitting with a pen out—well before the bell rings—can't catch up and will miss out on important information. Verbal passive-aggressive communication is very common in America's schools.

## Nonverbal Active-Aggressive and Passive-Aggressive Communication

Nonverbal active-aggressive communication and passive-aggressive communication both rely on facial and body actions to deliver aggressive messages. No words are used. They sound very similar but differ significantly in the degree and the type of nonverbal facial and bodily involvement.

### Nonverbal Active-Aggressive Communication

Even though there's nothing to hear, nonverbal active-aggressive communication is very easy to see. Without the use of words, actions are often more exaggerated than when words are used. Active aggressive is, by definition, an attack that is directed toward another person through some action. We've probably all seen some nonverbal active aggressive behaviors very recently. Most pushing, shoving, bumping, and otherwise touching someone in an offensive manner without the use of a language is nonverbal active-aggression.

It's common in the classroom. Teachers walk around the room and take things from students without saying a word. Sometimes this can be a test paper. Sometimes their active-aggressive nonverbal behavior is directed toward someone who is caught cheating on a test; at other times, it's because they don't like the student. One teacher said, when questioned, "The student was looking around the room, and I didn't like it."

Teachers remove cell phones, water bottles, paper, pencils, and all other imaginable personal belongings of students without saying a word. Sometimes that's for a good reason; sometimes it's just because they choose to be active-aggressive. Removing students' lunches when there is no money in their lunch accounts is nonverbal active-aggressive, especially because the students have nothing to do with lunch accounts but are nonetheless treated aggressively by a school employee.

## Nonverbal Passive-Aggressive Communication

Nonverbal passive-aggressive child neglect and child abuse are fairly easy to see when we talk about rejecting and ignoring. When someone ignores you or rejects you, you might wonder if anyone else has noticed that it has happened. You might even think that you didn't really experience the nonverbal abuse or that you were mistaken about being passed over, but there's a feeling that comes with nonverbal passive-aggressive behavior. That feeling is that you are separate and not a part of what's happening around you; it's as if you are alone and even invisible. Nonverbal passive-aggressive behaviors seem invisible and make you feel invisible, but they are strongly felt. It's a busy world and classrooms are very busy places. There may be a feeling you've been attacked, but did something actually just happen?

So much is going on around you. But you don't see anything. No one rolls their eyes, and no one even comes near you. You don't hear anything. There isn't any groaning or even sighing. What is that? Look closely. What you'll see is that nothing has happened. Nothing has happened, but something should have. You should be part of the action in your classroom. Or so many students have said to me over the years, "It's just like I'm not there!" In the world of nonverbal passive-aggressive communication, behaviors are powerful and palpable.

## Complicating the Picture

Teachers go to college, completed a bachelor's degree, do their student teaching and land a job that remains fairly well respected. They can be smart, articulate, and even funny. Teachers are generally seen as socially appropriate. Some, but certainly not all, have a good command of the English language. Like most adults, they are often loved by their family and friends. A teacher may also have an important role in the broader community.

On the flip side, having the wonderful attributes just listed doesn't mean that the teacher is a good person. There are many charming, articulate teachers who are admired by other teachers, lauded by administrators, and are abusive and neglectful to their students.

Conversely, teachers might be good people even if they fail to achieve their work goal of educating children. Failing to reach a work goal (e.g., not teaching a student an assigned topic) is a form of educational neglect. While most teachers are likely to be good people, it's absolutely clear that there are a substantial number of teachers who are either not good teachers or are not good people or both. This may seem complicated, but we know that people who have many positive attributes may also behave badly. In fact, assets may be used to hide child abuse and child neglect.

It's just a good reminder that we don't all see or experience the same things. Because one person or one student is not abused by a teacher doesn't mean another student isn't. One student may see an intelligent teacher; another may see that the teacher is cunning. This is especially true if the child abuse is nonverbal and the perpetrator targets only one student at a time; maybe even one student each school year. We don't all have the same reality or experience, but that doesn't make your reality incorrect.

## Summary

The various traits and behaviors described in this chapter are an introduction to tactics that teachers and other school personnel use to abuse and neglect students.

Abusive and neglectful systematic and systemic behaviors are likely the most dangerous teacher and other school personnel behaviors that students are going to be exposed to during their educational years. The perpetrators of these behaviors are frequently reinforced by their successes. It is very difficult for anyone but the victim to catch them in a pattern because of the way teachers work. They are independently in charge of their students for most of the day. There is generally only one teacher in a room. The teacher is the ruler, and it's difficult to differentiate between what is ruling and what is abuse when the teacher is the only adult present. It's difficult to catch someone in systematic child abuse and child neglect and equally difficult to prove. There's no visible trail of blood, there are no fingerprints, and the student's word against the teacher's word is rarely considered.

Differing types of communication, ranging from usual verbal communication to nonverbal passive-aggressive communication, can be difficult for students to identify. Practicing labeling communication and being familiar with how they sound and look and what they mean allows students to be prepared when they encounter any type of aggression, especially nonverbal.

Chapters 10 through 12 will help give you names for the many ways teachers escape responsibility for their abuse and neglect. It might be that a child in the neighborhood who bullies other children can be called to task by a group of older children or some of the parents. But the teacher who commits abuse or neglect belongs to an enormous brotherhood of supportive professionals who protect him or her from responsibility. Even when the behaviors are habitual and systematic, verbal and aggressive, the members of the brotherhood are protected and cloaked by a bastion so powerful that change is disturbingly unlikely. Understanding communication and behavior can help students manage in the face of abuse and neglect.

## CHAPTER 11

# Teacher Tactics for Child Abuse and Child Neglect

> "The man who lies to himself and listens
> to his own lie comes to such a pass
> That he cannot distinguish the truth
> within him, or around him,
> And so loses all respect for himself and for others..."
> —FYDOR DOSTOYEVSKY

Teacher tactics for child abuse and child neglect are dissected and labeled in this chapter. These tactics cover a wide range of destructive behaviors. It's written in a way that readers of almost all ages can utilize the information. Knowing the tactics used by abusive and neglectful adults will help victims identify and then describe their experiences in their own words. Even children at the youngest of ages can learn to identify their experiences.

The teacher tactics for child abuse and child neglect described in this section are emotional and psychological abuse and neglect. Whether the abuse is sexual or physical, the neglect is educational, medical or physical, each is also emotional and psychological. The abuses and neglects that are visible are specific and definable. The abuse and neglect that is emotional and psychological can happen in concert with those specific abuses and neglects, or they can stand alone.

For many years, I've worked to understand student avoidance, dislike, distrust and disinterest in schools and the resulting anger and even failure. Psychological and emotional abuse and neglect in Americas schools is the single thread that pulls together each of those responses to education in the last decades. It weaves through students feeling hurt and hate, bored and belligerent.

The resentment and feeling of betrayal students disclose in response to their teachers and other school personnel is epic in its proportion. Perhaps students rarely comment, or infrequently complain, verbally. There are multiple forces simultaneously working within each person, each student, that moderate the time we invest in verbalizing our struggles. Students are working hard to manage their social and emotional development. They are working to succeed at their personal goals. Each young person is learning to navigate the experiences between youth and adulthood. Each of these, and multiple other individual personal, familial, and extra familial endeavors occupy time and space in the students' life. Because you aren't hearing the words of anger and frustration doesn't mean it isn't happening. Most young people believe they are powerless to deal with adult abuse and neglect of any kind. That, and the many challenges in this critical span of life account for the attitude which is reflected in such comments as, "Leave it alone", "If you say anything it'll just get worse", and "I don't want to deal with it."

None of the student's struggles, known and unknown to the teacher, stop the abuse or mediate the neglect. Students need to know which behaviors don't belong in a classroom. If they have been taught to recognize inappropriate adult behavior, they'll know it when they see it. Understanding inappropriate or abusive and neglectful behaviors saves a student from fear and confusion. When we don't understand negative experiences, at the very least we feel fear and confusion. If we teach our children to understand the teacher tactics of abuse and neglect, we reduce their risk of victimization. Fear and trauma, avoidance and anger, hopelessness and helplessness can be replaced by comprehension and awareness. Students will begin to think and ask questions rather that struggle with distress. Students are then able to begin a dialog using words and terms that have become a part of their vocabulary. Then they will better recognize and understand how they feel, and they will know why they feel this way.

Students who are selected for abuse or neglect may be marked by the perpetrator for having a particular characteristic. That characteristic can be positive, negative, or even neutral. The characteristic may be unidentifiable to bystanders, but it's likely that it has some meaning to the abuser. The perpetrator could choose a student to abuse simply because of his or her hair color or eye color. Perhaps the student is very smart, or maybe he or she is not very smart at all. The child victim could be a male or a female. But it's not really the characteristic of the student that is in question here. We must learn to understand the characteristics, methods, patterns, and tactics of the teacher who commits these acts. Our children need to understand when something in their school environment is abusive or neglectful.

The habitual problems of the perpetrator show us that child abuse and child neglect patterns can be predictable. In other words, a teacher might always abuse boys instead of girls. Perhaps only children on one end of the educational ability spectrum are the target. Maybe the teacher particularly doesn't like the child's parents because the parents are wealthy. Perhaps they have a powerful voice in the community. Maybe the family is receiving some government subsistence. Perhaps the parent is in law enforcement, or maybe the perpetrator has an issue with the student's ethnicity. I believe that many perpetrators choose a victim who they believe they can either easily break down or beat with their abusive behavior or a victim they see as an adversary and they want to beat in a power struggle. The first abuser preys on the weak, and the second plays with the strong. In both cases, the teacher is going to win because he or she comes to the task from an already defined position of power.

Keep in mind that the target choice is entirely the decision of the perpetrator and not the victim. The victim is simply the unsuspecting recipient of behaviors from the perpetrator. The victim's behavior is in response to the abuse; the victim's behavior is not the cause of the abuse.

The most important reason to name or label teachers' dysfunctional tactics of abuse and neglect is for the welfare of the students. For all the ways we can talk about the trauma some students experience in today's schools, it serves no purpose unless the students themselves can talk about it. The students are the primary victims. Parents need a functional vocabulary that they can have in common with their children that describes what these children face if they are in an unfriendly environment. The names I've applied to the teacher tactics of child abuse and child neglect aren't meant to be cute or curt. Rather, these named behaviors are explained to help enable students to finally understand the dysfunctional behaviors to which they can be exposed. The names are created to be easily remembered and used by the victims—the students. Students of every age need to talk about the trauma they have experienced at the hands of the otherwise untouchable authority figures.

As you read through this chapter, be sure to relate what you read to your own experiences or experiences someone has shared with you. Ask your family and friends if they have experienced any of these types of abuse or neglect.

There are as many ways of abusing and neglecting students as there are people. It's difficult to categorize every type of dysfunctional teacher or school employee who is a perpetrator. Like our fingerprints, our style of communicating and our style of dysfunctional behavior is unique. There are probably tactics of abuse that aren't covered here. But, this is a start. Here are the offences and the descriptions that will help you to recognize them when they happen.

## Selected for Punishment
An ugly, common, but easily understood abuse technique used by teachers is selecting out one or two students for punishment. The tactic is easily

recognized and truly evil. The teacher begins by picking a target that fits the abusers needs. Then the perpetrator waits for the opportunity to pounce. That opportunity often comes the first time when a student talks at the wrong moment. Everyone else in the room could be talking, but the teacher has eyes on one particular chosen victim.

There doesn't have to be a special incident that triggers the teacher to select one particular child for punishment. All the students might be working quietly and the selected victim gets called out for some behavior that he or she may or may not have committed. No one is looking because all the students are working. It's easy to start the punishment parade.

From that point onward, the teacher has established the target. Everyone in the class has heard the name of the student who has been called out by the perpetrator. Now the student is singled out for punishment at any opportunity the teacher can conjure up. There are endless ways to single out someone for punishment, but there are a few common scenarios, which are as follows:

- There is too much noise in the classroom, and you're sure to hear the victimized student's name yelled over the roar.
- The students are working in groups, and the victim is admonished to cooperate and do his or her share of work.
- Tests are in progress, and the student is told to keep his or her eyes on his or her own paper.
- Feedback is given; it's always negative or sarcastic even if the student has gained an A.
- Students are moving to another spot, and the victim is told that he or she is too slow, even when there are many other students moving around.
- Papers are handed in, and the student is called out for being last or first, or some sarcasm ensues, such as "Well, you have got it done, haven't you?"

The teacher-child abuser makes up anything he or she wants. The terms "have you finished yet," "don't," "finally," or "be sure to" may be added to any comment. There is likely no honest or real basis for the comment, no basis for being singled out or even addressed by the perpetrator. In fact, if the student really is a mess, then the teacher would have accomplished nothing by stating the obvious. In fact, it's the teacher's obligation to address a student privately and set up a useful plan of intervention if a student is really having management difficulties in a classroom. But it's more of a game for the abuser when he or she can see a student fall apart for no reason at all.

## Rejecting

Rejecting is passive-aggressive behavior. Passive-aggression and active-aggression are both aggressive behaviors. They differ much in the way they sound. Active-aggression is easy to see, for the perpetrator commits an action that is meant to harm someone or inflict damage using visible means—an overtly hostile action. Passive-aggression is a form of aggression that is a non-action.

Both passive and active aggressions are harmful. They both intend to inflict injury or harm. Aggression is an overt social interaction, acted out with the intention of inflicting damage or other unpleasantness upon another individual. Both active-aggression and passive-aggression are intended to be adversarial or painful.

Passive-aggression, however, is often silent or nonverbal. It is a form of rejection, and that is a type of psychological abuse. And child psychological abuse is very destructive. Passive aggressive behavior is a form of non-communication that communicates a message in a very strong way. And what it communicates is pretty ugly. For a thorough discussion of passive and active-aggression, reread chapter 9.

Teachers communicate throughout the day with their students. They give assignments, explain concepts, and relate ideas, facts, and instructions.

Teachers teach discipline, set limits, make demands, demand compliance, clear boundaries, and do much more. All these actions require communication. *Non-communication* is obvious when a student is left out of the communication loop.

*Rejecting* is one name for the passive-aggressive non-communication of a teacher toward a specific child or children. Rejecting communicates a world of information, none of which a student should be subjected to. The rejecting behavior can make students feel isolated and even invisible.

The act of rejecting or passive-aggressive rejecting behavior has identifiable signs. Some common aspects of rejecting behavior in the classroom are explained below:

1. *Not calling on a student.*
   Examples of this include the teacher calling on anyone else who raises their hands and saying no more questions if the rejected student is the only one with a hand raised; not answering a question when the student asks one; not calling a student up for a work group; not calling up a student who has asked the teacher for help; and not calling a student who the teacher knows needs help.
2. *Failing to give a student a handout that the rest of the class has received.*
   Examples of this include the teacher walking past a student while handing out something; ignoring a student while handing out notices; passing by a student while handing out candy; avoiding a student when handing out hall passes; not handing out homework packets to that student; and not handing out lists of instructions.
3. *Never using the student's name; the examples of this include the teacher referring to the student as "you".*
   When there is an absolutely necessity to interact; giving orders without using the student's name; and rejecting a student by using the names of other students when they are called on but only saying "Yes?" when calling on their victim.

4. *Never choosing that student for special tasks.*
   Examples of this include the teacher deliberately skipping over a student for line leader, making deliveries to the office, helping the teacher, sharpening the pencils, choosing group members, picking the sport at PE, selecting special things for the classroom, and having a say in some optional activities.
5. *Missing a student when something special is to happen.*
   Examples of this include the teacher forgetting that a student qualified for a fund-raiser; not sending a student for some special award that he or she has earned; and not calling out the student's name in front of the class when he or she has done some exceptional academic work.
6. *Seating the student where he or she will be invisible to the teacher.*
   Examples of this include the teacher seating the student in the back of the room, behind the teacher's desk, in a corner, facing away from the teacher, far away from the teacher, away from the board, and behind much taller students.
7. *Using descriptors that infer that the student has negative characteristics.*
   Examples of this include the teacher referring to the student as a problem or a poor student as being too short, too tall, too late, too early, overweight, slow, quiet, or any other trait that obviously refers negatively to the victimized student.
8. *Excluding the student by not including that student's positive characteristics in some reference;*
   Examples of this include the teacher talking about certain students in a positive way that excludes the victim student, such as the tall boys, the blond girls, or students with nice new clothes.
9. *Working it out so that the child is always the last.*
   Examples of this include the teacher compelling the student to be the last to have lunch or the last to leave the classroom; making him or her sit the last in his or her row; making him or her stand the last in line; making him or her the last to turn in homework; and

ensuring that he or she is the last to get his or her grade, the last to present his or her report, the last to go to the restroom, the last to get his or her belongings, the last to go to the locker, and so on.

It's easy to see that these behaviors are rejections. It's also easy to be convinced that the well-educated and sometimes admired teacher didn't do anything. The rejection of a student results in pain often accompanied by anger or depression. Rejection is an experience that we all struggle to escape throughout our lives. Yet the student is rendered helpless.

Rejected students don't speak out for the fear of retaliation. Maybe the other kids will laugh. Maybe the teacher will become actively aggressive when everyone can see. Kids don't know what to do, how to handle rejection, and even what to call it. For many children, it's their first experience with rejection. And that first experience in the hands of a teacher, in an inescapable situation in a room full of peers, contains a lot of messages directed right at that child.

To a child, rejection means that there is something wrong with them. They did something wrong. They are disliked. They are offensive. They are unwanted. They don't belong there. There is something wrong with their family, color, hair, the way they speak, or the way they dress, sit, or even smile. Maybe the teacher thinks they are stupid. But for sure, they know that there is something seriously wrong. Very, very wrong.

When children know that something is very wrong in the classroom and it's about them, they fail. They can't concentrate, they feel sad, and they feel bad. Students may begin to try to fade into the wall because they don't know why the teacher finds them so offensive. They stop working. They stop trying. They stop everything. The feeling doesn't go away. They often begin to avoid the situation altogether. They give up. They fail.

The vile act of rejecting a student in a classroom is pretty astounding. It's clearly child psychological abuse. The teacher obviously has a *systemic* problem that has led him or her to this severe pattern of *systematic* psychologically abusive behaviors. Some would say that rejecting is racist. But the definition of racism is not broad enough to include all the children who are chosen for rejection. Certainly, a teacher who rejects could be prejudiced. But rejecting may happen to a student who has a learning disability, who comes from a powerful family, or who is the child of an unpopular school board member. But remember, rejecting, like other kinds of abusive behavior, is really all about the perpetrator; it really has nothing to do with the child. It could be any child. The reason it happens could be so bizarre that no one will be able to figure it out. The child is the victim.

## Labeling

Labeling is an everyday fact. We label everything. It's really the same as naming. Labeling or naming is using a word or words to convey a meaning or message. When we say a word like *shoe* or *ice*, or any of the words that come from the human brain and are produced by the vocal cords, that word has a small range of specific meanings. Without some agreement on this range of meanings or labels, communication would be impossible.

In the classroom, as everywhere else on the planet, labeling is essential. There is too precious or too little a time in school days for learning new material. Much of the day is occupied with moving from class to class, packing and unpacking, outdoor recreation, lunch, and myriad activities. We use shortcuts, labels, and names for moving the process forward. We have to pull a red card when we're naughty and a green card when we behave well all day. We're in the STEM classes, the remedial classes, the college prep classes, or the SPED classes. We label all day every day. Mostly, we do this for convenience, a sort of shorthand to manage the grouping and movement of countless humans.

What happens when a teacher labels a child? How about your child? You probably don't care too much if the label is neutral and accurate, such as timely, passing, or performing. But what happens when a teacher labels children on a more personal basis? For example, the teacher might say that Sally is pretty or June has a nice new dress. Those are positive things to say, but you might already see where these positive labels are going.

By calling out to one or more students in a positive way, the teacher is labeling the other students by omission. That is, the student (or students) who get no nonacademic-related positive recognition assumes that the teacher sees nothing good in him or her. That student is labeled by the fact that he or she was left out.

Recently, I've heard an argument that there should be no labeling whatsoever. Students shouldn't get special recognition for their high performance in academic subjects or for their overall academic standing. The same is true for sports. Everyone should get a trophy, no matter how well they play in the baseball tournament. This is illogical. The extension of that reasoning is that anyone can join anything, just show up, and receive the same recognition, trophy, award, or scholarship as anyone else. No effort is required. Anyone could be the teacher because we don't have to perform.

How are these types of labeling different? If I give a plaque to John for being the top student, why shouldn't I tell Sally her hair looks nice? The answer to that question, once again, is simple in its logic. This is school. It's all about academic performance. Students are in the classroom to study and learn. If they work hard and stay engaged, they should have a better performance than those students who don't work hard and who don't stay engaged. If they complete their assigned work, their grades will be higher than if they don't complete their assigned work. If teachers are any good at teaching as they like to say they are and if every student does the assigned work, they should all be able to perform at a high level. It's the job. It's the student's job, and it's the teacher's job.

Other types of labeling are inappropriate in the school setting. Commenting on how well-dressed a student is doesn't belong in the classroom. The only comments about dress should be limited to dress-code enforcement, whether the student does or does not go to a school with uniforms. Labeling students, even positively, in areas of the student's personal attributes other than their academic attributes is out of place. This includes haircuts, vacations, book bags, and almost anything nonacademic or non-school related.

This brings us to direct negative labeling. Teachers use direct negative labeling to neglect and abuse. Teachers who use this form of victimization can make it quite an art. They develop cute names for students who give them trouble, act out, or fail to perform. Names like slowpoke or Mr. Tardy are common. Some teachers label several students negatively and then use the label to substitute for their name. Kids get known as the chatterbox or the hummer or any other term that we might think is endearing or well-earned, but it is not.

What happens when the labeling is both negative and personal? Victimizing a student with words is easy. This is when the line is crossed between playing and verbal abuse. Verbal abuse is common in the teaching profession, even though it's sometimes unheard by the student and confined to the teacher's lounge.

There's a long list of words teachers use, all aimed at students who aren't doing what the teacher believes they should do or the students the teacher doesn't like. But these labels are sometimes aimed at one student who has been chosen as the victim and actually hasn't done anything wrong. Here's a short list of examples:

- Lazy
- Useless
- Stupid
- Bad
- Ugly
- Dumb
- A waste of a seat
- A waste of my time
- Sloppy
- Not smart
- Dirty
- Failure
- Sad

- Loser
- Embarrassment
- Ugly

Labels hurt. They stick. And being singled out with negative labeling affects the student in more ways than what we might at first notice.

Besides the obvious feeling of anger, the targeted student is likely to develop feelings of learned hopelessness. Learned hopelessness is a disabling psychological problem. A person feels hopeless when he or she cannot find a way to win or succeed in a particular situation. It's a no-win condition when someone is labeled negatively, no matter what he or she does. You might have heard or used the term learned helplessness. For students who are continually chosen to be the victim for an abusive teacher, the feeling is more hopeless than helpless.

Some years ago, I was in a position of support to an administrator. He had followed a well-loved, easy-going old-timer into an important role with a failing economic picture. The new administrator had to make severe cuts and enormous changes to the operation of the organization. People's duties changed. People were dismissed and new faces arrived. Paperwork demands were put in place. And people fought with him in every way possible. People decided that he was responsible for their life changes and their misery. In the end, he resigned.

While the administrator had done everything allowable to salvage the organization, when the economic picture was finally positive and stable, he was hated by all. He began to feel hopeless. He believed that even though he had done what was correct, he would always be treated poorly. We discussed all his options. In a moment of levity, he said that he would be accused of trying to poison the staff if he invited everyone to a free lunch. He was absolutely convinced that the situation was hopeless, and so he left. Perhaps it could have been described as escaping. He was so unsure of himself and so hopeless that there wasn't anything he could do to succeed; in fact, at the end of the two years, he wasn't clear if he would even apply for another job in the same field. This person had learned hopelessness through repeated labeling.

Students feel locked in a classroom and learn that they are hopeless when they cannot escape abusive, repeated, labeling. Unlike the administrator who quit his job, students have few or no options. The psychologically abusive teacher is in a position to carry messages about students to other teachers. Because of the teacher's position, what they say to their peers carries some weight.

Don't forget the loyalty that the brotherhood members have for one another. They are willing to support one another's messages and opinions even when the abusive teacher is wrong. In turn, they expect to gain support for their own needs and wants in the future. While influencing other teachers and administrators, abusive teachers also influence the students who witness the abuse. Students have to live with their peers; sometimes, for many years, they have to move along with these peers to new teachers in new grades. When one student is repeatedly negatively labeled, everyone remembers. The student's peers might not see why the teacher is labeling and might even understand less that this is psychologically abusive behavior. There will always be a residual reputation that will move with the student throughout the school years. The damage having been done, the teacher faces no consequences, moves on to the next victim, and collects a paycheck.

## Death Threats

In some districts around the country, eleven-year-old children are moved to middle school. These are pre-pubertal boys and girls who, for the most part of their lives, have been protected by their families from a world of awfulness. They find themselves moved from the innocence of an elementary play school to a new and strange world. Certainly, some sixth grade children have been exposed to what goes on in the middle school years. What students and parents alike find in the middle school environment is often startling and assaulting to their senses.

In the middle school setting, teachers often model abusive behaviors under the guise of teaching children how to behave. These teachers should, instead, be modeling strong and firm behaviors. Helping young people—the students—to learn appropriate behavior in an educational setting is an admirable goal. Discipline is an important tool for managing a classroom. Being a disciplined person is a major factor that leads to success in life. Apparently, there are teachers and administrators who cannot differentiate between discipline and abuse. And on the other end of the spectrum, there are teachers who cannot even discipline themselves and are therefore guilty of child emotional abuse and child educational neglect.

Thankfully, most eleven-year-old students already know how to behave; they behave like eleven-year-olds. Thankfully, at eleven, young people still have a foothold in childhood; eleven-year-olds are familiar with some freedoms. They retain a playfulness that accompanies age eleven; that playfulness is a healthy behavior within their young social groups. Normally, functioning families treasure this last period of childhood. We still kiss our kids goodnight, play silly games, share silly movies, and watch as they stumble in their social graces. As parents, we pick them up, brush them off, and encourage them to learn to fly on their own.

This transition into the middle school's regimented semi-adulthood is very difficult. The transition into middle school will mark the beginning of failure for some of these students. As the school recess disappears from the school day, social expectations leap from paying attention and playing by the rules to a hectic and often confusing schedule of changing classes and the maze of expectations of six unique teachers. Homework can take up several hours each night, and freedom can be curtailed. The pressure to perform can be a death knell for young people's grades and behaviors if it isn't managed properly by the teachers.

None of these concerns stop teachers who love to abuse students. These special perpetrators use death-threat techniques at every opportunity to get their sad, abusive needs met. Death threats are classic behaviors for teachers who abuse. Almost every teacher, at one time, has gotten in the face of a student who is chronically obnoxious. Teachers are human. They have bad days. We all get that. But death threats are used regularly by a particular type of teacher who is abusive. Defined as in your face, screaming, or character assassination behaviors, death threats by abusive teachers are dangerous.

A local teacher is famous for death threats. Here's an example of a death threat that occurred when a student forgot to bring his book to class. On random days, the students were told to bring the textbook to class. There is no schedule. This is not a recurring practice. Books come to class only when the teacher says to bring the book on a particular day. Somewhere in the classroom process, the teacher says, "Bring your book tomorrow."

What happens when a student forgets the textbook? Is the student admonished to remember next time? Is the student penalized by being given some type of demerit? Are the students' extra credit points for being prompt, getting the work done, or not talking in class diminished? No, none of the above. This teacher creates a spectacle for the entire class. He disrupts the classroom and wastes valuable time with death threats. This is how that happens. This adult professional rushes like a man on fire toward a student who is without a book. He looms over this sixth-grade student with an evil and threatening glare. He screams and yells for him to get out of the classroom. He orders the child to the OCR (on campus detention). This is an angry, vile, and threatening behavior. The student is stunned for a moment. Then with this man still in his personal space, intimidating him, yelling at him to get out, he hurriedly grabs his backpack and papers and flees the room.

The school where this teacher was or is employed allowed him to send students to OCR if they didn't obey his rules. Never mind that there is no OCR for most of the school day. It doesn't really exist. Never mind that the eleven-year-old doesn't know what to do and is reduced to tears, wandering around feeling lost and traumatized. Wandering into the office, feeling dazed, the staff asks him to take a seat.

At the beginning of the year, most young people are already in a stimulus overload mode. They are often anxious and on edge because of having to absorb so much change in a short time. They have six or seven changes of class each day, not including lunch. Each student has to learn the rules of six different adults, all of whom are strangers to the student, each wanting that student to meet different sets of goals and objectives. Some of them require students to take notes. Some of them may allow students to talk. Some of them want students to line up outside the door. Some of them allow the student to have time on computers. Some of them allow the students to address the teacher. And the list goes on. Then there are separate sets of rules for lunch. Then there's PE. And dressing out. For the first time, many young people are undressing in front of strangers. Stress. Changes. Seven, eight, or (maybe) nine people in a day at school teach discipline each in their own way. When was the last time you had eight or nine bosses, all with different rules to answer to all day, every day? Welcome to the world of an eleven-year-old child, a sixth grader.

In the example of death threats, the student has been humiliated and subsequently is confused about what to do next. Of course, no one who has made this rule about sending a student to OCR for not having a book has any concern for this student missing the lesson. Why care about having a book? The punishment is missing the *whole assignment* for a simple act of forgetting. Like catch-22. The rule is all about some person's idea of discipline. Education seems to take a backseat or, in this case, no seat at all.

Here are the rest of these teacher-child abusers' rules and behaviors. The child can return to the class only when the student can find a phone and call a parent to get the book from home and bring the book to the office. This is a classic double bind. This punishment is a missed lesson, some missed assignment instructions for the next day, a missed test, and so on. The eleven-year-old is made to believe that there is really some solution but is crushed when he understands that it was a trick.

The class is only fifty minutes long. Twenty minutes have already passed. Even if the parent is at home, holding the book in his or her hands, he or she cannot deliver the book on time to be used in the class. Some students are so afraid and so anxious that they might need a book that they carry all their books with them every day. Middle schools in our area don't allow students to use lockers. At eleven years of age and weighing maybe eighty pounds, their backpacks weigh about twenty-five pounds. They carry this weight on their backs all day, loading and unloading with bells ringing and papers flying, to avoid the humiliation and failure dealt to them beyond description.

Most good teachers simply keep a set of classroom books. One of the local high schools understands that carrying all those books is unhealthy; bad for the students' growing and developing necks, shoulders, and backs; and a waste of time. They don't want the books to be carried back and forth for 180 days. That high school keeps a set of books in every class for use that day. Unfortunately, not all schools use that kind of logic and reason. But the problem of books in some schools never really exists. In others, the book-day demand is a golden opportunity for the perpetrators of death threats.

The difference between good teachers and abusive teachers may be a difference that stares at us, but we have trouble seeing for what it is. Long after the incident, standing in a cool shower on a hot summer night, thinking about death threats at the hands of a middle school teacher is likely to send an electric shock through us from foot to head. Now, it's too late to change the outcome and too late to help our children and ourselves. We are now unsure of how we could have addressed the abuse, even if we had understood it sooner. But there it is. The book debacle is a sly way of having a readily available opportunity to abuse when this teacher needs to feel important or ventilate some rage, not to mention that long list of other reasons for which a teacher might like to perpetrate child psychological abuse and child educational neglect. The perpetrator can be certain that at least a small percentage of student will forget their text on the random 'book day' and has, therefore, a built in guarantee that he can play his death threats game. It serves no purpose for the student, there is no education, and the result is one more wedge between the student and the school.

Death threats are very common. In every group where there are good teachers, other teachers are abusive. Death threats are used at every level of education. Some educators suggest that in-your-face tactics are useful for training in the later years of secondary education. No administrator, so far as I know, has been able to present a shred of evidence that there is value in treating or managing another human with this horrendous behavior. We will not behave toward our peers in this way. We will never allow a neighbor or a relative to treat us so shabbily. If we treat an employee in this manner, we are likely to be fired and maybe charged with harassment or assault. Who could possibly believe that behaving this way with a school student is anything but the worst kind of child psychological abuse and child educational neglect?

So, we see that school becomes the perfect setting for chronic teacher abuse or a death-threat incubator. The result of death threats is a serious *game on!* When teachers are abusive, they engender resentment from the students. Once this chess game begins, it's very difficult to stop. For many young people, this kind of resentment means the end of focus, lack of interest in the work, and loss of interest in school. The focus becomes to avoid or get even. Unlike adults, the student has no viable response. Unfortunately, the teacher has all the power and is free to abuse that power. The brotherhood has protected this abusive teacher for as long as he or she has been part of the bastion. Students lose when they are targeted by the abusive and neglectful teachers who use death threats. Should death threats by teachers be prosecuted? Death threats are child psychological abuse and child educational neglect.

## Creating Fear

Creating fear by using some kind of spoken or inferred threat is an old form of abuse. It's been used all over the planet, probably since the beginning of humankind, by people who are unable to manage their roles in a normal way. Management skills are required if someone in a position of leadership wishes to be successful in their efforts to reach a goal. Whether you're running a tour group in the Balkans, leading a band, supervising a processing line, raising children, or teaching a class, management skills are required.

There are people who have signed up for a job, but they really have no management skills or maybe don't want to manage. There are people who don't really care about making it to the finish line; in this case child education. These inept or unwilling managers still want to get paid to be in the position, despite not taking the job seriously.

In a job like teaching in a public school, the teachers are set for life. They are not obligated to reach a goal, and they cannot be fired for failing to produce results. Even in private or religion-based schools, teachers who fail are often retained because of some connections or obligations of the board or body that has oversight.

In the classroom, these poor managers often resort to using fear-engendering tactics to get behavioral compliance. It seems that there is a fallacious belief that behavioral compliance results in improved goal completion. Behavioral compliance may or may not result in getting the student to learn anything. Student learning is the collective functioning of many elements. But the use of fear to induce students to behave in a certain desired and perhaps questionably necessary manner definitely results in student distress, which is a deterrent to learning.

Child psychological abuse generally includes the chronic use of threat simply because of the power differential. Yet, despite its recognized illegality, the use of threat to induce fear to achieve compliance is pretty common. Some adults or managers do not know the difference between threat and discipline. It's the same problem with almost all types of abuse tactics. The common theme is that the job requires the manager to discipline his or her followers. But what does discipline have to do with fear or threat? Absolutely nothing.

Discipline requires that the followers know the rules and the consequences. Discipline requires the leader, the manager, or the teacher to state the rules and the consequences; this is followed through with role-modeling adults into well-disciplined individuals. That is, the manager's behavior has to be disciplined enough to manage the followers according to the rules and consequences that he or she has clearly stated. No more, and no less.

In the classroom, students naturally know that not performing or performing inadequately results in failure. Or do they? If the goal is simply to get out of school, in most public K–12 organizations all you have to do is show up. If you show up, you can do nothing and continue to be passed from grade to grade until you're old enough to choose not to show up. That's true for both the student and the teacher. The teacher just has to show up, tell the students to do something, and wait until retirement. There are lots of teachers who do nothing but hand out assignments. If the goal, as seen by the student, is learning or getting educated, that student doesn't need to be motivated by fear. So, what happens to student compliance and performance when the student is managed by threats resulting in fear? There is no discipline; there is only fear. There are no consequences. You get out of school one way or another, and being held back just isn't done anymore. Students who are self-motivated have self-discipline; they achieve success despite the teachers' behavior. For that select group of students, the teacher's behavior is academically irrelevant. But teachers don't necessarily discriminate between motivated and unmotivated students when they choose their victims to pander fear. Fear is unnecessary and injurious; it comes at the high cost of the student's physical and mental health.

Fear causes hypervigilance. Hypervigilance is critical for survival in a hostile environment. Fearful responses are the body's way of reacting to a hostile environment. The business of being ruled by fear is circular, which is described as follows:

- Human perceives a threat
- Human feels the fear

- Human body reacts with physiological and psychological changes
- Human becomes hypervigilant
- Human focus is on self-protection, and hence the body is ready to fight or flee
- Human concentration and memory as used for learning ceases

The physical and mental health consequences of entering and surviving a hostile environment are enormous. These consequences alone create stress. The body experiences psychological and physiological stress when hostile environments can't be readily escaped or when threats are random. That stress is not only continuous but also anticipatory. As a student approaches the time in which he or she is under threat, the anxiety rises.

So how does the teacher in a classroom create fear through threat? Does the teacher issue a threat when he or she clearly states that any grade below a C will result in extra work? No—that would be a stated condition with stated consequences. Does the teacher threaten by saying that a call to the student's parents will be the result of talking excessively in class? Maybe, but only if the word *excessively* is not defined.

So, we say that the words that make up a rule must be defined. The example here shows that *excessively* needs to be defined. If the term is not defined, that rule of not talking excessively can be randomly defined based on a teacher's whim. The meaning can change if the teacher is having a good day or a bad day or if the teacher is setting some vague rules that can be used as a threat on a random basis. Ill-defined rules that can be easily altered are fodder for the abusive teacher who is looking for a way to issue a threat.

Here are some examples of the behaviors of teachers who threaten in order to create a rule by fear. Notice that consequences are not stated; this increases the student's anxiety of what these consequences might be. At the same time, it protects the fear-mongering teacher who can deny that there was really a threat.

Spoken vague threats include the following:

You'd better watch it!
Don't push me.
You don't know what you're asking for here.

Spoken direct threats include the following:

You all get zeroes today.
Don't come to my class wearing too much jewelry!

Random unplanned orders include the following:

No more bathroom passes for this class.
Stay for three minutes after the bell (forces students to run or be late).
Tomorrow there is a test on the last three chapters.
You can leave when you've copied the six pages from your book.

Unspoken threats (passive-aggressive) include the following:

Assigning students to computers that aren't working properly.
Withholding anticipated extra-credit work.
Grading a practice test without notice.
Asking questions orally on a chapter the class has just begun reading.

Indirect or inferred threats include the following:

Cookie sales will give you ten extra-credit points (you'd better sell cookies).
Parents at open house, you leave early (parents no show—you stay late).

Good students are always two minutes early (the bell doesn't count now).

Joining my after-school group is good (not joining is bad).

The message in all these threats is, "You'd better jump through all my hoops whenever I say so. If you don't or can't, you're in trouble." It doesn't matter how impossible the hoops might be. It doesn't matter how randomly the hoops are thrown in front of the student or students. It doesn't matter that the hoops have nothing to do with the academic materials. It is a case of "When I say jump, you jump. If you don't, the consequences will be an unpleasant surprise."

What happened to management with clear rules and clear consequences? A reign of fear perpetrated by the class ruler doesn't need to be managed in a logical or predictable way, right? After all, these students function better when they are chronically stressed by the unpredictable whim of an inescapable ruler.

Threatening children is a form of child psychological abuse. It doesn't matter how old they are; a threat is threat. Threats stop working after some period of time. Students really aren't stupid. They will figure out that responding to threats is a losing battle. In the end, the teacher can't fail the class or even a high percentage of the students. That would negatively reflect on the teacher. There are teachers who are known for not giving any A's or setting a particular number of A's that will be allowed. The goal is to keep the students fighting for the A grade. To some students, that A grade is very important to their future plans. That teacher has carefully developed a scalloped curve for reward and punishment. Just like gambling. Payouts are carefully set to increase with the number of times you put money in the machine. But how much is paid and the interval at which money is paid is random. In the classroom, the random, unpredictable behaviors of some teachers are more frustrating than Las Vegas. The student can perform all semester and still not escape from a management run by the teacher's threats. There may never be a payout. The student has only stress and fear that *not* jumping through random, unpredictable hoops *may* bring great unnamed peril.

The abuse from threats is psychological, but it also causes physiological consequences. Problems in memory and concentration co-occur with chronic anxiety. Chronic anxiety interferes in academic performance across the board, not just in the stressful, fear-driven class. Chronic fear puts enormous strain on the developing organism. The body's immunity system can be compromised, and the gastric, the cardiac, and the pulmonary systems are all affected. We worry about how much smog will affect our children's lungs when they go out to play. Who assesses how much school stress, induced by fear, is injuring our children?

Child psychological abuse has no place in the educational systems. Parents and communities support educational systems, and they expect these systems to be safe, not destructive or guilty of child psychological abuse. Teachers who can't or won't manage without appropriate tools need to move out of management before they injure more students, causing more failures.

## Ridiculing

Ridiculing means treating someone with contempt. When a teacher in a classroom ridicules a student, the message is "You are less then human," or "You aren't worth my time." When an abusive teacher ridicules, the student gets the message that he or she is useless as a person. The use of ridiculing by the school personnel is a behavior that is both demeaning to the student and to the school personnel themselves. Ridiculing is a fast and dirty way of being just plain ugly. It's an obvious form of abuse; so obvious, in fact, that anyone two years or older knows how to ridicule. The ridiculing requires practically zero intellectual functioning. An American proverb reads "Even a dog knows the difference between stumbled over and being kicked."

There are lots of other words that mean ridiculing. People might say scorn, poke fun at, mock, or taunt. Sometimes, ridiculing is thrown at a student but hidden in humor. So, when a teacher pokes fun at or razzes a student, it may sound like play, but the student knows that he or she has been ridiculed.

Because of the enormous power imbalance between teacher and student, the victim is once again rendered helpless to respond. If the student doesn't laugh and act as if the ridiculing is all in fun, it makes him or her look weak in front of his or her peers. And because of the power imbalance, the student can't confront the teacher. Even if he or she confronts in the nicest way, with extremely appropriate manners and good communication skills, the student risks being accused of defiance. Even worse, when an adult in power has a habit of behaving in this ugly way, even a very young student knows that there is a risk of retaliation if he or she dares to respond.

Ridicule can also be inferred. Labeling is pretty overt. So is ridiculing, even when it's indirect or cloaked in humor. But ridiculing, like ignoring, is one of the forms of child psychological abuse that can easily be communicated through nonverbal language. That is, ridiculing may be seen and not heard.

Anyone who has a teenager at home already understands nonverbal communication. A teen rolling his or her eyes can show strong contempt for his or her parents or the parents' directives and is often used when teens want to ridicule the parent or the parents' opinions. One of the most obvious and petty forms of ridiculing another person is staring. Small children use this tactic, but some people forever remain small in their behaviors.

Ridiculing is probably the exact opposite of respecting. Disrespecting is currently a term that is widely used. The kids call it dissing. Now, Hollywood can't seem to have a conversation without using the term one or more times. But ridiculing, like other forms of child psychological abuse, is a one-way street in America's schools. Teachers believe that they get a pass when they ridicule or disrespect their students—the power imbalance makes an immature behavior look even more foolish.

When a young, developing student who is looking for good role models is ridiculed, the teacher has made a bad decision. Everyone in the classroom, in the auditorium, and every student who sees this obvious form of abusive behavior knows what it is. Ridiculing is not some secret means of communicating contempt.

The outcome of ridiculing is also pretty easy to predict. How is it that a well-educated professional can't see it? How is it that the teacher doesn't realize that he or she is the single person in the classroom who believes he or she will be given a pass for ridiculing? In the end, the teacher will wind up being ridiculed, laughed at, mimicked, and used as a parody by all the students behind the teacher's backs. The ridiculing shifts, and it's now carried on by the students. They have easily seen the teacher as dissing them or another student, and the teacher is looking pretty foolish. A caricature. No respect. The teacher becomes a parody of him- or herself.

The impact of ridiculing on a student is that he or she feels embarrassed. Then the student begins to feel hurt. Sometimes, depending on the personality of the student, he or she jumps right into anger. Others do a slow burn. The feelings of hurt and anger affect everything young people do. I've heard young people say, "I just brush it off." Many people still use the word *bullied*. I've even heard adults say they were abused by a particular teacher, and they brushed it off. Now, we find that childhood abuse by teachers and other school personnel behavior is still affecting these adults years later. Somehow, we can't see that we don't really brush things off; these offences against us stay with us. Child abuse and child neglect stay with us. Everything in our lives gets woven into who we are, and this is not going to be the one exception. Who we are is ever changing in concert with every experience throughout our lifetimes.

Don't ever make the mistake of thinking, or, even worse, saying that it's the student's own fault. There is no acceptable justification for a professional to behave so childishly or so cruelly. Adults who behave badly regardless of their self-righteous excuses are role modeling exactly what they are reacting to. After ridiculing students and putting themselves dangerously close to the edge, there is no possible return from the cliff that teachers try to hang on to.

Worse is that there is no possible reason, no matter how conjured up the reason is, for ugly acts aimed at students who are managing or struggling to manage their school lives in an age-appropriate manner. Being dismissive to a student who is merely being a young person is reprehensible. In these formative years, every insult, slight, or crass behavior is permanently recorded in that victim's brain and becomes a part of the decision-making process for the remainder of life. Trust is quickly eaten away by the constant belittling, shaming, and humiliating a child or making negative comparisons to others. The teacher becomes the enemy. In a highly influential position of responsibility, shirking one's role of mentor, teacher, adult, and professional, and yes, caregiver, is inexcusable.

Ridiculing is an egotistical and self-righteous behavior. It conveys the message, "You're not as good as me..." or "You're not as good as (anyone)..." Developing minds integrate that information. Students react with shame. And what a preposterous scenario that becomes. Here is an example of how ridiculous this sounds:

"You're the student; I'm the teacher. You're a minor; I'm an adult. My job is teaching; your job is being a student. I have something to teach, and you have something to learn. I'm paid well for doing my job so that one day you can get paid well for doing your job. I'm going to use my time to ridicule you and cause you to feel shame. You can learn from my role modeling. Being ridiculed and feeling shame is a valuable tool that you can use to succeed in life."

There are daily instances of teachers shaming students. I ask all my clients about their childhood and adolescent years. They relate the experiences that stand out. Some of their most painful life moments were at school because of some ugly teacher. Ridiculing young people is a form of child psychological abuse with long-lasting consequences.

## Grade Manipulating

The sneakiest, most underhanded form of teacher-child abuse is grade manipulating. Yet it's a single weapon against students that I believe to be extremely common. In grade manipulating, teachers raise or lower students' grades based on how they feel about the students. This doesn't mean how they feel about the student's work. Grade manipulating is easy for teachers to accomplish and very hard to defend.

There are some signs to look for when a teacher is manipulating grades. First and foremost, the student will tell you that he or she believes the grade is not fair. They may do this using various wording, such as "I know I did better than this" or "How did I get such a bad grade? I did exactly what I was supposed to do." There are some work-related signs that grades might have been manipulated. These are as follows:

- Marking things wrong when they are correct
- Not assigning a grade to well-done papers that would ordinarily be graded
- Assigning grades based on excessively marking down items that were not related to the assignment
- Grading very low when there are few errors
- Not assessing the work at all and assigning a grade as low based on random items
- Assessing work that is not usually graded and assigning a low grade
- Not even reading the paper, just assigning low grades and throwing away the papers
- Grading classroom activities low that have no basis for a grade
- Assigning competitively based group grades low

There was only one time when the problem got so bad with one of my own children, that I stepped in behind the scenes to double-check the assumption that grades were being manipulated. This grade manipulating was going on in an English class. So, I took the extra time to correct each paper before it was turned in and made sure the papers were redone until there were no grammatical mistakes. This may seem excessive, but this is a great learning tool for students as well as a way of checking on what's happening with a teacher. I've always spent extra time looking through science papers. From early on, during my children's school years, I made sure science papers were all done in correct format, with no missing steps, with correct wording, and checked grammar and spelling. If there were errors, they all had to be corrected before the paper was turned in. This child was very interested in science and the practice of correct formatting paid off when the research got more complicated. So now the English papers got the same scrutiny. But that same scrutiny and time with corrections didn't make any difference in the English paper grades.

I asked a friend who was an emeritus English professor to evaluate a couple of papers. The grades still didn't or any more consistent. There was an average of three essays, short or long, assigned each week. One or two were returned in any month. The few papers that were returned graded were drafts that were to be redone for a final grade. The final, redone papers were assigned a grade, but they were never returned. There was no way to know the basis for the grades, whether the papers were really graded or even looked at. It's possible they all went immediately into the trash can. This is an example of how easy it is to grade manipulate in middle and high school.

The problem of grade manipulating is not as easily accomplished in elementary school. Papers are very simple, and the answers are straightforward. The most obvious case of elementary grade manipulating I've seen had to do with graded cursive writing. The student whose cursive writing grade was manipulated was certainly not the teacher's favorite. The child, who struggled academically and had some overactive problems, was repeatedly given failing grades on the quality of the cursive alphabet. The mother brought the papers to me and asked what I thought. There didn't appear to be any obvious errors. I went to school in an era and a place where cursive writing was ritually corrected. All the letters had to hit in certain places on special three-line rows. OK, this child's teacher may have been very old school, and there's certainly nothing wrong with this form of teaching. After all, we all got educated and graduated from high school successfully literate. However, this child's teacher severely evaluated what was a pretty passable cursive writing, gave failing grades, and ritually assigned this student more cursive homework each week. In this case, grade manipulating was likely a poorly constructed attempt to teach discipline through punishment.

It becomes easier for the teacher to grade manipulate when the work evaluation is subjective. But even the manipulative behavior of down grading is difficult to remediate. To have an incorrect grade corrected, the student has to take an action that is time-consuming and complicated. They have to catch a teacher when there is available time. The teachers are often not available. The students operate on a system of bells and tardy slips and are afraid that if they try to catch a teacher between classes, they'll be penalized for being late to the next class. Many teachers do not have any availability during lunch and before or after school. Some teachers faithfully have hours set aside to be helpful to students. Others disappear the moment their last class is ended and are never available outside of class hours. This, despite most contracts setting their work hours to extend beyond the last class. So, getting a grade corrected is made difficult, and if this occurs frequently, the student gives up.

Pointing out to a teacher that he or she has marked items wrong when the item is correct is also dangerous. If the teacher continuously marks items wrong, and the student continually has to bring the paper back for re-correction, the abusive teacher will simply find another possibly worse way of being abusive.

It might amuse you to know that many high school students calculate the value of each grade that requires correction and weighs that against how much time they have for assignments, which are worth more points. Don't make the mistake of believing that most students don't know what's going on with the teachers.

Teachers also manipulate grades to make students grades look better than they are. If a teacher likes a student, he or she may be given breaks on his or her grades. This happens everywhere, but some obvious examples are when the student is important to a school sports team and when the student is the child of a teacher, administrator, or a well-liked school employee. Some examples of up grading are:

- Grading high when there are many errors
- Not assessing the work at all and assigning a grade as high based on random items
- Assessing work that is not usually graded with a high grade
- Not even reading the paper, just assigning high grades and throwing away the papers
- Grading classroom activities high that have no basis for a grade
- Assigning competitively based group grades high

Neither assessing grades high nor assessing grades low is OK. It's probably illegal, as grades dictate such things as college admission and scholarships, team participation, and awards. Proving grade manipulation is almost impossible and very hard to tackle. With the brotherhood present in every individual school and the bastion supporting any defense of teacher child abuse and teacher-child neglect, parents are fortunate just to get their children through the system intact.

## Other Teacher Tactics of Abuse and Neglect

Teachers can invent very sneaky ways of discriminating against students and clever methods of abuse and neglect that are superficially invisible. For instance, there was a teacher in our area who marked students absent from his class when they were present. He did it routinely enough that it became obviously targeted at those he had already shown dislike for or had chosen as his victims. An occasional absent report can be considered a mistake. Sometimes when students are very tardy, the roll has been taken and the teacher doesn't want to be bothered with changing the absence to a tardy. That's understandable, especially for teachers who plan to accomplish something and want to get right down to work. But when a teacher simply marks the student absent because he or she likes being abusive to certain students, the problem is systemic and the behavior is systematic.

So how does the student correct the absence? The student must go to the main office when an attendance clerk is present and available and the student is available, and the office is open. Any idea how hard that is? But wait. The attendance clerk hears what happened and then gives the student a special form with all the information. The student must then go to the offending teacher and ask the teacher if he or she will please sign the form so that the absence can be corrected. This opens up the student to all kinds of other abusive remarks; comments; and derogatory, degrading possibilities if the teacher chooses to continue the abuse. If not, at the least the student is still left with the problem of having to nicely ask the perpetrator to take back the abusive behavior of marking him or her absent when he or she was clearly there. And it doesn't end there. The teacher may say no. The teacher may want to deny the student's presence in the class. I recommend that no student ever see any teacher alone for many reasons, and this is one of these reasons. The student should take a student along who is in the same class. This can backfire for the other student, however, who then may him- or herself become a target. If the teacher says no, that's the end of the chances to have the intentional absence removed. If he or she signs the form, that's still not the end. The student must now go to the office again, find and wait to see the attendance officer, and turn in the form.

This very simple tactic of abuse causes much misery for the student. My experience with this scenario and variations of the absent tactic is that teachers don't use this tactic frequently or with any regularity. But if they use this tactic two or three times a year, it reminds the student that they are being manipulated by a teacher and can't do anything to stop the abuse.

I was sitting in an airport, reading a book, and looking out the big window onto the tarmac in New Orleans waiting for a plane that was very late. It wasn't crowded or noisy, but a group of young women who were traveling together sat a few seats away. They seemed cheerful, articulate, and were probably flying on the same plane I was waiting for, going to Dallas. Although I didn't attend much to their conversation, a few words got my attention.

One young mother was talking about what she was going to do when she returned home. It all had to do with her child's abusive teacher. She described the teacher's behavior to her companions, what she had done to date, and the administrations usual nonresponse, the same things I've been hearing for years. Apparently, the child had been chosen for punishment and was the subject of discrimination and labeling. She laid out the steps she had devised to trap the teacher in her own web of abuse. I silently cheered her on for being an assertive and protective parent. Still, now I wish that I had intruded on her conversation and given her encouragement. But my social training from early in life kicked in and I missed the opportunity to help.

There are endless devious techniques used in America's schools to abuse and neglect students. Coaches are particularly discriminatory and are famous for choosing teams based on personal preference or favors owed rather than the skill levels. They also use covert methods of eliminating certain students from teams they want to play on, especially if positions are very competitive.

When your student says that there's something wrong with a class or teacher, listen to him or her. Try to figure out exactly what the issues are. Ask questions.

## Summary

This section on teacher's tactics for child abuse and child neglect describes the methods that abusive teachers use in the classroom. The teacher who gets in the face of a student, screams, humiliates a child, and then banishes him or she to some nonexistent remediation is guilty of serious child psychological abuse. There is no justification for a teacher or other school personnel ridiculing, ignoring, or injuring a child in any other way. Those dysfunctional teacher behaviors lead the student to resentment, anger, and even worse. It deters the child from seeing this teacher and this classroom as a place to learn, and the child begins to see school as horrible, a punishment.

Any and all of the behaviors described here are criminal offences. Think not? Talk to anyone who has been involved in a child custody battle. The very behaviors described here are behaviors cited in courtrooms and weigh heavily in custody decisions. Is this parent fit to be a caregiver? What would you do if your boss behaved this way? Ridicule, harassment, humiliation, and embarrassment are all workplace violations. You would be entitled to file both criminal and civil charges and collect for damages and possibly long-term compensation for the traumatic injury. There are rules that allow schools to punish, even expel, students who behave in these very ways. Where is the compensation for the student who has been injured? Where is the justice?

All the teacher abuse and neglect tactics result in strong and sometimes lifelong reaction from the student. None of those tactics are positive or healthy for the young person, despite some pundits' claim of toughening up the child or managing the classroom. So, just what is the point of abusing or neglecting a student? As you know, there is no point. Child neglect and child abuse by members of the educational bastion nets very negative returns. The only reason child abuse exists in the schools is because the perpetrators feel like doing it and no one stops them.

## CHAPTER 12
# Teacher Child Abuse and Child Neglect Defenses

> "So, when we're lost, we humans strangely start running.
> There are an infinite number of directions to run.
> What are the chances when we're running
> that we're going to find our way?"
> —D. P. CALLIN

Well-known bastions, including enormous organizations in the fields of sports, religion, politics, and law enforcement, are described in the introduction to this book. The members of these and other bastions, the brotherhoods, behave in similar ways when problems arise. The protection a bastion offers its members, those of the brotherhoods, supports the freedom to abuse and neglect without consequence. In each bastion, the members of a brotherhood can easily avoid any offensive confrontation with their victims. Each brotherhood member acts in self-defense, using tactics that fit the situation, the perceived weakness of the victim, and the personality of the neglecting or abusing member. The behavior of the members of the teaching brotherhood is no exception. Fleeing to self-defense indicates running away from accusations. Similar to fleeing the scene of the crime, the guilty party tries to escape the consequences of their bad, abusive, or neglectful behaviors. Teachers and other school personnel, along with many other people from all walks of life and in other bastions, each have their own way of fleeing to self-defense.

Make no mistake here; every teacher tactic for defense is just another form of child abuse. Teacher-child abuse is cumulative. With each affront, each instance of abuse and its subsequent defense fits into a pattern in which the student suffers abuse repeatedly. We label these tactics as teachers' defensive tactics, and they are the defenses that abusive and neglectful teachers use. The defenses reinjure the student who has already been abused or neglected or both, and the injuries pile up over one another. Cumulative trauma is the result of such behavior.

Patterns of fleeing to self-defense in various brotherhoods have some commonalities. For instance, almost all abusers answer a complaint or accusation with denial at the very first. Then, when that doesn't work, they display some form of defensive aggression toward the victim. We've all heard the expression, "The only good defense is a good offence." When abusers are confronted by their victims, they deploy a series of steps or defenses. When one type of defense doesn't work, they move on to the next. The perpetrators' defenses begin with simple denial and quickly become increasingly more aggressive: first passive-aggressive self-defenses followed by active-aggressive self-defenses. Abusers work hard to protect themselves.

Accusations of child abuse or child neglect are very serious. If proven guilty, the perpetrator has a lot to lose. It's possible that I've missed reading some of the accounts, but I've never heard of a teacher who was accused of major offences or confronted by a victim who just admitted upfront, "Yes, I did it" unless he or she was caught in the act.

Once we understand how teachers and other school personnel turn the defense of themselves into offense aimed at the victim, we can begin to predict the perpetrators' responses. We can even predict what types of defenses to expect from the abuser. This is a great advantage when dealing with an individual or group who are practiced at defense and offence. The tactics are almost scripted. The perpetrator is generally in a hurry to deny and then flip the accusation back to the victim. Victims can be prepared by providing them knowledge of such patterns, which leads them to anticipate and address all possible defenses *before* the first confrontation. Get prepared before the perpetrator has the first opportunity to deny. Be prepared to handle what happens when the denial is over and the victim blaming begins.

Listen carefully to the perpetrator. There is no rush to respond. Don't let him or her rattle you. You can respond now, later, or even much later—that's up to you. Engaging in a battle of words is a very bad idea, especially when the perpetrator is practiced and has the support of the whole bastion. Take your time to notice which step the perpetrator uses in his or her defense. The perpetrator may switch between tactics or entirely skip one level altogether.

This section describes passive and active means with which teachers respond when confronted for their child abuse and child neglect. These responses are common and often predictable. The first responses are generally passive. That is, the teacher either ignores or directly denies any wrongdoing. If that doesn't work, the defense becomes active. The defense changes its focus back to the victim, and the defense becomes offense. Carefully review the defensive tactics and offensive tactics you will encounter when confronting child abuse and child neglect perpetrated by teachers and the other school personnel. Think of other ways in which a perpetrator might defend against the victims' allegations.

Defending abusive and neglectful behaviors usually, but not always, occurs in stages. It begins with a simple response; that is, it begins with no response at all. The primary response to an accusation is just blowing it off or ignoring the accusation. This isn't direct denial; it's very passive. The perpetrator pretends that the complaint isn't important and isn't worth his or her time to respond. This tactic gives the perpetrator time to think about how to proceed while hoping that the complaint just goes away because no one pays attention to it. There are two general types of *passive* defenses: ignoring and denial.

## Ignoring

Believe it or not, silence is a powerful tool. The first usual step for lodging a complaint is to talk to the guilty party. Ignoring a complaint puts the problem back into the hands of the victim. The victim must now muster the courage to go beyond the normal complaint procedures set up by the bastion, already aware that the odds of getting any kind of acknowledgement are slim. Worse yet, the problem can escalate with the teacher retaliating with further abuse and neglect while the student and parent struggle for safety. Often, there is no safety in the face of an abusive member of the brotherhood. Safety is only reserved for the abuser.

## Denial

The second likely defense on part of the teacher is a surprisingly difficult defense to overcome—blatant denial. This isn't a complex tactic, but it's very difficult to negotiate with in the school setting because, once again, the power differential is too hard for a student or parent to navigate. When a parent or a student brings a complaint about a teacher to the administration, a frequent response is denial. The teacher flatly says, "No, that didn't happen." Some teachers then go on to add one or more of the other types of teacher defenses. But even by itself, straight denial defense is a real challenge. The perpetrator openly challenges the victim to prove it. The burden of proof is thus always put on the accuser; in this case, the burden of proof lies with the victim or the victim's family.

Once again, the victim must act to stop the abuse or just give up. On the surface, denial looks quite straightforward. But denial, in fact, has many facets. For instance, both the student and the teacher know that the complaint is genuine, that the latter is lying, and the challenge is a very aggressive game that forces the victim into a corner and dare he or she escalate his or her actions to the next step. Ignoring and denial are passive-aggressive defenses. The teacher denies that the abuse ever happened. The administration denies the presence of any evidence. The school board drops the matter. These problems occur constantly in schools around the country. All the school administration would need to do is ask the other students in the room and one at a time. But the other students are often not asked because everyone already has knowledge of the occurrence and don't want to provide any evidence.

Denial's passive appearance is pretty unattractive. However, denial often takes on increased *affect*, a word for the many expressions in nonverbal communication. In other words, the abuser who denies becomes animated in some form. He or she might appear outwardly aggressive. Sometimes denial is laced with sarcasm and threat, which sends the underlying verbal or nonverbal message, "I dare you to take this any further," or "You'll be sorry you're doing this."

So, what happens when the victim's complaint doesn't go away? What if the teacher ignores or denies, and the victim doesn't give up? If ignoring or denying doesn't work for the teacher, and the student doesn't give up trying to stop the abuse, the escalation begins with the teacher going on to active forms of defense.

Teacher defenses are readily available. Teachers have all the power that their position provides them as a member of the brotherhood with the support and power of the bastion behind them. Moreover, they have experience in setting up and using teacher defenses. The offending teachers and other school employees have used defenses and watched their peers use the same for as many years as they have been employed or longer.

Escalating defenses happens with the perception of increased threat. In many cases, the perpetrator skips the ignoring stage and maybe several levels of defense. But if the abuser has been ignoring or defending the problem, and those tactics don't suppress the complaint, the teacher defenses escalate; the defense transitions into offense. There a many possible forms for an active defense to take; there are ten types defined and discussed in the next section.

When a student, a young person, is adequately prepared and displays typical age-appropriate behavior, there is no particular reason to regularly focus on that student in any unordinary way. There are teachers who do notice good work and make an effort to hand out praise when it's deserved. Otherwise, both teacher and student go about the daily business of the school with a simple nod of recognition, if anything at all.

But when some teachers or other school personnel are abusive or neglectful, they may be called out for their behavior. When they can't defend themselves by ignoring or denying, they start flipping the blame. Flipping is the primary tool for all *active teacher defenses*.

When people are caught doing something wrong, they often become defensive. Rather than just saying they did something irresponsible, they deny and ignore, and when that fails, they flip it back to the victim. Flipping is the most basic and predictable tool of offensive defense mechanisms. It's used by bullies and abusers in the world over. Look at politics. There is nothing more common and obvious than blaming the other guy, the other party, or the person who preceded you. When the victim is a student, victim blaming is relatively easy. As you read earlier, the position of teacher in a bastion the size of the public-school system is formidable. Students and parents alike find it difficult to stand their ground and confront wrongdoing. Thus, the teacher has the upper hand. The teacher has all the power, age, experience, and position to hide behind. He or she also has an endless taxpayer purse to defend him- or herself, all at no personal cost. Most families have no resources to fight even one member of the vast bastion.

There are several forms of flipping the accusation back to the victim. Some of these flipping tactics may appear to be silly and far too simple. But they are actually quite effective. Even the simplest flipping of responsibility back to the student casts doubts over the student's accusation and brings into question the complaint's credibility.

Read through each type of teacher defense that relies on putting the blame back on the victim. Remember that flipping is active-aggressive. The aim of the teacher is to use the accusation of the victim to form the base of their offensive attack. The acts of the abusive and neglectful perpetrator, which have been exposed by the victim, become the material for the perpetrator's defense. Suddenly, the injured party is reinjured or re-traumatized by the very person who created the injury. Only this time, the perpetrator has the whole bastion to help him or her in his or her vicious agenda.

It's pretty common in courts to use this tactic. This flipping is the reason why many rape victims don't come forward. They are often accused of causing their own rape. How can that possibly happen? How can a student be responsible for an injury caused by a teacher? Here's how this magic trick works.

## Arguing Reality

To some extent, we've all participated in arguing over objective reality. Witnesses to any event argue over the details of what actually happened. The result is a contradiction between what two witnesses say: two people perceive an event differently. We also argue over issues of right and wrong. When we argue over an objective reality, this is generally based on our beliefs, preferences, or prejudices. We often find it hard to understand why the other person cannot see the situation the way we do. Even more so, we are amazed that he or she sees a situation in the way he or she does; we label that person with various terms generally meaning unintelligent or uninformed.

Arguing over reality is often a fruitless endeavor between peers, friends, or even foes. It happens in the courtroom where both parties are represented by attorneys. But those are examples of more or less even playing fields. The teacher and the student are not in an equal position. A figure of authority who argues over reality is fully aware of his or her position of power and that he or she is likely to win in any disagreement. The only probable situation where a student's word is considered over that of the teacher's is when there is undeniable evidence.

When denial is used, the resulting attitude is a simple "it didn't happen." Arguing reality in the student-teacher conflict occurs when the teacher refutes the accusation as untrue and that the incident didn't actually happen the way the student presented it. In arguing reality, teachers don't deny saying something, but rather they flip the blame back onto the student with a simple response, "That's not what I said." This implies that the student is either mistaken or lying.

With students, especially elementary schoolchildren, this is a pretty common teacher defense tactic. Children don't have a fully developed distinction between reality and fiction. It's often hard for them to tell a lie from the truth. The teacher is someone they have been asked to hold in respect. Teachers are the ones in charge. Children have little capacity to argue with an authority figure even if they *do* understand that the teacher is abusive.

You know that someone is arguing against your reality when he or she says things like, "That's not what I said." Some of the hundreds of variations of arguing reality include such things as, "It didn't happen that way," "You misunderstood what I said," or "You took it out of context." Generally, students don't respond when teachers use this method of arguing reality. They don't know how to defend themselves and feel that the teacher is too powerful to argue with. Students also know that they can be accused of disrespect. They may have been cautioned by their parents at the very beginning to respect the teacher. Confronting any teacher behavior can escalate with the student being re-victimized.

Remember that being silent after the teacher flips the accusation back to the victim doesn't stop the victimization. It doesn't solve the victim's problem. Silence may stop the abuser for the moment. However, there are times when a perpetrator uses that student's silence as a victory and begins to exhibit an entirely new aggressive behavior. In fact, the student should expect that silence worsens the problem. The abuser may actually gloat at the silence. This may be as simple as the teacher lecturing the victim about being careful what he or she says or sarcastically suggesting that the victim should be a better listener. But it may also move into another type of defense that is harder to overcome.

## Rewriting History

Rewriting history is a variation of arguing reality. The perpetrator redefines the actual occurrence. This is sort of a bait and switch behavior. Instead of saying, "I didn't say that," which is denial, or "That isn't what I said," which is arguing reality or redefining of the actual content, the perpetrator rewrites the entire incident. It's done in a sequence, with the perpetrator in control of each phase. Here are some examples.

1. Teacher chooses student victim and baits him or her.
   - The teacher walks in front of the chosen victim while lecturing.
2. Teacher psychologically abuses the student.
   - The teacher stares at the victim while lecturing.
3. The student confronts the abusive teacher.
   - The student becomes uncomfortable and finally gets brave enough to ask, "Why are you staring at me?"
4. Teacher engages in active aggressive rewriting of history.
   - In firm, accusatory terms, he or she says, "You're not working," "I told you to put that away," "Don't speak unless you raise your hand," or even, "You aren't paying attention."

The student is thus being psychologically abused. When the teacher denies what actually happened, the student is faced with a decision: "Should I confront this teacher? How can I do that without making this abuse worse?" Can you imagine a way in which the student can stop this teacher? Can the student stop the teacher from denying every action that takes place between them? Students are always in a subjugated position compared to the teachers. The system is set up that way for several reasons. However, the system fails to police those teachers who take advantage of their positions to victimize young people. Look at another example.

- Teacher seeks out the chosen victim and baits the student.
  - Teacher makes an accusatory remark, which is obviously intended for victim.
- Teacher abuses victim.
  - "There are actually some students who think they don't have to get started working until the last minute."

- Student responds to abusive teacher.
  - "I was listening to your lecture."
- Teacher active-aggressive rewrite of history
  - "I'm not talking to you," "That wasn't meant for you," "You always think it's about you," "That's not what I'm talking about," "Try to keep your mind on what you're doing…not what I'm saying," or "Everyone else heard it, and they didn't think it was about them."

The abusive teacher has thus successfully set up the victim. The victim has been baited. When the student tries to respond or defend, he or she gets verbally walloped. The pattern is maddening and widely used. The rewriting reality defense generally includes a new story or a statement like "That's not what I'm talking about" or "I wasn't talking to you…"

The student is aware that the verbal denigration was intentional. But it's confusing and embarrassing to deal with. The student can't win, no matter what he or she does. If the student argues, he or she is punished; if the student does nothing and take the punishment; he or she looks and feels helpless. Many parents try to move their child to another classroom when their student is chosen as a teacher's victim. But that isn't always possible, and at times the school doesn't cooperate.

## Creating a Fictional Reality

Creating a fictional reality is related to rewriting history. But instead of baiting and switching with the events at hand, the abuser creates an entirely new fictional account. "This is what really happened" is the beginning of a tall tale of creating a fictional reality. Again, this is active-aggressive, unlike denial, which is passive-aggressive.

In the previous example, creating a new reality happens when the perpetrator simply uses a scenario that did happened. Then the perpetrator distorts it. However, in creating a fictional reality, the storytelling has little relationship with any facts. Look at the following examples:

"I was walking by and smiling at each student."
"We were having a great discussion."
"I give each of my student's positive attention."
"I always make eye contact."
"I was giving (the victim) attention because he was clearly following the lecture." "[The victim] is really a good student; I was encouraging participation."

None of these are probably true. Creating a fictional reality puts an imaginary spin on what's really happening by making up a fairy-tale scenario. It may start with the same baiting as rewriting history does, but when confronted, the teacher tells some extraordinary tale about his or her great student. This makes calling out the abuse difficult. When under threat, the perpetrator may act as if the victim is actually his or her favorite student. Maybe the abusive teacher infers that the student is so wonderful that he or she is like a friend. Some ridiculous stories include entirely fictitious depictions of a relationship where the teacher tells a tale of how he or she depends on this student and can always count on the student. The perpetrator hints that there may be some indication that this student is a really special person, perhaps exceptionally smart or wise.

We've heard it all before. Countless innocent victims were chosen by God and the local priest. They were special, they were to serve, or they were called by the church. The abuse was often cloaked as the young person's obligation to God, as something that God directed. There is no difference here. These are well-used lines and well-practiced scripts. When your child tells you that a teacher is abusing him or her, be very skeptical when the teacher starts telling you that your student is a special person.

Conversely, the abusive teacher might invent a horrifying story about the chosen victim. It can be either elaborate or simple, but it will for sure be fiction at its best and worst. For example, the teacher might accuse the student of lingering in the classroom and behaving in insulting and aggressive ways. The perpetrator could hint at not wanting to complain in the past, but with the complaints the student has lodged, he or she has no choice but to disclose how awful and miserable the student really is. And there are infinite variations of these fictional realities just waiting to be created by some perpetrator who has been called out for his or her own abuses.

Rewriting history and creating a fictional reality are implied threats. They are very similar, but they differ in whether the perpetrator simply redefines the event, changes the meaning of the event, or completely writes a new, often elaborate story. The perpetrator sets up the challenge and thus gives notice to the victim. The perpetrator implies that now that the victim knows that when he or she fights back, he or she will face retaliation.

What happens when the student is determined to hold the teacher accountable regardless of the implied threats? When rewriting history and creating a fictional reality all fail, when the victim continues to fight back despite being warned that it would hurt him or her, the abuser embarks on another more aggressive approach. The abuser turns from denying or redefining the event to directly blaming the student. This is where the aggression becomes intense.

## Making the Student Look Bad

If the abusive teacher can't change the reality, the student is made to look bad. Again, the student is held accountable for the perpetrator's actions. Judgmental statements are made that have the intent of causing the student to look responsible for the problem and make the student look bad.

Notice that the word *you* appears in almost every aggressive accusation, but especially if the perpetrator's intention is to make the student look bad. "You have some kind of a problem," or "Why would you even say that (or think that)." One teacher even yelled at a student in the middle of a classroom, "What's wrong with you?"

Making a student look bad works as a teacher defense. This defense is offensive, and therefore puts the entire responsibility for the event back in the victim's lap. The active, aggressive act flips the guilty teacher's behavior and directs the accusation of wrongdoing on the student. It's no longer that the perpetrator denies the event or says that the student misunderstood, misheard, or even misinterpreted in some innocent way. This isn't making up some halfway pleasant or horrendous fairy-tale. Unlike the horrendous fairy-tale, making the student look bad is a more direct attack on the victim.

There are many reasons for which making the student look bad works for the abuser. If the victim has been repeatedly abused, the other students are already aware that the teacher can get away with it. When the teacher makes that same student look bad again and again, it negatively reinforces how other students see the victim. They may think that there is something wrong with the student that they just can't see or understand. They can also understand that the teacher is abusive and wonder why the student puts up with that.

Making the student look bad also reinforces how the other students see the teacher. Their own level of intimidation is enhanced. Other students may be fearful of speaking out. Possibly, they themselves may have had complaints about the teacher, and they learn that there is no support for them from any figure of authority within the school system.

Responding to the teacher who has made the student look bad is risky. Once the teacher begins to use the word *you* in an accusatory way, the stakes are higher. Remember that the abuser has already likely tried several means to get out of the situation. Perhaps he or she tried ignoring or denial or maybe even resorted to creating a fairy-tale. All these have failed to silence the victim.

It's also true that the perpetrator may have started the attacks at the elevated *you* defense mode, entirely bypassing the denial and changing reality strategies. This happens for several reasons. First, the abusive teacher is well versed with abusing and doesn't feel a need to deescalate the problem. Second, he or she has been toughened by his or her repeated abusive behaviors that have no consequences and is emboldened to jump right in, starting his or her defense with a direct attack. Third, the abuser may also feel challenged by the student and feel that the student is being self-righteous in his or her determination to get the abuse to stop. Fourth, the abuser may be angry that he or she is called out, and it causes the abuser to be more aggressive. Last, the abuser may be surprised by the student's assertive response to try to stop the abuse, so he or she begins the more powerful aggressive defense—he or she attacks.

Just remember that making the student look bad is only the first of ways through which an abuser leaps into the aggressive *you* as their response to being called out for their abusive behaviors.

## You're Disturbed

Abusers often defend themselves by saying that the student has some kind of a personal problem. In this case, the teacher is not denying that something happened. He or she is not rewriting history. Rather, the teacher blatantly stating that something happened and that indeed there was a problem. But the problem occurred because the student was overreacting, overemotional, or incompetent in some way. The teacher may go on to say that he or she understands and that what happened was nothing at all or unimportant. This leads to the inference that the teacher has the higher moral authority as he or she tries to not take it personally or that he or she has been blamed for something that happened because the student was disturbed. The teacher may act as if he or she feels compassion for the student's problem. The teacher's dismissal of the complaint then goes one step further and placates the student or the student's parent by inferring that the student needs some kind of help, that the teacher, the professional, has been in this job for years, has seen it before, and that intervention might be useful.

This is an aggressive flip. In this situation, the perpetrator hands the complaint back to the student with an added feature. The inference is that the victim is not only responsible, but that the victim's family should now take some extensive action to evaluate their child's personal functioning. Again, the defense says, "I'm not going to get angry with this student's accusations because I understand that he or she needs help." The aggressive message is, "You are sick or broken, and that's obvious because you accused me of doing something wrong. Ha-ha, I'll get even with you." Don't forget that both the student and the abuser are keenly aware that the teacher is lying.

In essence, the victim is dismissed along with the victim's complaint. The victim is sent away to seek help for his or her problem. This is very much the same as the abuse cases where priests tell children and their parents that the victim is possessed by the devil or is evil. The aggressive defense takes the focus off the accusations and places it firmly in the laps of the victim and the victim's family. It's an amazing kind of flip. How does a family who might not even speak English deal with that? It's likely they run the other way and vow that they will live with whatever horrible abuse goes on because they have been made to fear the consequences of speaking out.

## You Overreact

Saying to a student or his or her family that a student overreacts is a variation of "you're disturbed." Shifting the blame for abuse by saying the victim overreacts is usually done through innuendo at this stage of aggressive defense. In some variety of words, the abuser infers that the student, who has been a victim, is deficient in his or her observations, also inferring that the student is actually an emotionally excessive human being. This type of flip may sound parental or concerned. But the underlying message is that of "I pity you," "Get a grip," or "Chill out." In much the same way, women have, for decades, been labeled as hormonal or PMS-ing. Men are overly aggressive when their testosterone is said to be raging. They can't be counted on to be reasonable and use good judgment because they are too emotional. It comes out sounding like the student is too emotional to possess good judgment. After all, to think a teacher would behave badly is quite excessive according to behavioral norms. It does fly right in the face, however, of the expectations schools have of their students' capacity to manage their own behavior and produce a steady and excessive amount of work, class after class, year after year. I suppose that being over reactive is reserved only for those students who accuse their coaches, teachers, and other school personnel of abuse.

The abuser may argue that the student has one or many issues because he or she cannot manage his or her emotions. You may hear comments thrown in, such as the following:

"Being overemotional gets in the way of judgment and common sense."
"You're too sensitive; you imagine everything to be more important than it is."
"Maybe there are other problems that we haven't yet recognized."
"You overreact because your emotions cloud your judgment."
"This overreacting interferes with your comprehension."
"I've noticed when I'm grading his or her papers that there are some things…"

None of these statements are new. They have been used in defense of abuse cases time after time. They can be heard across the country in courtrooms where victims fight for justice.

Students accused of overreacting to a teacher's abusive behavior have been doubly victimized, as are all victims of abuse. They are first victims of the abuse, and then victims of the lies, and then victims of accusations of abusers who again the student in an effort to defend their abuse.

The student has already endured some kind of teacher abuse and has faced the source of the problem. It's made to look like the student may always have these kinds of problems; but hopefully, he or she will outgrow the problem, grow up, and get ahold of his or her emotions. As with all teacher-abuser defenses, this shifts the problem back on to the victim and takes the focus off the perpetrator. The inference drawn from such statements is that the problem is with the student who is too overemotional to know the difference between right and wrong, between normal interactions and inappropriate interactions, and is thereby overreacting.

## Attention Seeking

Has anyone ever accused you of seeking attention after you have complained of being injured in some way? Just when you have the courage to try to resolve an issue, suddenly it gets made to look like the problem is all about you needing attention. The inference here is that a real problem does not exist. Accusations of attention seeking are pretty nasty. They evoke angry responses in people who are genuinely in need of getting help with an issue.

It's difficult to pin down attention seeking in action. Using the dictionary definition is fine and dandy, but in real life, the term *attention seeking* is thrown about carelessly and acts as a substitute for some more substantive opinions or observations. Calling a behavior attention seeking is also an easy dismissal, which enables the avoidance of the problem.

In the classroom, the teacher always knows that one or another student may act out because he or she is seeking attention. All the students may recognize that some of their peers will at times display attention-seeking behaviors. They know that there are times when everyone needs attention, and acting out is one way to get it.

Because attention seeking is a common behavior among young people, it's an easy transition for the perpetrator to make. This is a common but pretty aggressive defense. Teachers can point to a multitude of attention-seeking behaviors they deal with every day in the school. This may confuse the victim's peers. The victim's peers know that attention seeking is common among children and young adults, but they might not have necessarily seen this behavior among their peers.

Accusing or attacking someone who has been already been injured by labelling him or her as attention seeking often succeeds in stopping the action against the abuse. It takes some time to process this shifting of the blame coming from a new angle, thus construing a new attack. Remember that the victim is already speaking up because he or she has been abused by the teacher or other school personnel. The student has already been the victim of death threats and has been singled out for punishment or other forms of child abuse or neglect. Once the student's words are changed to label him or her as attention seeking, the victim and anyone who observes the interaction may need to regroup. A new element, the accusation of attention seeking against the victim, is thrown into the pot along with the existing problem of the teacher's abuse, and this further muddles the picture. No one, especially the victim, expects such an accusation, an accusation that is completely unrelated to the victim's need to get a teacher or other school employee to stop the abuse. The accusation, however, is completely related to the abuser's need to throw out some defense that contains a *you* message. Attention seeking is an easy deflection back to the victim.

Unfortunately, there is very little irrefutable evidence in the cases of teacher abuse. So, the young person lives with the reputation, the anger, and the resentment, and leaves with the undeserved and untreated injury.

We see here how other people are often involved when an abuser denies and defends. Many of those people are also victims themselves. They have been duped into playing a role in the abuser's game. Some of them stand up for the perpetrator because they themselves have something to lose or gain if they don't. This topic will be covered more thoroughly in chapter 13. When a student is accused of attention seeking and others are involved, those who have been involved likely have to stop and take a breath and reexamine their support of the victim. After all, there is a lot of attention-seeking behavior from students in the classroom; there is, in fact, a lot of attention-seeking behavior in the world. How can anyone argue with that? Students who have not been bullied may be more confused than the student who was bullied. The student who has already been abused and is now trying to stand up to the perpetrator may be surprised or confused. But at least he or she knows the perpetrator is guilty. Those around the victim may not be sure. In yet another way, the victim is reinjured by being questioned and evaluated by others.

We do know that accusing someone of attention seeking works to quiet the victim; he or she fears that his or her persistent search for justice might *appear* to be attention-seeking behavior and therefore make matters worse. It's important to mention that the accusation of attention-seeking behavior may come from someone other than the teacher. The abusive teacher may ask some other school employee to intervene and therefore involve that person in the abuse. There are common responses from other members of the brotherhood who are called on to step in to defend the abusive teacher. They often come in the form of, "You're overreacting" or "You're attention seeking." Try working out a defense against someone accusing you of overreacting or attention seeking. With lots of practice, it's possible to handle these new, flipped accusations effectively. But for the average young person, or even their parents, this is a difficult task.

## Problem Student

Some students do have personal issues. They may bring them to school in any number of ways and for many reasons. Students can be depressed, lonely, unsuccessful, rejected, stressed, or have myriad other problems. They are likely to bring these problems to school just as adults bring their problems with them wherever they go. Having difficulty coping and spending enormous time mentally sorting through one's life problems is part of being human.

Grouping students with problems with students who complain about teacher abuse isn't unusual. It is sad and perhaps even sadistic. But unfortunately, teachers who are abusive and neglectful are happy to find that a student has personal problems—the abusive teacher can conveniently shift the focus away from him- or herself. This is what makes students with problems prime victims—they're easy to victimize. This misuse of an individual's private struggle is common fodder for desperate attorneys looking for a way out of consequences for their clients. We see this kind of low-blow tactic coming to surface with every low-blow individual in politics and divorce and injury cases, some even going so far as to blame a murder victim for being killed.

Students who are being abused or neglected by some teacher or other school personnel are often called problem students. This label can appear after some recent teacher abuse, or it can be slowly developed as the perpetrator systematically targets the victim. But the first time it's probably heard outside the brotherhood is when the abused student actively defends him- or herself.

Telling a student that he or she is the problem is an outright form of defensive aggression. The perpetrator defends by declaring a student as a problem student. The responsibility for the abuse is denied and shifted in one easy step. There are some typical statements used when this flip is used, as listed below:

- "You're a problem student."
- "You see everything as problem even when there is no problem."
- "There is no problem, except you're the problem."
- "You just want to create problems."

A lot can be learned about a teacher who uses the problem-student defense. There's a certain kind of laziness inherent in the demeaning behavior, just as there is in the denial defense. But the denial defense is passive; it doesn't include any active accusation from the perpetrator. In the problem-student defense, the perpetrator actively blames the victim. But, like the passive-denial defense, saying the student is a problem doesn't require any creativity, or likewise, any effort. In fact, the perpetrator has likely not even thought of how the or she might create some circumstances to support this sloppy, aggressive defense. At least the student can easily understand what the teacher is doing. Everyone knows that an authority figure can simply suggest that someone is a problem, and it seems to hold ground because of the accuser's position. The student's peers probably know all about the victim and probably understand that the teacher is at fault. Even other teachers sometimes know that the student in question is not a problem student in the classroom. But those teachers are highly unlikely to ever take a stand for a student against a member of the brotherhood.

So, although the flipping of responsibility for their abusive behaviors by calling a student a problem is a frequent aggressive defense, it's not one that has as much substance as the other teacher defenses. Unfortunately, victims are often encouraged to stand up to this type of child abuse. This may sometimes work when a bully and a victim are peers, but it definitely has no chance of turning out well when the perpetrator has all the power. So, even though the aggressive defense of flipping by calling the victim a problem student is pretty obvious, it's still hard to live with and hard to respond to. Remember, the student has already been victimized, and all these teacher defenses are cumulative injury.

## You're Part of It

A somewhat more complicated type of aggressive defense is to accuse the student of being part of the original abuse or neglect. When the perpetrator or the teacher infers that "you're a part of it," the resulting problem is more difficult to dissect. "You're a part of it" implies that the victim played a major role in his or her own abuse or neglect. The shifting of responsibility from the perpetrator to the victim is complex, and the victim struggles to understand the same.

"You're a part of it" implies that the victim was party to his or her own injury. This is a direct assault, very aggressive and painful. The victim's reaction to this message can be multifaceted. The reaction may be confused and angry, but it can also lead to a physical reaction. In this situation, there is a struggle to understand how an abuser can accuse a person of hurting him- or herself. This struggle is powerful, and it causes the body to react so strongly that it can briefly immobilize the victim. Feelings of anxiety, confusion, anger, or even guilt or shame might be present simultaneously.

It's hard to see that a student might participate voluntarily in his or her own injury. For one, the power imbalance is too enormous to allow that a student has that much say over any decision he or she might make in school. The students are monitored at all the hours they are in elementary school and even more so in middle school and high school; bells ring, names are taken, they are watched, evaluated, judged, and overloaded beyond the capacity for performing tasks that any average adult has. In fact, if they aren't watched and someone gets into trouble, the question of why they weren't supervised arises. Very few behaviors are chosen or voluntary on part of the students. They spend almost their entire day doing as instructed. They line up, sit down, open up, unpack, read, write, calculate, exercise, jump, run, fetch, listen, complete an assigned task, close up, pack up, get up, move to another preassigned place, and do this all over again every day. So, when some abusive, neglectful perpetrator says that the student willingly participates in self-injury, the result can be overpowering.

These feelings are so strong that there is a physical response as well as the cognitive and emotional response. This is the whole-body response to danger discussed in chapter 11 in the section titled Creating Fear. There's a good reason that a victim has a physiological, whole-body reaction.

When someone tells you that you have been responsible for your own suffering, red flags go up and the brain signals spell trouble. Physical reactions can include such things as difficulty in breathing, increased heart rate, clamminess of the skin, perhaps a sudden queasiness in the stomach, or maybe a rush of adrenalin to the brain that awakens you and puts you on alert.

The body is an amazing messenger that alerts us to many kinds of danger. If you run down the street and suddenly there is a terrible pain in your ankle, the pain is a messenger that says, "Stop running!" The pain is really not the problem; it's a healthy human reaction that warns us of danger. If you keep running, the pain tells you to stop running because your ankle is damaged. If you persist in running, you may permanently damage your ankle. The pain of being the victim can stop us the same way. We sense danger, which triggers some physical reactions, and we stop what we're doing. We should make a new plan.

If there is any doubt that abusive haters will tell others that they participate in their own injury, look no further than to politics in America. Quite recently, several politicians were attacked, some critically. Members of the opposing political party were quick to say it was the victims' own fault for being in that particular political party. Others went so far as to say they deserved to be shot (Ross 2017).

When there is an abuse or neglect problem, the student, and perhaps also the parent, prepares to confront the teacher or other school personnel. They've all talked about the problems. The student has tried to work on his or her own behavior. They've worked at understanding whether the student has a role in the problem. Nothing seems to make the abuse go away; in fact, it appears to get worse. There's a meeting set with the teacher. You're already on the edge. But it has never crossed your mind that the abusive teacher would tell you that you are part of the problem. The perpetrator has stopped you in your tracks; any plan you may have had is road blocked. All the energy, the worries, and the planning how to handle the problem, and what you're going to say, is wasted. You've hit a wall.

Victims are always labeled as part of the problem for the perpetrator; some perpetrators vocalize this more straightforwardly than others. You can't treat someone appropriately or honestly once you've started abusing or neglecting him or her. Why? Because the victim already knows you're abusive. The victim doesn't like you or trust you. So, the abuser just keeps going until something stops him or her. Being stopped by a student or a parent is unlikely. The following lines illustrate what actually happens.

You've gone into the lion's den with trepidation. You know you can't trust this teacher. After being painfully psychologically abused, you've now been accused of being responsible for colluding with the perpetrator. In essence, the perpetrator is saying that you've gone along with a horrible interaction between the two of you. Furthermore, the insinuation is that you could have stopped it anytime you wanted, but no, you chose to participate, and now you say you're a victim.

Does it seem as if these are just theories are too out there to believe? Not at all. These are the very words, the very lines and scripts used by sexual abusers. A predictable excuse for sexually molesting a child is that the child wanted it, liked it, or asked for it. Even more horrifying is the message that the victim could have stopped the abuse any time he or she wanted but didn't want to stop, or rather, was enjoying it. When an adult role model decides to take control over the mind of a young person to injure or use him or her, the adult often defend him- or herself by including the victim as a co-perpetrator. Teachers sexually abuse students. They also psychologically abuse students, play mind games with them, use them, and then accuse them of playing along with them. We see this easily with sexual abuse; it's just as true with every kind of abuse.

But you've decided to talk to the offending teacher, and this accusation levelled back at you is the result. Your body reacts, sending the brain some serious messages. You're in a dangerous situation. The psychological abuse and now the aggressive *you* messages and the flipping of responsibility are not going to get resolved in this manner. It's best to stop the conversation and develop a new plan.

You might have predicted before you even set the meeting that you would not stop the abuse. You might have predicted that there was absolutely no chance of a positive outcome. In fact, if you had asked yourself to spell out a positive outcome, you wouldn't be able to because you realize that the perpetrator was never going to take responsibility for his or her behavior. No one will make the perpetrator apologize. No one will tell him or her to do the right thing. The brotherhood, once involved, will advise and support the abuser to protect themselves and the bastion in every way they can.

Trying to meet with or reason with someone who is methodically and systematically victimizing your child is a bad idea. Once the abuser has stated that the student is co-responsible for the very thing you are now disclosing, you know that the teacher's denial, transfer of blame, passive and aggressive defenses for the child abuse he or she has committed will not be punished or stop.

Rational adults know better than to think that a student wants to be abused or neglected. And rational adults know that the minor is not the responsible party. Regardless of the student's age, there are laws that set limits on what a minor can and cannot be responsible for. And there are laws that set the boundaries on what an adult can and cannot do. Handing off adult responsibility to students is a dangerous undercurrent in the United States.

Students are not "part of" teachers' child abuse and other illegal behaviors. It's a sad truth that the great bastion of American education closes ranks and stands behind almost any member of the brotherhood who abuses a minor; the bastion fights to protect the perpetrator and allows one of its members to transfer the blame onto a student. If each member of that brotherhood examines their own conscience rather than be fearful, trembling members of the herd, they would not be guilty of colluding in the collapse of education in America.

## It's Your Own Fault

Finally, the ultimate flipping and re-injury to the victim is being told that he or she did it to him- or herself. "It's your own fault that I abused you" is a clear, see-through defense of child abuse. The student didn't misunderstand; the victim didn't co-participate with the perpetrator either. No, the student was definitely not the cause for the adult's abusive behaviors. It's a long road to travel from pretending nothing happened to aggressively accusing a student of enabling child abuse or child neglect. We see this "It's your own fault" behavior as an explanation for every kind of child abuse. Whether the abuse is psychological, physical, or sexual, the perpetrator is never responsible because he or she knows that he or she will be defended. Teachers and other school personnel are backed by the power of publicly funded deep pockets of the bastion.

The reasons perpetrators give for victims being responsible for their own abuse, their own injuries, vary from abuser to abuser. Recently, there was a teacher who made the news when she said that she was the victim of sexual abuse, not the student. We've all heard that girls and women are raped because they are dressed in a way that caused the rape. Child abuse and child neglect have been a part of every society.

The most common and vile defense that perpetrators use is that the victim is responsible for his or her own suffering, as if he or she is doomed to suffer because he or she exists. Whether the student is possessed by the devil or is the devil is irrelevant; there is no distinction and no reasoning this through. No amount discussion can change a teacher who argues that the child has somehow been gifted with the original sin for being in the world. The abuser says that the students themselves, through some quality of their very own, caused the teacher to be abusive or neglectful.

This blaming the victim is the single most disturbing recurring theme I see when working with special education students. Teachers and administrators regularly ignore disabilities of every kind. They act outside the students' needs and treat disabled students as if they are a constant, miserable reality that the unfortunate teacher is forced to tolerate or is burdened with. This has long been an insidious problem with teachers who dismiss minority students. And if the minority student is also disabled in some way, the consequences can be even more severe and heartfelt.

Over the last few years, blaming a student for his or her own abuse has become less visible, but it's really an undertow that sucks the entire system into a mire of failure. The fact that we see more of the abusive behaviors with disabled students simply distracts from the less visible, better cloaked child abuse and child neglect of minority children. When the child is not a minority and not disabled, the "it's your own fault" defense seems as if it might be less probable. But no, it's an easy-to-use label thrown at the victim. It immediately casts doubt about the victim's behavior and takes the pressure off the teacher. The defense is pathetic, ugly, and vile.

It's your own fault means more than the ridiculous idea that wearing something provocative is the cause of rape. It's your own fault that you're black, don't speak English, and have a disability. If you talk too much, wiggle, make a joke, forget a paper, you deserve to be treated abusively. The variations of seeing and treating students as being at fault for their own abuse are archaic, endless, and obvious. But there is absolutely no way that a student or parent can change that kind of thinking or abusive behavior. The only way to change this kind of abuse in the American educational system is to start anew with real teacher education and real teacher screening. That isn't going to happen until the system completes its current pathway toward collapse. Out of the ashes, we may once again consider that excellence in teaching and behaving in education has some meaningful value for our country and our future. None of this abuse is going to stop because there are no consequences for the perpetrators. In the meantime, the only escape is to get out, as we see happening all over the country, and go to the press.

## Summary

In schools where young people grow, develop, and change every day, accusations flung at them from defensive and offensive abusers can have permanent negative effects. Young people are impressionable. They mimic behaviors and attitudes from television, movies, books, their peers, and their adult role models. Think about the consequences for the student who has been the victim of teacher child abuse tactics and teacher child abuse defense tactics.

When teachers use child abuse defense tactics, both the student and the teacher know that the teacher is lying. The student knows that the teacher is lying. The teacher knows that the student is well aware of the lies. This mutually held truth is a critical underlying cause for the long-term damage inflicted by the teacher's defense tactics. Lying is one thing every one of the defenses has in common. It seems hard to say those words. The abusive teacher, who is now lying to defend him- or her-self, is dangerous. The teacher abuses and then lies about it using teacher defense tactics. Other members of the brotherhood protect the teacher. The student is caught in a trap.

When a student and an abusive teacher look at each other, the student sees someone who is toxic. The student feels hopeless, helpless, angry, and sometimes sick or depressed. Lying, supported by other authority figures and having no consequences, makes the student's attempts to stop the abuse look foolish. The student believes that he or she is a target. The student fears that others may think there is something wrong with him or her instead.

There's a secret that passes between the abusive teacher and the victim student. They are the only two people who know for sure that the teacher has caught the student in a web and there is no escape. The first and probably repeated teacher abuse causes serious psychological injury. The student is trapped. If the student is strong enough to attempt to stop the abuse, he or she is again seriously injured by the lying and flipping. Helplessness and hopelessness increase. Then the student realizes that part of the pain is the fact that only the two of them share the secret of the lie.

Young people often go through schools with the same peers for all thirteen developmental years, from early childhood through adulthood. When they are neglected or abused by some teacher or other school personnel, the result can have a permanent impact. For the rest of their school lives, their peers know or believe something about that student. They may not be sure what that is, but for sure something happened that they don't understand.

When our children are bullied by another child and there is no help, we feel angry and helpless as parents and caregivers. But when our children become victims of an adult, especially an adult who is in a position of authority, the repercussions can go on forever. Every type of child abuse and child neglect used by teachers and employees of educational organizations is damaging. And all the myriad ways in which these same members of the brotherhood defend themselves is outrageous.

Just imagine how insane it is to tell a child that he or she is participating in a teacher's neglect or abuse! Having a teacher say that the child is responsible for his or her own abuse is like saying that the minor is able to fix this problem if he or she chooses to. This is very much like saying that it's OK to send a child to fix a car. Students don't have the tools required for the job.

Having the terms used in the text to describe the abuser's behavior helps both parents and children when they open a discussion. Words make events and feelings more concrete, more understandable. Patterns are easier to see when they are thoroughly defined. By now, it should be easier to look more objectively at child abuse and child neglect at the hands of teachers.

# CHAPTER 13
# Guilt by Avoidance

> "We men and women are all in the
> same boat, upon a stormy sea.
> We owe each other a terrible and tragic loyalty."
> —G. K. CHESTERTON (1874–1936)

When one of my sons was in elementary school, he was bullied mercilessly by his female teacher. I wasn't prepared for this chronic and sly behavior. She was menacing at times. It took me by surprise. We had meetings and we met with the principal, but it occurred only in hindsight that this was practiced behavior and that she fully intended to continue her horrific behavior. The meetings were agreeable. She was very polite. This woman repeatedly asked about what we thought we should do about my son's complaints. She was playing with abuse, entertaining herself.

This teacher enlisted minions, both adults and children. It took months for me to figure out that she was amusing herself by dragging out her game and stringing me along. That was quite a revelation for me. My own work requires that I constantly mediate and negotiate. Well, that's what I was doing here—negotiating, suggesting, and mediating. And, of course, it didn't work.

Very slowly, there was a dawning realization that there was to be no end to this. She never had an intention of stopping. She singled him out, cautioned him regularly when he was simply at his seat, and humiliated him in front of his classmates. Eventually, she enlisted the minions, which included the other innocent children, who got her attention by following her lead. Then she enlisted the yard helpers who looked for him and corrected his every move. My son said to me, "The only place I feel safe is when I am with my advanced class teacher."

But my son had friends, and those children were the heroes. One in particular, a girl who really liked him, started my brain working in an entirely new direction. She was waiting for her ride after school while I was waiting for my son. She looked at me and hesitated before asking, "Why is the teacher so mean to (my son)?" I was actually speechless for a moment. I suppose she noticed my surprise, my silence, or even my odd expression. She quickly followed up with, "You didn't know that? She's mean to him every day." By then, one of her friends joined her at the fence. She chimed in with, "Yeah, and he doesn't even *do* anything!"

I was absolutely sick. What wasn't obvious to me was always obvious to the kids who weren't caught up in being minions themselves. All the time and effort spent talking, meeting, and negotiating—none of that had made a dent. Then two more events had me burning mad. I was talking to another therapist about this situation when an adult standing nearby approached me and said, "Well, she was accused of that a few years ago, but they got her off!"

That evening I let her know I'd be in to see her before school the next day. She didn't show up; she said later that she never got my message. While I was waiting for her, my son's advanced class teacher stopped to say hello. He asked what I needed. The end of the story and the moment in which the lights were fully blazing in my brain came with his response, "Is she still up to that stuff? I thought she had quit doing that!" He flatly recommended that I moved my son elsewhere.

There were months of events not included in the telling of this story. There were many days of exclusion from getting treats in class. He didn't say anything. Then there was a day when I had donated the candy that this teacher so loved. When he raised his hand to say that he hadn't gotten a treat, she ridiculed him and accused him of lying. She didn't miss a chance to neglect and psychologically abuse him. But at the end of the same day, I learned that she had a history of these unconscionable behaviors of bullying and abuse. So, I met with the principal. When I walked into her office, she already had the transfer paperwork finished. Her last, and probably most useless, comment was, "Well, some teachers and students really don't hit it off!" This statement, I've learned, is part of a scripted line used on almost every parent who dares to stand up to an abusive teacher or administrator.

The anger I felt then is the same anger I feel now thinking about children being abused by teachers. But now that anger is highly directed. I've learned how to help the families who come to me when their children are being abused or neglected by a teacher.

Children are frequent victims of child neglect and child abuse in the schools. But, the number of children and families that one person can help is limited by the hours in a day and the days in a year. Who could better help the parents and the students who suffer abuse and neglect by a teacher? Who should be policing the failures among those who are employed in the school system? Is it possible that an organization could police itself? Will there ever be a time when individual good will takes precedence over the self-serving wants of the brotherhood? Could focus on an individual value ever happen in any brotherhood, where the members are honor bound to protect those whom they serve? Who could and *should* help students who suffer abuse and neglect?

There are good teachers and good school personnel, but they are guilty by avoidance. They see the crimes and remain silent. They could and should act to stop the abuse and the neglect perpetrated by all the school personnel. These good administrators and teachers who do not intervene are not adult minions, or are they? They simply wouldn't be abusive nor would they neglect any child personally. Is that really so?

The school personnel, in every role, should be held accountable for the failure to protect the children who are being abused. School personnel are legally mandated reporters. It is their job to keep the children in their care safe. They are told to act, intervene, and keep their eyes open. Yet the best teachers are often the least involved in what's going on around them. Perhaps that distance they put between themselves and the crimes and failures occurring around them keep them on the job and provide a buffer for them against a toxic environment. Blinders are passed out with the paycheck. Many school employees have said to me that they are afraid of the system and are afraid for their own jobs, using excuses like "I don't want to make any waves," or "I can't get involved." An adult outside the system recently said, "These teachers don't want to be seen as making trouble for the school. Making trouble for the school is making trouble for themselves. That's why they don't say anything." Same old brotherhood! Same old bastion!

The principal in this brief vignette, not surprisingly, moved on to be a district administrator. She was headed to be a true leader of the brotherhood. We used to call people like her "The Organization Man," after a book that described her very behavior but in a corporate setting. In this famous work written by William H. Whyte and first published in 1956, Whyte discussed the incentive for not taking risks and supporting the status quo. The way to survive in the corporate world is to cooperate and do nothing to negatively affect the organization. The reward for taking no risks, he said, was the very absence of consequences. The incentive for falling into the step is the survival of the organization and the guarantee of permanence. Sounds familiar? But corporations aren't directly responsible for the lives of our children. School principals are, and they, nor should anyone in America's schools, be accessories to the crimes of child abuse and child neglect.

The teacher who told me to move my son was one of my all-time favorite teachers. He was truly one of the good guys and an excellent, committed teacher. But he had fallen off his pedestal because, in the words of John Stuart Mill, "Bad men need nothing more to compass their ends, than that good men should look on and do nothing" (Mill 1867).

Is it understandable that he was guilty by avoidance and hence an accessory to the crime? Yes, it is understandable, but it's not acceptable. Loyalty to the brotherhood in the face of child abuse is criminal. The fear of retaliation against this teacher by the same abusive teacher who uses retaliation on children is a real possibility. So what? Is it OK to keep the silence? Do adults in this bastion always have to pull together and close ranks? Are they so fearful of losing their voices? Have they lost their honor, judgment, and sense of right and wrong?

Teachers, administrators, and other school personnel belong to the same form of brotherhood as priests, law enforcement officials, sports coaches, and others. When hopeful, good people decide to join a brotherhood and owe an allegiance to the bastion, they have to choose whether they will give up their own principles or stand firm against corruption from within. The saddest reality, which I know, is that most members of the brotherhoods lose their honor. They trade their right to do right and be right for the unspoken contract of protecting themselves and protecting the bastion. These people are guilty by avoidance. They are guilty of child neglect and complicit in child abuse. They are guilty of accepting the blinders with the paycheck.

This incident was one of the major seeds that eventually sprung into life and resulted in the book you're reading now. I don't want to be guilty by avoidance any longer. Knowing how teacher-child abuse and child neglect works can be a blessing and a burden. So few people understand, in all parts, what their children are experiencing. Almost no children and a few college students are safe and able to protect themselves and stop the abuse and neglect. It's a common belief that any individual is powerless to confront the great bastion when a member of the brotherhood is guilty of child abuse and child neglect.

The only great movements of the last decades have been grassroots actions. These movements come from mothers sitting around drinking coffee and trying to imagine how we could stop repeated offences, such as drunk driving and the revolving doors of our prisons. In the case of the American school system, there aren't any heroes. There isn't much done except for throwing around money and putting new demands on students. None of that is working. Innovation is not reformation. Problems in the schools have to be addressed, but not with worn-out accusations of racism, discrimination, lack of money, or any other common way. Rather, the people responsible for the problem must be held accountable. By everyone. Including me. Including you. And they must hold themselves accountable.

## CHAPTER 14

# The Minions

> "People saw nothing holy in this spring morning...
> inclining to peace, good-will and love, but worshiped their
> own inventions for imposing their will on each other."
> —Leo Tolstoy

Child victims of psychological abuse are often isolated with pain. They feel alone. They have been singled out from the other children, and they can be left without a peer group. The response to the abuse and neglect of a child in a classroom has far-reaching results. There are many layers of victimization occurring when a teacher is an abuser. These layers begin with the primary victim. But everyone in the classroom is affected when one student is being abused or neglected.

When child psychological abuse happens in the classroom, there are some perceptive children who know what's going on. They may secretly learn to distrust the perpetrator, or they may join with the perpetrator. Children who witness victimization of one of their classmates may feel that they want to help that child, and hence they stand up for the victim when they can. Yet other children reject the concept that their teacher could be abusive. It's possible that they cannot see what's wrong with the picture, at least not at the time the wrongdoing is taking place.

There are distinct groups of children in any classroom who see that primary victim abuse and neglect are occurring. In these two groups of children, the children know what the teacher is doing to one of their peers. These children who see and know that their classmate is a victim of child abuse or child neglect are called primary minions here. I've named students, who do not recognize immediately or delay recognizing the abuse and neglect of their classmate, as collateral minions here.

Primary minions are students who know what's going on and then follow the lead and model their own behavior after the teacher. Collateral minions are students who see the wrongdoing from a distance and do nothing. Lastly, but infrequently, there are students who can watch the teacher's wrongful behaviors, do not understand what they see, and become delayed collateral minions. There is also likely a group of children who see nothing, hear nothing, and do nothing, and that doesn't change. They are absent from anything that occurs outside of the self, and this is a rare occurrence. Our main focus here is really on the primary minions and the collateral minions. But the delayed collateral minions and witnesses also suffer in ways that are predictable and, at times, devastating.

Teachers are role models for child neglect and child abuse. The teacher is always, by definition, a figure of authority and a role model. This is especially true when the child or student is in pre-elementary and elementary school, but the modeling extends far into the middle and high school years and finally into the college years. Teachers, as role models, continue to be who they are and hold enormous power, whether they are working in the preschool system or the college and university system. Whether we call them teachers or professors, they can be equally capable of harming those in their care because of the inherent authority of their positions.

The dynamic, or means, of abuse or neglect by teachers can change over the years as society and education evolve. But rather than improving or disappearing, abuse in the classroom is often becoming more brazen because there have been no consequences. The more the union or the bastion grows and extends its range of influence, the less accountable the members and the brotherhood are to their local authority. They also accrue more power, which makes them untouchable and unaccountable for their crimes. The types of threats to the students may change. The threats may become more systematic. The threats are clearly more calculated at times as the society, the community, and the individual understand that they are helpless of defense against the bastion. After all, the bastion has access to unlimited public tax money and can fight with no consequence for itself and no consequence for the offending teacher.

But child abuse and child neglect only *begin* with the direct victim. The reverberation begins with the obvious victim and ping pongs around every student in the classroom. The direct victim is severely injured by the perpetrator (the teacher) and is further reinjured by the responses of many peers and other school employees, who now see the victim as different, singled out, bad, tainted in some way, or even worse, as an opportunity to garner some favors to be owed to them when they commit atrocities of their own. The bounce doesn't stop there. The children who have become caught up in the minion role have their own crosses to bear.

## The Child Minions

The child who is victimized by the teacher is alone and develops a belief that there is no help for them. He or she begins to feel isolated and depressed. But what happens to the young people who share this small classroom or peer environment with the victim? What happens when one member of their peer group is singled out and ridiculed or otherwise neglected or abused by their teacher? They follow the lead of their role model; they learn to do what they see is done. They frequently become mimics of their role model; they become the primary child minions.

## Primary Child Minions

The metamorphosis from peer to primary minion is frightening and ugly. A group of the victim's peers become quickly aware of the fact that one of the students is always in some kind of trouble. They hear the teacher calling out this single child. They hear the child's name in a negative voice as a regular event. Their authority figure and role model, the teacher, is spending time and energy on one child, and that time and energy is very negative.

Being in the classroom is very distressing for children when the teacher focuses negative energy on one or more of the students. Students are uncomfortable and generally unclear as to why their friend and peer are being treated badly. Maybe this student did talk too much on Wednesday! But so did everyone else! Is their friend really fidgeting more than the other students? Is he or she really too slow, or sloppy, or careless? Maybe the teacher can see something that they can't see. Maybe the teacher knows something about this problem child that they don't know. Maybe this child really is a problem. Students begin to see the victim as a problem. Why not? After all, the teacher knows what's going on better than they do. The teacher doesn't treat *them* badly. It has to be the child (victim) who is troublesome. Many children who witness the neglect and abuse of one of their classmates fall into step with the teacher and become primary minions. How does this happen?

Children are told by their parents that they are to show respect to their teacher. Respect for a teacher includes an unspoken message that the teacher is always right. There are probably only a few parents who have never said things like, "Listen to your teacher; she knows what she is doing," or "Teachers go to school for a long time to know how to handle things; just do what you're told."

Parents are concerned when it comes to their children's success. Sometimes without thinking about it, parents believe that their children's success in school is dependent on the teacher's liking of their children as much as the parent likes the child. A common and probably accurate belief is that children who are liked are given more positive attention and special privileges and have better grades.

As for children, they perform better when they are positively reinforced. Like all of us, we want to do what an authority figure tells us to do when we want to be like that important person. We do this because we want someday to have what they have—power and admiration. To get that positive feedback from an authority figure and to be like they are, we copy the authority figure. Just as ducks imprint on their mothers, small children copy the behaviors of their teachers. The teacher can be the source of positive feedback and reinforcement. Teachers give stars, good apple awards, student-of-the-month awards, special helper roles, and the ever critical report card that goes home to the parent. The teacher is the role model.

Being liked by the teacher is universally important to school children. They seek the approval of adults who they see as important. Children around the world spend an enormous amount of time away from their parents and in the hands of schoolteachers. It's a natural tendency for children to sense that they are safe with someone who likes them. While it is true that children are safe in most adult-child relationships, we also know that these young adults or small, trusting people can also be the major targets of abuse and neglect by the very person they trust. But we sometimes overlook the students who witness the victimization of one of their own peers. These onlookers are also victims. And these victims often become minions.

When a teacher abuses a child in the classroom, that abusive behavior is made available for every other child to see, hear, and mimic. These teacher role models not only teach the abused child to be both victim and bully, but they also give their approval to the children in their care to be their primary minions. Primary minion students mimic the teacher who commits child abuse and child neglect and begin to act out against the victim in similar ways. These classroom peers are known by children who are abused and neglected as the teacher's minions. The term *minion* was probably made popular by one of the media productions in the last decade. But the word, which is of fifteenth century French origin (*mignon* or *mignonne*), has been translated to English and defined in the *Oxford Dictionary* as a follower or underling of a powerful person, especially a servile or unimportant one; a loyal servant of another.

Children act as minions for many reasons. As you read at the beginning of the section, this is often to get the attention and the approval of the teacher; in fact, it is a case of "Do as I do, and you become my special little minion." Minions act to support the abuser's position. Students can easily become teacher's pets by following the teacher's modeling. Teachers are likely to reward or reinforce minion behavior.

When students become minions, they can also avoid becoming the object of abuse and neglect and avoid the teacher's negative attention. When a child sees another child—whether a peer, a classmate, a friend, or just some kid they don't even know—being abused by an adult, they become fearful. At the least, they are puzzled or confused. For certain, the feeling that comes from watching someone else—someone like oneself and another student—being abused by a teacher is highly disruptive. The primary minion child suffers along with the victim.

Aside from learning to get attention from an authority figure in the wrong way, child minions also are likely to repeat the abusive behavior in other settings after having tried it on, so to speak. When we see children act out abusive behaviors, we call it bullying. When bullies grow up and continue to injure children, we call it child abuse. Modeling is a very powerful tool.

Even worse than this is when the children, who are somewhat perceptive, have an instinct of what they are doing is wrong but they nevertheless participate in abuse, mimicking the abuse, and become the teacher's primary minion. When a child understands what he or she is doing is wrong, it can greatly affect the child's self-esteem.

The child who understands that he or she is a bully toward another child may not understand the effect it has had on his or her own esteem for a very long time, maybe for years or well into adulthood. Perhaps when the child was young, he or she tried to talk to a parent or another adult who also didn't understand what was happening to the child (the primary minion children). That trusted adult could have advised them to stay away from the primary victim. Parents can fear that their own children will become identified with a child who is often in trouble with the teacher.

Other children stay away from the abused child so that they are not left out by their good friends. There is, sometimes, an exodus away from the primary victim. This may result in feelings of guilt and confusion that haunt a child when he or she abandons another child. These feeling of guilt, confusion, or shame may go on for years. But at some point of time, maybe much later in life, primary minions realize that they hate what they have done, and they hate the person who modeled the abusive behavior and rewarded them for doing it. It's devilishly easy to teach children to mimic abuse. Most children do exactly what an authority figure tells them to do or models for them. Child sexual abuse victims attest to this every day.

In 2012, two elementary school teachers were accused of bullying a student. On June 15, 2012, Richard Oppenheim wrote an article titled "Another School Bullying Case—This Time the Teacher Is Accused." In his article, published in the California Business Litigation Blog, he reported that one teacher instructed her students to line up and hit a classmate who was a bully, or so the teacher had claimed. Even though there was no evidence to support the teacher's belief, the students nonetheless lined up and in turn hit the child in question. The second teacher stood and watched, only stopping the directed abuse after a particularly hard hit to the child's back.

While the entire incident is unfathomable for all healthy adults, it easily demonstrates the obedience to authority concept so well documented by the researcher and author Stanley Milgram. The author and researcher's famous work explained how Hitler was seamlessly successful in turning one segment of the German population against an entire religion and culture of the time. Systematic desensitization by successive approximation is a powerful tool used by evil people to achieve dangerous goals. When people are desensitized to hearing the same negativity repeatedly, they tend to no longer react negatively. The world changes when desensitization is followed by systematic reinforcement for actually participating in the negative behavior. We are reinforced into accepting something that we thought was unthinkable in the past. There are hundreds of readily available examples in history to illustrate this principle.

Abusive teachers don't have to work hard with children to get them to change their beliefs. Children's natural trust in all adults, in this case teachers who are supported by the children's parents, is all that is necessary to turn children into cooperative participants in the teacher's child abuse. Just as in the classroom where all the children lined up on the teacher's orders to hit their classmate, children may participate in the teacher's abuse any time they are reinforced for doing so. They are fearful that they themselves may be abused if they don't do what they are told. They become primary minions.

By the time the student reaches high school and college, there is some movement away from abuse mimicking. Older children who are nearing adulthood are passing through the individuation stage of growth and development. By the very nature of this stage, children move from obedience to questioning and finally to separation from their adult role models. They cut the umbilical cord and no longer feel that the adults in their lives are absolutely necessary for their survival. Slowly and steadily, authority figures seem less like the looming giants they once did. With increased exposure to the outside world, other families, the media, and extracurricular activities, developing children begin to have their own concepts of right and wrong. They act on their own. Children go from asking permission to trusting that their view of the world is correct and, therefore, they empower themselves to act.

Thankfully, the individuation process moves the child into a position where he or she has the self-confidence to strike out on his or her own. Without this important change, no one would leave the safety of their childhood. Parents would not let go of their beautiful, adoring, and obedient children. Children would continue to adore and obey their parents and teachers.

This normal individuation process allows and supports high school students in their quest to think for themselves. Yes, this often results in very young adults, middle, and late age teens getting into conflict with their elders. But without this stage of separation and deindividuation, the young person would never leave home.

But primary minions are not only young children. You would think that coming out of the rebellious middle school and high school years of deindividuation, college students would be far beyond the risk of becoming a primary minion. However, at the university level, professors—who are seen as gurus and gods—are chronically guilty of proselytizing with the goal of making students change their world views to align them with those of the professor, to become their primary minions, and to carry their message to others. The more alignment, the better chance that student has of being handed what he or she needs or wants. This can come in the form of grades, perhaps a teaching assistant position, a badly needed recommendation, or perhaps admission into graduate courses. Thankfully, there are mature college-age students who have the wherewithal to question the behaviors of their professors, regardless of the potential consequences.

## Child Collateral Minions

So, now we see that there are multiple levels of student response to child abuse and child neglect in the American school system. The direct victim's plight creates the opportunity for making new student victims, the primary minions. But victimization doesn't stop there. Collateral minions are those students who are in the environment along with the perpetrator, the primary victim, and the primary minions. They are the students who watch and understand and do nothing. At least, they look like they do nothing. All of the action that occurs with the collateral minions happens internally. And that internal action or response to the surrounding abuse and neglect events varies with the individual student.

The collateral minion may be angry with the teacher who is abusing the primary victim. It's also possible that the anger could be directed at the primary victim, believing that the victim is actually the cause of the problem and all the trouble in the classroom. Another possibility is that the collateral minions see themselves as collateral victims. This minion may feel stuck in a problem that someone else made—either the perpetrator or the primary victim—and can't do anything to get out of the situation. The collateral minion may be angry because the action in the classroom is negative or unpredictable and interrupts his or her necessary role as student.

The collateral minions may be truly and silently going along with the action, which they fully recognize and understand. They may be silent because they aren't sure which action is best for them. They may choose to become part of the wallpaper to avoid all notice because they themselves may be victimized if they are too noticed. If they speak out, they may face the scary unknown consequences of one or more adults. Rather than being angry or unsure, they may be afraid that they will take the wrong action or that they will make the problem worse. They may believe that there is no one they can trust to go to.

It's plausible that one could make the argument that passive inaction is better than active action. That doesn't hold true when the collateral minion is an adult. However, in the case of child victimization, children other than the primary victim believe themselves to be equally powerless. That powerlessness is for all the same reasons as above, namely confusion, fear, and helplessness.

Don't forget that all minions are also victims. Being a minion doesn't mean that the child necessarily has an intention to harm. It *can include* students who have an intention to harm, but that's another subject that fills another volume. Generally, primary minions and collateral minions are both trying to survive but are ultimately going to pay a heavy price for having been in the environment with a teacher who is guilty of child abuse and child neglect.

## Delayed Collateral Minions

Not all children are psychologically minded and therefore may not understand that abuse can be something you can't touch or see with your eyes.

Yes, they will recognize abuse if a teacher hits a child. Children consider hitting as abusive. They may refer to the abuse as bullying, which is the incorrect term in this circumstance, but they have generally not been taught the difference.

Behaviors that are visually apparent are easy to see. But children who are not treated badly or unfairly in their homes, families, and other groups may not be able to recognize many of the complicated and self-serving behaviors of child abuse. Conversely, children who are neglected or abused in their home environment might see that the behaviors are routine because they have become desensitized.

At times, children have uneasy feelings but are fearful of the feelings and block them out. At other times, they are afraid to do anything that is different from the other children or from the teacher. In general, they may have been fortunate to have many teachers who have been appropriate, teachers who have liked their job, and teachers who have behaved as appropriate adults in the classroom. Teachers talk to them, help them, and care about their achievements. But then the abuse/neglect occurs, and they continue to hold the teacher in a good light. If their peer is treated badly, then it must be the fault of their peer, the victimized child, and not of the teacher who is a professional and who they look up to.

Children in the group called delayed collateral minions really don't understand what's happening around them and to them. These children really don't know what they are seeing when they see it. It isn't because they are self-absorbed. Rather, they are generally psychologically immature, inexperienced, or naïve.

Problematically, the delayed collateral minion will likely understand what he or she has lived through sometime later in his or her life. They will wake up in the middle of the night or have a sudden memory from their childhood while standing in a shower or trying to relax. What they saw, what they felt, and what really happened back then will all come together in a cognitive Nano moment. The delayed impact can be a small, "Oh, that's what that was!" or the impact can have life-altering consequences.

At times, there are events that children are subjected to in school that are so horrendous that the child simply blocks them from the memory. Never heard of an event in school that bad? Then you haven't investigated or read relevant articles.

In Florida, a teacher told an autistic boy to stand in front of the class. The teacher then requested each of his peers to criticize the student. They called him names and voted to have him excluded from the class. Only two students did not participate. Do you think it's possible that some of the students have blocked this from their minds? Do they think about what happened to that child later in life? Do they think about the effect it had on them? Do they wonder if it altered their lives? Were they duped? Were they used? Did they understand at the time the impact it would make on their lives and the life of the autistic child? How would you be affected if you were there?

## Fostering Minions is Child Abuse and Child Neglect

In the earlier chapters, you learned that child neglect is an absence of action in a situation where an action is required. Caregivers must actively anticipate the needs of the child and provide for these needs before any problem arises. A parent, a caregiver, or a guardian who notices that the child in his or her care is not eating pays attention before the child begins to lose weight. A parent, a caregiver, or a guardian notices when the child in his or her care is withdrawn or appears sad. Responsible adults notice when the children for whom they are responsible are behaving in inappropriate ways. In each case, the adult is expected to provide for the child's needs. The adult in charge may not create the problem, but care for the problem he or she must.

But what happens when the parent, guardian, or caregiver creates the problem? When do we cross the line from child neglect to child abuse? Let's say that an adult is a smoker. The child who he or she cares for may witness the adult model smoking and seek out ways in which he or she too can smoke. The adult does not directly invite or force the child to smoke. But the modeling is very powerful, and the children are great mimics. They need to be mimics; this is how much of human learning takes place.

Jump back to the minion problem. What happens when the guardian of a child not only models smoking but also allows the child access to smoking? How about when the caregiver thinks it's funny or cute when a child picks up his or her cigarettes and pretends to light and smoke one? This is active reinforcement or encouragement for the child attempting to smoke. Is this child endangerment? Is this different from telling a child how great he or she is or rewarding the child in some way every time he or she play-smokes or smokes. It's a case of "Do as I do," or "Do as I say." In this situation, we're past the part of even being a role model with mimics.

Creating minions to assist in and justify the abuse and neglect of a student is both child emotional neglect and child psychological abuse. When a parent encourages and allows a child to smoke and creates a small minion for him- or herself, it is abusive. When a teacher abuses a student and creates an entire classroom of minions, this is systematic child abuse and evil. Knowingly manipulating children to act in some illegal or immoral way is evil. Manipulating multiple children for one's own evil or devilish ends is serial abuse. Ignoring their confusion, fear, and anger after you have used a child for your own illegal or immoral acts is also child neglect. Members of the last great bastion and the brotherhood of teachers may not now be successfully prosecuted. But that's pretty irrelevant to the facts. Teachers who use children and create minions for their own awful ends are guilty of child abuse.

## The Adult Minions

Most of the child abuse and child neglect focus has so far been on the abuse inflicted by the teacher perpetrators and the minion peers of children who have been victimized in some way while participating in America's educational system. The perpetrators, both teachers and their minions, logically have an enormous effect on the victim, which is exacerbated in part by the prolonged and intense time they interact for each of the 180-day school years.

But there are other employees of the American institutions of learning. There are two other large identifiable groups of adults in the school setting who hold power in the system and interact with students. Their influence on students is sometimes overlooked. This is likely because of their limited presence in the classroom, which narrows their time with students.

The administration and the support personnel play a large part in the ebb and flow of the school's business and are essential to the success of the teaching staff in the current educational configuration. Administrators and other support staff are the school employees who are thought of as the background to the educational mission. Our children's education and welfare are connected to their teachers and somewhat to their peers; the teacher is connected to these background personnel.

The administration and the school support staff members of the brotherhood may not be directly involved with the students, but they are highly connected to our children's teachers. And at times, the relationships overlap, and the lines of authority change or are blurred. Both groups interact with every teacher, and both groups have roles in our children's education and welfare. One has only to sit in a teachers' lounge or the private sections of a school's operations to begin to see the complex set of relationships between all the members of the brotherhood.

When visualizing these school personnel, you might be imagining some television documentary produced by a reputable institution displaying a case of intelligent educational forethought. Project that to a television sitcom that espouses the many skills and sacrifices of the noble teaching profession and the revered institution of education. This image is inspiring, maybe even pulse racing. But the reality of daily banter between the school personnel in America's schools is rarely movie magic.

There is very little that is not said out of the reach of students' ears about students. Well, maybe the thing that is little talked about is how wonderfully a student is performing, a special child's talents, or the joy of waking up each day to hurry on to their classrooms. Most of what is bantered about is personal perception, which is usually negative and often based on personal biased experiences. The rest is based on gossip or the repeated negative statement of some other school employee.

It's not unusual for a student to ask why a certain person at school doesn't like him or her. Recently, a middle school boy was yelled at and treated rudely by a first grade teacher who happened to see him. He only knew her by sight and didn't even know her name. They had never had a word pass between them. He didn't know anything about her. But she acted as if she knew him. She definitely knew his name, and her behavior toward him was accusatory and psychologically abusive. The only explanation was that she was imprinting on another teacher, administrator, or support staff that had already victimized the boy to set an example.

Often, there is slapstick humor among the school personnel at the student's expense, which is generally sarcastic. At other times, an acute administrator or support staff observer will ferret out the abusing teachers' sad needs to define and label a student in advance as their own defensive move. That is, the offending teacher or other school personnel (be it a teacher or a yard guard), having been guilty of some inappropriate negative interaction with a student, rushes to spew out negative comments regarding the student in the hope of preempting any potential complaint. This is a manipulative setup. They are flipping in the anticipation of needing to defend themselves. The teacher's defense, "Make the student look bad," becomes a working tool for all perpetrators in the system and that includes all the adult minions.

Schools are like small colonies or villages. They have their own societal rules and their own mores. An often assigned eighth grade Language Arts assignment is a short story called *The Lottery*; written in 1948 by Shirley Jackson, it tells the story of towns where people participate in an age-old, superstition-based ritual of holding an annual lottery to choose one adult who is stoned to death to assure a good corn harvest in the coming year.

As the story evolves, we find that the same man who is responsible for the festivals and other holiday events is also in charge of the lottery. The boys gather first in the town square to collect piles of rocks as part of their morning play. The town residents are in a hurry to get the lottery and stoning done before their afternoon chores.

We learn from the story how people can be unaffected by their own horrific or bizarre behaviors. The behavior of the village residents has become ingrained; they hardly notice the patterns that had evolved. Communities become communities because they have commonalities, they benefit mutually because of the associations, and they take care of one another to assure that they remain a part of the group that is looked after by the community. So, we see that villages or colonies and communities develop their own ways of taking care of business and protecting themselves and their future.

So it is with schools. They are closed communities, and the members of that brotherhood work together to protect the future of the bastion. Many schools have the same employees for twenty to thirty years. Their closed societies, their territorial imperatives, and their methods of protecting themselves are so self-defensive and so inbred that they are invisible to even the participants.

It's likely that within the tenure of any one school employee there has been, at a minimum, one experience where he or she has needed to use the "blame the student" form of preempting any backlash against his or her own bad behavior. So, the strike first rule of self-defense is theirs to use when they need it. They can call it in, just as their own village brotherhood has required them to act out like the annual lottery in which the villagers fall into place and each play their roles. Word spreads about a student, negative rumors, negative attitudes, and use of the words like *bad*, *disrespectful*, or *lazy* begin spread like maggots. Game on! Full participation of every brotherhood member is expected and given without exception, including administration and support staff, and with that, the adult minions of America's schools are out in full force.

The two groups, the administrative minions and the support staff minions, come to the lottery in different ways and therefore make different but equally negative contributions. Let's look at how they're different and what to expect from them.

## Adult Administrative Minions

Adult administrative minions are in a unique role. They often appear to be struggling, as if they are a dealer at a roulette table. They count on the house to win but always know that the other people at the table may call them out. Like the roulette wheel, their dealer's role is exceptionally circular with allegiance to few and all.

Teachers can make or break an administrator. The teachers' successes and failures reflect on the administrator's performance. Administrators get stuck between protecting the members of the brotherhood and protecting the bastion to which they owe many loyalties. Unfortunately, it's a chess game where the pawns, namely the students, often get sacrificed. The students are the last, or maybe never, to be protected. Like the roulette dealer, administrators are always betting that they can be safe and win with their house, the brotherhood, and save the bastion on which they depend for their careers.

What that really means for the primary victim is that he or she will never get support, never get safety, and can expect to be abused and neglected as long as he or she is in that setting and are the chosen victim. That neglect is primarily educational neglect and is a major root of educational failure. The only way a student who is a victim can be helped or rescued is if he or she has power and money, and sometimes these are interchangeable. Truth be told, very few primary victims ever get help. They may get moved around, but they take the accusation of abuse against one of the members of the brotherhood with them. The pawns can never accrue enough power to save themselves, no matter how badly they are abused. Pawns are, after all, the most powerless piece on the board. They can be used to the advantage of those in power if they are in the right position, otherwise they are sacrificed. And so, the very people who are the essence of the educational system, the students, fail. With their failure, so goes the failure of America's public education system.

There are countless examples of students and parents who have made complaints; they have filed complaints with everyone in the system, and they are all whitewashed or turned around and used against the victimized student and his family. Administration acts on behalf of abusive and neglectful teachers to prop them up when their failures threaten the bastion.

In another version of the administrative minion problem, consider what happens when the teachers and the local administration don't perform at a level acceptable to the board. The board is highly aligned with the bastion. The ultimate power of the bastion, which holds the purse strings, maintains control whenever the board, the administrator, and the teachers are not meeting certain evaluative goals that have been set by the bastion. In this case, the administrative minions are caught between the bastion, the board, and the teachers. Chaos ensues, and the students' welfare becomes a negligible concern to any of the three power groups.

I recently witnessed a situation where a school board fired the administration and most key personnel during a school holiday and put themselves in charge. It was a comic shock when the students returned to school. There was no lead time, no notice was sent to parents and family, the students were confused, and the remaining employees were in fear for their jobs. The entire business was so badly handled that it could have been the opening scene of a very dark film. But to offer up a truly sophomoric moment, an e-mail was sent to the parents containing a copied letter, which was supposedly voluntarily signed by the remaining staff, swearing their support for the school and for the new administration. The new administration had become minions to the board, and the board was responsible for making sure that the funding kept flowing. Then the remaining employees, teachers, aides, and clerical staff became minions to the administration. The signed letter was embarrassing simply in its reading. But imagine the humiliation and subservience, as it suggested, being suffered by the signers. It was certainly an ultimatum, but it should have read under the signers' names, "John Doe, Minion." Unfortunately, the atmosphere remained dreary and tense for the remainder of the year.

What was the cause of the eruptive and disruptive behavior of the administration? Questions were declined. The obvious changes in the school's atmosphere and the children's feelings about the before and after effect were glaring. The children who would discuss the changes and how they were affected generally indicated that people who were at the school before really cared about them and that was greatly missed.

The first administrator encouraged sporting events between students and teachers; projects, such as the yearbook and plays; and after-school tutoring. The atmosphere was student centered. After the change, there was absolutely nothing but increased work assigned by the teachers and increased pressure on the new and remaining teachers to increase discipline and apply more stringent rules. Even the parent-teacher group was disbanded, as were their efforts to work with the teachers and do fund-raising.

The teachers became minions for the administration, which was kept in line by the board; therefore, the administration had become minions to the board. Who the teachers and administration are and how they operate in relation to their audience, in this case the students and the parents, changes to fit the needs of the board and not the needs of the students.

The action that occurred, the firings and the changes, were likely the result of the administration being under fire from the board that were responsible to the bastion in order to continue funding. The administrator did not meet the board goals in the current normal configuration and so simply started all over with something the board felt that they were able to control more fully. They reverted to a very punitive and driven system. They equated success with discipline and drudgery. Everyone became the board's victims. The students or the pawns suffered.

When a student is singled out by an abusive teacher, support staff minion, and child minions, the damage is hard to miss. Most families slowly understand what is happening, watch the changes in the victimized child, and attempt some action to alter the destructive course of events. Unfortunately, the first line of complaint is to the site administrator, often called the principal. This administrator always has seriously divided loyalties. He or she is accountable to some higher administrative group, usually a board. Any problems at the administrator's site needs to be handled at the administrative level so as not to draw the attention of superior bodies, namely the board and the bastion. These superior layers of management don't want to hear about problems and don't want to be bothered in general. The more a site administrator is seen or heard, except for some great awards that bring joy to the hearts of boards and the bastions, the more trouble the administrator is seen to be.

Each of these levels of administration sling around mission statements, mottos, slogans, and other tantalizing, pleasant-sounding phrases, reassuring the community and the family that the "students comes first" and that "education is our goal." We all know how ridiculous that is, judging from the glaring, repeated annual reports of America's failure to educate.

But worse is the overall lack of interest in protecting students from child abuse and child neglect by school personnel. Administrators hear the serious complaints of students for whom they serve as guardians in loco parentis. Unlike real parents or guardians, however, they owe too many loyalties to other adults in the system that can cause them to lose their jobs. Administrators become administrative minions to the abusive teachers, who put them at risk and expose them to the boards and the bastion.

When an issue comes to the office of the administrator, the first and most usual response (if there is any response at all, for some complaints are ignored or sidelined) seems to be some sort of in-house query. This pretty much amounts to asking the adult accused of abusive behaviors if he or she has been behaving inappropriately. To my knowledge, parents have neither the right to hear the conversation nor the right to know the administrator's real findings. In fact, when any organization or group is self-investigating, we can accurately predict the results.

The next step might be either a full dismissal of the complaint or a supervised meeting between the teacher and the parent. These meetings often wind up being an opportunity for the teacher to tell the parent everything that's wrong with the student. And sometimes the teacher uses this audience to tell every wonderful thing that he or she is doing. It doesn't matter if the student has been a model student to this point; a handy comeback is that students "change as they get older." You'll likely hear one or more of the teacher tactics of defense covered in chapter 12. There may later be a repeat of this meeting, where the new offences of teacher's abuse are discussed with the same outcome.

All the while, the administrative minion is weighing the probable outcome of each response. If the teacher is abusive, the administrator wants to control the consequences for him- or her and the school. They often drag out the meetings and discussions, hoping it will go away; either the abusive teacher will go on to another student, or the parent will get tired of complaining and just give up. They can hope that the parent will leave the school and suggest that the student and the teacher are not a good fit, something of an understatement, and move the primary victim to another classroom.

The minion administrator can't sacrifice the teacher; that would infer that he or she had no control over the situation and force a higher level of administration to get involved. That's bad for the administrator's career, and so he or she protects the abusive teacher. That's a win-win for the administrator because the abusive teacher now knows that the administrator will cover up his or her wrongdoing, and he or she becomes the teacher minion to the administrator; in fact, the teacher now owes the administrator some favor in return that the administrator will call in when he or she needs supporters.

As we know, betting with the house is safer than going with the outsider, and the administrative minion is reassured that the bastion to which they belong will come through and protect them from any liability. So, the student is sacrificed. Nothing changes and it never will. So much for mottos and mission statements! The student in each case comes in dead last.

There are endless examples (in the thankless, but critically important media) of schools where complaints about an abusive teacher went on for decades. America's public schools get to ignore the complaints or they pass the trash onto another school. This enormous bastion of public education has unending funding from our public money to settle cases, defend abusers, defend themselves, flip accusations, make threats, and countersue families who dare to try to hold them accountable.

## Adult Support Staff Minions

There are adults in the school systems who participate in child abuse and child neglect just as willingly as teachers. These support staff minions include classroom aides, secretarial staff, yard guards, school bus drivers, lunchroom personnel, and other school personnel. More rarely, the janitorial staff is included in this group. They actually have less direct negative influence than the teacher or other support staff on a student within their daily roles, but they are sometimes named as bullies, mean, or evil by the students. However, the janitorial staff seems, in my experience, to be the single adult group in any of America's schools who the majority of students like and praise, with the head janitor being frequently named by students as a safe person to talk to.

These support staff minions serve in their roles as yard guards, lunch ladies, classroom aides, and in other functions as long as the present administration and the teaching staff of the school choose. Their survival depends, in large part, on learning to do their jobs, staying out of the way, and keeping everyone in the food chain ahead of them happy. And in fact, everyone is ahead of them in the food chain, save perhaps someone new to the campus and unproven in the brotherhood.

These support staff minions have little power when compared to the chain of adults above them. If there is a problem in the village, they must call on another employee higher up the chain to make a decision. Any independent action they take is narrowly defined. Even those few acceptable actions appear not to be assumed, but rather have been given strict *explicit* approval by members of the school system who have power.

However, many of the actions of support staff minions in relation to students are really empowered by *implicit* collusion with the teaching staff and the administrators. Their jobs as support staff depend on how they work with other more influential staff. They observe, they study, and they watch those in power and slowly adjust their behaviors to fit in with the behaviors of the teachers and the administrative staff. So, the support staff minions act in concert with authority figures, regardless of whether the authority figure acts to support the student or acts to abuse or neglect the student.

How does the support staff become support staff minions? The support staff minions take their cues from the more powerful members of the brotherhood. Non-credentialed employees in schools are empowered by the teachers and the administrators. So, here are some examples of how this works.

A teacher targets a child for any one of an infinite number of reasons. We could begin a list, but there aren't enough pages in a book to cover all of them. However, there is neither a good nor acceptable reason for a teacher to target a student. Nevertheless, support staff sees, hears, or learns in some other way that the teacher is targeting a particular student. Maybe the teacher has privately complained in a simple schoolyard conversation about a certain student. Or maybe they see each other in the lunch room, the teachers' lounge, or at a staff meeting. The opportunity presents itself in endless ways.

For unacceptable reasons all their own, that support staff employee sees an opportunity to buddy up with a teacher. Perhaps that support staff minion is just looking for an opportunity to exert some control in a job in which he or she has little control. Perhaps it meets his or her need to elevate his or her status in a caste organization, where power lines are very cut and dry. The more the employee looks for and finds opportunities to report some behavior to the teacher, the more positive feedback the employee gets from the offending, abusive teacher. This collusion can be rewarded with recommendations for full-time work, promotions, or other desirable outcomes where there is enormous competition for position. They may even be rewarded with a social relationship or a friendship of sorts; as it is said, like minds fit well together.

For example, an elementary-age child who complained of being singled out by a teacher and was verbally abused got the same treatment from one of the yard employees. Multiple incidents occurred where the yard employee would follow the child to the classroom lineup when the bell rang and yell to the teacher some complaint about the student so that every student in that line as well as everyone else were sure to hear. The teacher would yell back, "Not again," then look at the student and loudly say, "What's *wrong* with you?" Then the teacher would make some highly affective gesture of sound and say, in an exaggerated and exasperated voice, "I'll deal with it." This is a scenario that actually occurs more than once; it helps us to understand how everyone gets into the picture.

During recess on a hot day, a child got a drink from the water fountain. The water was very hot and had a foul taste. Not wanting to spit out the water back into the fountain, the child leaned over and spit it onto the cement. The child minions (the classmates of the student) ran to the support staff minion, a yard employee, and in chorus cheerfully said the child spit water onto the ground. The bell rang and the yard employee told the child to follow her and marched all the way to the classroom lineup. The yard employee yelled the complaint and the child's name, standing at a few feet from the line. Everyone in the class lineup and the lines of students from other classes looked at the child primary victim. The teacher yelled the predictable response to the regularly victimized child, something like, "Not you again!" in an angry and exasperated tone. The other children laughed. The child was humiliated for the twelfth or thirteenth time. No one ever asked the child what happened.

Why didn't the two adults who were involved ask the child what happened and why water was spit on the cement? Well, there might be a jaggedly illogical and enormously sad explanation. The explanation is an example of a sort of backward reasoning, which supports this kind of self-justification that we see every day. So, it's like this. If either one of the adult perpetrators asked the student victim in this situation what had happened, it would end with an explanation that someone would have to listen to. The explanation, being reasonable and acceptable, would interfere in an opportunity for child abuse and child neglect. There would be a missed opportunity for the collusion between the two adults, a missed opportunity for teacher child abuse, and therefore there would be no opportunity for support staff minions to be rewarded.

The behaviors are predictable. The collusive, unspoken, relationships between the abusive teacher and the child minions and the support staff minions are already set up. No one gets out of a collusive relationship without some negative consequences. Even if the support staff minions want to stop the abusive collusive behavior, they don't dare as it might result in them being targeted by someone who has always had more power in the collusion, namely the abusive teacher.

A lot of time and effort goes into building up the whole abusive teacher, support staff minion, and child minion coalition. Teachers who bully and abuse and their minions don't want to confuse a good thing. Every role of the three groups—abusive teacher, adult minion, and child minion—is rewarded and reinforced in some way. It's like a game. It's a very serious game. It's a criminal game.

This game takes a lot of time and energy. Choosing victims and looking for opportunities, setting up opportunities, exaggerating circumstances to create opportunities, and making up circumstances to create opportunities are all time-consuming, and they occupy a significant part of the mental energy of the participants. The primary victim begins to feel like a rat in a maze that really doesn't have an exit. The results are extremely damaging. If all that energy went into education, imagine what could have been accomplished. But for many members of many brotherhoods, business as it should be done just isn't their goal.

## Summary

There's sadness in understanding the reverberations for all the children involved in child abuse and child neglect perpetrated by teachers. Children who are subjected to witnessing child abuse and child neglect eventually develop the knowledge that they have been used as minions. With that comes the awareness of their responsibility for hurting another child. The torment of being a child victim is life-long. The minion is no less a victim than the primary victim. They can be tormented by what they have learned, what they have been encouraged to do, and what has been done to them by adults they have trusted and have seen as role models. Like ripples in a pond, the reverberations are endless.

For primary minions, collateral minions, and delayed collateral minions, the impact of the recognition of their roles in relation to the direct victim and the role model teacher can be life-changing. People have said that realization of the abuse at the hands of school teachers and other school personnel has opened their eyes. The nagging subliminal feeling and the chronic anxiety, which they have never understood, finally has a home; it now has a center of gravity. Some people are furious when they understand that they were duped as children. They are resentful that they were put into awful and sad roles. They feel shame. They feel used. They feel guilty. The minions' experiences, as part of their educational years, are often whirling memories without names and without any language.

Just as so many adults and children were the minions of the Catholic Church and played into the abuse of countless scores of children, the past is with them forever. And finally, they feel relieved that they can clearly see their own past and the painful school experiences suffered at the hands of abusive teachers, coaches, and others. They can see their burdens in an honest and concrete context.

People can grow from recognition that they actually have played a role, a horrible role, written and directed by a trusted and honored authority figure. All the words they did not know and could not find in childhood now become part of their adulthood. Child primary minions, collateral minions, and delayed collateral minions grow up and, hopefully, grow wise. If they can recognize their roles and experiences in childhood and their parts in someone else's evil, they won't pass it down to their own children. They will listen and understand the next time a student asks for help and the next time they see the signs and symptoms of child abuse and child neglect in the classroom.

In the case of all adult minions and the child minions who are dragged into the mix, the relationships are truly symbiotic. The system is closed, has no accountability, and is historically well established within circumscribed sets of defenses. The individuals who play their parts know their limits within the great bastion. The members of the brotherhood know that they are free to fail to educate, to do nothing as they choose, be abusive and neglectful, and to injure scores of students and never be held accountable.

Schools have set themselves up as self-policing bodies. From special education to advanced classroom content, the tight community of the American school has very little to no accountability. From the obvious failures to educate, from educational neglect to the glaring criminal behaviors of child abuse, the doors are guarded and the system is protected from within. The bastion is so enormous that every attempt at change and accountability from outside is stonewalled.

# CHAPTER 15
# Retaliation

> "It is as if a man, who was given a blade so marvelously keen that it would sever anything, should use its edge for driving in nails."
> —Leo Tolstoy

Retaliation, retribution, revenge, reprisal…it's all the same, and it's going to happen whenever one dares to call out America's schools, teachers, and employees for child abuse and child neglect. The business of retaliation can be a knee-jerk reaction or a well-planned, highly evolved set of behaviors. In both cases, retaliation is a getting even, getting back at, or I'll show you response.

There are different types of retaliation. When one is deprived of something, he or she may believe he or she has a right to react with an eye for an eye. That is, "if you take something from me, then I'll take something from you." Under certain circumstances, we might agree. For instance, if I take your car, you may believe that you have a right to take my car. The law upholds this form of retaliation, not directly, but through a complex legal system where someone else gets to judge the legitimacy of the claim and settle the question of what the perpetrator loses and what the victim gets back. Pretty much, we all support this system to keep the payback fair.

The other type of retaliation is a lot more complicated. Let's say that I paid you for a car, and the car doesn't run. I call you out for taking my money under false pretenses. We begin a legal argument of sorts about how I can get my money back. You don't like me standing up for my rights, so you sabotage the car and claim that I did it. This is a pretty ugly way of evading the process of giving me my money back, but sometimes it works. Fortunately, there is still a legal system that may be able to sort it out, so that I am not too badly victimized. I may still get my money back, but at the cost of time, energy, and stress.

This gets us one step closer to the type of retaliation that we see in our school system. Retaliation by the brotherhood of America's teachers, which is supported by the great bastion of public education, is even more complex, uglier, and part of an underbelly that we loathe to touch. In retaliation, the original perpetrator—who has been called out for the wrongdoing—continues the offense, but with an insidious and sly progress, like something hiding in holes and around corners and grabbing at an ankle before ducking down and making itself secretive in the dark.

Every member of the brotherhood knows that every other member participates at some level in the child abuse and child neglect; only some of them get called out. But, although there is no due process for the student to seek justice in the school system, the cloaked ugliness has been brought to the light of day. The people involved must face the horror of seeing the underside of their own lives, a part of the bastion, even if only for a moment. As with the exposure of every bastion that has been cloaked for generations and (maybe) centuries, there remains a fight to defend evil rather than change for good. Having once again been forced to look the devil in the eye, the perpetrator is released and consoled; but the perpetrator, the victim, and everyone else involved—both in and out of the mainstream—know the truth. I know that. And you know that.

The guilty teacher absolutely can't and won't let it go. The payback begins. The only available target is the student. The perpetrator's peer group smile as they pass and make small talk when they meet; but that is all part of the effort made to enrich and solidify the bearable illusion that nothing is really wrong with America's schools and that they are wonderful, safe, and healthy institutions of learning.

For the victim, there are no smiles and no illusions! There are no depositions, no witnesses to be called before the public, and no witnesses who can be cross-examined by the defendant. So, yes. Just as there is no real due process in addressing child abuse and child neglect for the students who spend their days in America's schools, there is also no consequence for the abusive and neglectful teacher and no possibility that there will be any retaliation against the teacher. The only consequence seems to be the favors owed.

Then what are the retaliations? What do they look like? How will they come? Most of the retaliations by teachers and other school personnel are directed at students and the students' real caregivers, their parents. The retaliations are subtle and underhanded. They aren't usually noisy, grandiose, or obvious violations of students' rights. Because the school employee has already had to defend the original crime, the retaliation phase goes underground. Many teachers use the teacher's defense tactics as the basis for retaliation.

Grade manipulation is a form of retaliation. I once dealt with a student who had complained about a teacher. The complaint was aired and closed. Then the teacher withheld a student's high grade on a final paper until the next grading period to assure that the student got one letter grade lower for the entire current semester.

Retaliation often comes in the nonverbal ways that were discussed in the section on ignoring in chapter 13. The teacher ignores requests for help or explanation, he or she won't call on the student in the classroom, he or she pretty much behaves as if that student who dared to complain no longer exists and has been relegated to the category of lepers in the 1800s. At the slightest opportunity, the guilty student is grouped into class-wide complaints having nothing to do with whether they were even present.

But the most devious and injurious behaviors are attitudinal. We can all feel the attitude of others toward us. When the attitude is positive, there are positive smiles, facial expressions, and a wonderful, positive, encouraging energy. When the attitude is ugly, there is a palpable negative energy, almost a smell of a human who abhors the sight and presence of his or her victims and wishes for them to disappear, but not without punishing them first.

Retaliation occurs without any due process available for the victim because, as we've already established, the bastion that we call America's schools has created a system without balance, without due process, and without accountability. Its power over students and their families is out of control. New complaints are generally met with long, annoyed sighs and an intense tonal expression of, "Oh, no! Not you again."

We've discussed the problems that occur daily in the classroom. Chapters 6 and 7 delineate the types of child abuse and child neglect occurring in the schools. Chapter 12 covers the tactics of abuse and neglect. Chapter 13 covers the defenses that each member of the bastion uses when confronted. In part, these defenses are forms of retaliation. But in addition to this, there are subtler and more heinous forms of retaliation even beyond these defenses. The true underbelly of today's classrooms is the covert abuse of power and the increased use of child abuse and child neglect.

So, here it goes. After the first problems were brought to light; after all the complaints have been aired; after all the adjustments and accommodations have been put to pen and paper, signed, and delivered; after all the victims have been blamed and punished; and after all the perpetrators have been counseled and hand slapped—wait for it, wait for it—the retaliation will begin. It's a guarantee. It's without question. And it's what all the kids and the families mean when they say, "Telling is just going to make it worse."

Call it what you will—retaliation, retribution, revenge, reprisal—it's all the same ugly, dirty business of an organization that self-polices and self-perpetuates its self-interest. There's no "other" in this crime; the only "other" is the victim.

Retaliation is a form of whistle-blower's punishment; a kind of punishment that can go on indefinitely with no restrictions, no boundaries, and no consequences to the perpetrator. This form of retaliation occurs after someone fails to effectively deal with the first complaint, which emboldens the perpetrator and supports his or her retaliatory behavior. In this case, the teacher or the other school personnel gets called on the carpet. They get a hand slapping for the verbal record and, simultaneously, get a high-five from behind the scenes peer collusion regarding how disgusting it is that someone dared to complain. They believe that this is a private joke, and no one knows what's really happening. They believe that the students and their parents think that the complaint is taken seriously. They believe that the students and their parents don't know what comes next. They are wrong about all these beliefs. But they also believe that they can retaliate in such underhanded ways that they can get away with it. What they are right about is that they usually do get away with it. And that's why most victims of child abuse and child neglect in America's schools don't tell. And yes, retaliation can go on forever with no restrictions, no boundaries, and no consequences to the perpetrator.

Those whistle-blower's punishments often go on for years, even generations. A student who complained about a teacher's abusive behavior in the seventh grade is likely to be branded throughout high school by the brotherhood. Their siblings become fair game and get handed the same subtle underhanded retaliation. The staff may work at one school for forty years, and many are ensconced for at least twenty-five years, until retirement. This means that the children of the victim may also get the same punishments.

The only broad kind of help that may be useful against this retaliation is power in numbers. Any kind of power is built, in part, on understanding the problem and identifying it when it happens. So, to address the inevitable crime of retaliation, the students and their families must begin an open dialogue. Today, students across the country who have already suffered child abuse and child neglect in the schools are now continuously suffering retaliation, and currently there is no voice of help. The opportunities to access open dialogue have vaporized along with accountability.

The end of the real parent teacher organization/association (PTO/PTA) in the schools meant the beginning of the end of parent-parent opportunities to communicate. PTO or PTA meetings were a place to meet and greet teachers, staff, and other parents. Now, the PTO in our local schools consists of parents donating supplies and food to the teachers' occasion lunches held at the school; they do not even include the few participating parents who have arranged the feasts. In years past, when parents were welcomed on schools' campuses and in school classrooms, communication between the school personnel and the parents was open and free-flowing. Now, the schools are offensive fortresses, and communication is carefully meted out by appointment only, if at all. There is virtually no opportunity for positive banter, discussion, or interplay. As a result, communication with teachers is generally considered adversarial in that it occurs only when the parent reaches out to discuss a child need or problem. Communication is rarely initiated by the teacher or the school other than when the child and, at times, his or her parent, is summoned for disciplinary action. The exception to this might be an automated voice recording that announces trivial matter, such as the lunch account is low or that the student is absent or tardy.

The PTA was an opportunity to connect with other parents to discuss school events, school happenings, school progress, and school and classroom concerns. This missing piece of student and family involvement in education in much of America has come at a high cost to students and schools. But it also creates and supports the illusion that schools are untouchable in more than one way. Because they are out of bounds for all but the school personnel and the students, there is a suspicion that what goes on in our schools is out of our control and that schools have a lot to hide. Some of what we suspect is lurking within the fortress walls built by the great bastion and driven by the brotherhoods is child abuse. And there's no doubt about child neglect; what is left to be determined is only its frequency and timing. For anyone attempting to shed some light on the subject, there is also retaliation.

Walled and gated schools are main stream. But there are a few exceptions. There are some schools where parent involvement is part of the daily routine. One of the best schools in our area is a faith-based school. The parents are required to participate and volunteer. The students' education is exceptional in a town where even the elementary schools are failing and many score two out of ten on the Great Schools score. The teachers at these exceptional schools are hard-working, disciplined, and accountable. The parents are accountable for their participation in their child's education. The students are accountable to themselves, to their teachers, to their parents, and to their church. They are all great role models for one another. The school is part of a very low-income community, parents put in work hours at the school to reduce the tuition, and it works.

Another type of school that seems to be working is the schools in highly affluent areas. People often believe that this is because the schools have more money than the schools in the poverty-stricken areas. Whereas there may be some donated money, the schools in the poverty-stricken areas and the low-test score areas are the ones with the extra money granted due to their failing-school status. What is little understood is that these schools do have something that other schools don't: the parents have oversight. Are we talking about public schools? Yes, indeed we are. How can that be? It's pretty obvious, when you look at the composition of the parent's economic and social status. These parents have inserted themselves into the public schools where their children are students. They have committees, fathers breakfast clubs, the parents' involvement in athletic oversight, and the ear of the administration. How did they accomplish this? Is it because they have nothing to do, or maybe they have more time than the parent who has a day or night job? No. What these parents have is the wherewithal to group together and stand firm against any type of aberrant behavior on school campus. They are omnipresent. They use their power of numbers to hold everyone in the school accountable. They stand together.

How did this group succeed where the others failed? They know from their experience in business, industry, and other professions that they have to work together. They know that education in America is a business, and they know that it is a business out of control. They know how to get started to make change. They have the dedication to continue to work at this commitment for their children. They stay the course, even when they are required somewhere else. They don't get into petty causes and arguments. They demand what the brotherhood is accountable for: educating their children in a safe and nurturing environment.

So, what does this have to do with retaliation, retribution, revenge, or reprisal? Retaliation happens after child abuse and child neglect happen. Retaliation happens after the teacher is called out for abuse and promises to be nice in the future. If the schools are supervised appropriately and there are consequences for their failures, none of this would be happening. Angry, ugly, abusive, and neglectful teachers in the American education bastion should be confronted effectively with the truth about their failures. But the failures stay right where they are, and they are free to retaliate, to reinjure the student who dared to call out to them.

## CHAPTER 16
# Bottom-Up Change

> "To change something, build a new model
> That makes the existing model obsolete."
> —Buckminster Fuller

One of America's greatest historical failures cannot be fixed because the status quo will not address the problems at the root of the disaster. To understand a failure with the goal being to find a solution, you have to know how the problem started and what keeps it alive and sometimes growing. To know what to change to alter the course of an existing problem, you have to accurately identify the problem. But there's the rub! The problems leading to these failures are in the hands of probably the largest self-policing institution in America's history, America's school system, the last bastion of cloaked abuse.

Why has the public-school system, this last bastion, been impossible to change? The Boy Scouts identified the problems of abusive scout masters. The Catholic Church identified the abuse by the priests. The sports world identified the abuse of its coaches. Law enforcement has identified the abuses of its officers. The military has identified the abuses of its soldiers. Industry in America recognizes when a system doesn't work and makes difficult changes to keep the country running. But this brotherhood of America's teachers and the bastion that we know as America's school system has been impossible to change because they operate entirely on mandated public money that has no end and are accountable to no one.

America's school system continually invents new tests, new curriculum, and new (even bizarre) teaching strategies. Notice that in the NCES 2015 student test scores, the only area that is significantly impacted is the scores in technology. Only 57 percent of students are not proficient! Never mind that the extremely large majority of America's students are not proficient in reading, math, science, and history. It makes sense for now we have a new focus, namely STEM education. It's too bad about those irritating, failing math and reading scores.

All the frequent changes; fancy new programs; catchy new titles; and crisp, new money act like a smoke screen for the rotten roots. With such enormous and very lucrative smoke screens, to date no one has been called on or held responsible for identifying the problem that actually lays at the base of the failure of the American school system…the real bottom line. The real problem. There are many competing voices, all lined up inside the brotherhood and behind the bastion, which are willing to say, "Look here, I know what the problem is!" These voices echo out of their own agendas, offering solutions in line with the great bastion. There is no changing anything if you're not willing to tear at the roots of the failures. Despite every change processed to date, every fix mended, every trash truck stuffed with money, every new test, every new paperwork filled out, and every step taken, the problem of America's failed education system cannot be and will not be fixed!

The supporting characteristics of the structure of the public-school system are broken. The public-school system and its relationship with each and every employee are broken. The entire system has evolved to assure its own existence and to push students through its sieve-like structure at the cost of the health of the students and their education. The public schools' original purpose is obviously lost in the grind. Severely deteriorating educational positioning in the world population is now the face of our future with masses of students who cannot read, write, add, and subtract in thirteen years of schools, students who never even finished school, and students who are abused and neglected in the care of the brotherhood.

From the first moment that any caregiver is allowed to usurp the role of parent and use that role to injure America's children, the classroom becomes a free-for-all with no accountability. And it only gets worse. From the teachers who just don't teach (and therefore commit fraud in the form of educational neglect) and the teachers who rape and molest their kindergarten students to the professors who live to indoctrinate, America's educational professionals are an embarrassment for they have forgotten the definition of education and their obligation to educate.

The structure of education in the United States is likely the beginning of its own destruction. The current system has significantly worsened over the last seven decades. There was a time when young people who went to school learned reading and math and then acquired work skills that provided for them throughout life. Through a building block of sequential changes, that system has now failed. From some ridiculous proposition that all people should go to college, to a fictitious propagation that all people want to go to college, before climaxing in the fantasy that there would be no jobs for those who don't go to college, the piecemeal, slapped together, now failed system is a disgrace that has seriously damaged an entire generation of students. Yet this myth was created by the educational system to ensure its own longevity. The myth is funded with dollars taken from you and me. But the greatest cost is at the expense of the young people, who it does not serve.

We all know the structure. Thirteen years of lockstep education. But by the end of the third grade, educational failure is glaring on the faces of many students. When an elementary school scores three or four out of ten based on their students' evaluations, it generally means the majority of students are already behind. Yet they are pushed on (as if the scores just aren't true!), accompanied by a devious plotline that they will catch up when they're more mature. Does anyone actually believe that? There's not a high school dropout I've ever met and who believed that.

What has to be done to stop the child abuse and child neglect in America's public-school system? What has to be done can only be done from the bottom up. Hopefully, we know by now that new overlays of anything won't solve these problems. The essential changes that will take us all out of this educational mirage are hard to face.

The role of teachers, administrations, and other school personnel should include the following:

- Union membership optional legislation should be passed. This will allow teachers to distance themselves from broken systems and dangerous people. It will be at least one forum for teachers, who are now guilty by avoidance, to stand up to an abusive and neglectful system.
- Involve law enforcement when teachers are accused of abuse or neglect. Do not allow them to self-police. Do not allow secret consequences with secret statements like the secret police. That method of self-policing leads to no consequence and a greatly expanded network of employees who owe everyone in the bastion. That's a swamp. That's like Washington politics. That's an old boys' club! This is not a taxpayer-owned and taxpayer-supported organization with goals to meet.
- Prosecute all school personnel using the same criterion used for prosecuting the parents who abuse and neglect their children. Stop calling abuse and neglect bullying. Stop blaming the students. Stop passing the trash. Stop minimizing the full responsibility of the guilty party.
- Insist on personal liability contracts. Teachers are contracted. They should pay for their own liability insurance policies. The taxpayers should never have to pay for an individual's criminal behavior, his or her policies, attorney's fines, or court costs. Nothing should be paid by taxpayers if the contracted employee is acting outside of their contract. There are hopefully no clauses in teachers' secret

contracts that allow them to get paid for or defended against abuse and neglect.
- End the tenure. The tenure is the obvious pathway to "I can do whatever I want with your child and nothing will happen to me." Perpetual contracts are not a part of successful endeavors.
- Require teachers to complete an advanced level of continuing education, specifically in their own field, with periodic evaluation of their knowledge bases and fitness to teach in their subject areas. No more "take anything that vaguely applies" for continuing education and easy pay raises. Advancement should be based on evidence-based advanced and accredited education in their own field.
- Teachers should be mandated to grade any paper they require a student to complete. If the paper is important and useful enough for a student to spend out of school time completing, the teacher should certainly grade the paper, indicate what is correct and incorrect, and go over with students what they are doing incorrectly. No grades should be recorded without returned corrected work; the opposite is happening now. Teachers issue many grades where the content errors are never seen by the student, they are never corrected, and there is no re-teaching when the work has not been mastered.
- Teachers should be required to hold forums for parents where complaints can be aired, questions can be fielded, and the teachers have to provide examples of their own work.

The parents' role should include the following:

- Public parent bodies (and not hand-picked or permanently installed parent liaisons, boards, or panels) should inspect every aspect of education. These bodies would have access to disciplinary hearings; review complaints; and oversee the physical site, including cameras, water fountains, restroom, locker rooms, computer systems, attendance, and the compliance of teachers.

- Parents should have access to forums where teachers can field questions, complaints against teachers can be aired, and where teachers have to give examples of their own work.
- The now defunct parent-teacher organization should be replaced with a parent organization with regularly held meetings for any and all parents for open discussion on any relevant topic, no matter how controversial it might be.

The students' role should include the following:

- Students should receive some type of pay or reward for hours attended and work completed in the classroom. Grades are not a sufficient reinforcement for most students. With such an incentive, classroom attendance and the measure of work completed will skyrocket.
- Students should be given fifteen- to twenty-minute work breaks, just as those given to any adult in the workplace. Walking from one work area to another work area is not a break. There is too little time to use a restroom, eat a granola bar or a banana, or have something to drink.
- Students should take anonymous surveys designed by parent groups to evaluate the quality and appropriateness of teachers' performances.
- There should be regular student forums where students can attend meetings in groups of choice (based on the paradigms of teacher, subject, or problem), including groups that discuss teacher and staff abuse and neglect in their school. They should review both media and research articles on education and educational problems and learn what's happening around them and in schools around the world. They should offer feedback at both the parent meetings and the teacher forums.

- Students must have opportunities. They must work on projects that earn them respect and some other kind of reward. Students should be linked with communities, like those related to the arts, the sciences, agriculture, and electronics. It's hard to know who is the most bored, the students or the teachers. The teachers have made themselves boring. The students don't want to listen to them because they feel they don't accomplish anything by being in school. The fun they have in school is not related to their academic day, but it can be. Students can feel productive.
- Students must all be fed lunch. They should be fed real lunches. They must be given their lunch time and nourishing food. One slice of pizza, a small side, and a drink is not sufficient to nourish growing bodies. There must be enough food to not only get them through the day that would be grueling for any adult, but also into the afternoon of school and the night of homework, where the real learning happens.

The role of the schools and the curriculums should include the following:

- Cameras should be installed and working in every room in the publicly owned school system—classrooms, lunchrooms, offices, and hallways. Bodycams for all employees is a good option. Many schools already have at least a partial system where students appear on camera. The difference would be that the teachers and public-school staff would also be on camera. No one ever need see the videos unless something goes wrong. Teachers should love cameras. They blame the students for the problems, for the abuse, for the neglect; now they'll have proof. Or the other way around. It would be good to see what students mean when they say that their teacher does nothing all day but yell, hand out more work to do, and tell them to be quiet. Students feel they are a real inconvenience for some of their teachers; let's find out why.

- End useless curriculum. What do our students know after thirteen years of public school education? Not much. The required years of algebra, foreign language, and English language arts have done nothing to put millions of high school graduates to work. In fact, these graduates' test scores as a whole are so bad that they are not qualified to go into even a community college without taking remedial courses.
- Movement through the public-school system is a one-size-fits-all business for the convenience of the system, not for the student. Movement through the educational system must be mastery based, not age based. Throughout the world there is multiage learning that is highly successful. Mastery-based education will provide motivation for students to attend and learn. The current age-based, no failure, pass on without knowledge system is an epic failure. It is a transparent and unfortunate disincentive for student participation. It doesn't matter to the system if students do nothing; they will continue to be passed on without consequence. The system, however, has failed to explain to the students that the money the system collects for the filling the classroom seats keeps that system alive; the system doesn't care about what happens to them later. America's teachers and other school personnel have no interest once you no longer fill the seat. You're left on you own to struggle for the rest of your life with no education. Students cannot progress and learn until they have progressed and learned.
- Stop the repetitive and expensive waste-of-time testing. There are quizzes, chapter tests, unit tests, semester tests, comprehensive tests, MAP tests, state tests, national tests, AP tests, college entrance tests, high school exit tests, and the list goes on. There are so many tests that I see appear on the computer grades of students, and I have no idea what they are or why they're given and what the results are used for. It all would have been OK if anything was learned from the testing. But the teachers don't even go over last

night's homework and answer everyone's questions. They don't go over the test after it's taken and graded. The students have to learn on their own with very little feedback and a given grade. There is no benefit for anyone in saving the brotherhood and the bastion.
- Put in place rigorous job training courses. Return drafting, woodshop, auto mechanics, firefighting, law enforcement, roads and grounds, electronics, heavy machinery operation, cooking, business management, human relations, vocational nursing, sales, bookkeeping, and basic building. Make sure that high school graduates know what they want to do at age eighteen and prepare them to walk into those jobs. There are too many young adults who are failing because education has been meaningless to them, has wasted valuable years, and has failed them.
- Each and every class should have a full course syllabus with all required work, complete detailed directions, and due dates handed to the student at the beginning of the semester. This allows for students and families to organize and schedule student work hours and workloads. Students will have increased control over their school responsibilities. Students are no longer subject to the sudden whim of multiple classroom teachers which interrupts the students' life outside of the schools jurisdiction. Currently, students cannot plan, schedule, and organize, their lives. This every day, spooned out, poorly delineate information on teachers expectations is a major part of students failure to mature. College preparation severely lags because students are not allowed age appropriate control of their responsibilities.

Putting these changes in place should be required for any school to be granted continued funding. Child abuse and the child neglect will stop when schools are mandated to monitor teachers and other school personnel and there is basic educational format change in line with learning and achievement, not the student's age.

Child neglect has to stop for schools to be healthy learning environments. Physical neglect, medical neglect, emotional neglect, and educational neglect hardly make it to the news because they are part of the everyday life for students. With instances like leaving students with concussions on the playing field, medical neglect has become a safe move to protect the teacher and the bastion. Grabbing away children's food and physically neglecting their nutritional needs to punish parents is anything but benign; it's bizarre and archaic. Allowing students to quietly suffer emotional pain, failures, and embarrassment because of their disabilities and injuries in a system that is mandated to, paid to, and educated to seek out and find disabilities and injuries is the worst kind of emotional neglect. Educational neglect in the educational systems has to be the most ironic daily occurrence ever encountered in the United States.

Child abuse is illegal and should be prosecuted; America's schools can succeed if teachers are stopped from abusing their students. Sexual abuse, psychological abuse, and physical abuse are out of control in America's schools. There are waves of new teacher-student sexual abuse cases each year. Psychological abuse goes completely ignored and unpunished; like banging your head on a wall for years, hurting emotionally begins to seem normal, expected, acceptable, and even necessary to achieve an education. Physical abuse in unimaginable forms—from students dying in scream rooms to writing "loser" on students' foreheads—every day continues everywhere in America.

In the end, there's just no point in even continuing in school after the third grade if the student can't read, write, add, and subtract. Yet we pass students on with nothing to help them to succeed. The top-down change doesn't work.

Nothing is changing. The teachers aren't better educated. They aren't better prepared. They aren't better motivated. They aren't better at teaching. In the end, America's schools are failures as systems; its' teachers are failures as educators and the schools hire, support, and protect failed human beings who are free to commit child abuse and child neglect. Until the

American education system is revamped in ways that allow success, there will always be defensive, ineffective, and often dangerous teachers in the schools.

Teachers are contract workers. Teachers should be paid by the numbers. Contract to pay teachers for how many students master the material they are expert in teaching. Students should not move ahead until they master the material. This is a dual responsibility model; it puts the responsibility for failure and success squarely on the shoulders of both the student and the teacher. This will stop the disintegration of American education.

By initiating fully immersed, full circle, parent, teacher, administration, community, and student involvement in bottom-up participation, changes will happen. The recognition and the acknowledgment of child abuse and child neglect in America's schools can happen. We can begin a dialogue. We can make education and educators accountable. The changes must be bottom-up, they must be enforced, and they must be monitored. They must be effective. Most of all, we—which includes every one of us—must demand that education in America finally be held to its promise. We can all find our voices. And we must change now to save our next generations who are America's future, namely our students.

# EPILOGUE
## The Whispers Never End

> "When truth is replaced by silence, silence is a lie."
> —Yevgeny Yevtushenko

For all the publicity, all the public outcry over the atrocities of the world's most powerful bastions, the abuses go on. The horror of the truth is that, once again, discussions surrounding abuse might well be completely drowned in silence if not for our persistent media and now social media. In and around the bastion, there are whispered arguments against uncovering abuse in schools. Most of the whispers reflect dark fears that the shining crown of the mythical teacher and the time-honored school might lose their once precious but ill-deserved jewel: their reputation. America's schools count on respect and an untarnished reputation to maintain a high degree of power and control. No member of the brotherhood wants to be responsible for the tarnishing or the retribution that comes with the saying, "The emperor has no clothes." Hence, it's better to hunker down and hide in the dark.

Other whispers come from the inside and the outside of the bastion. There are those who slosh around in the circular and dizzying business of quantifying some conceptual number that represents an acceptable level of abuse. What does that mean? Perhaps some abuse is to be expected and is therefore unnecessarily dredged up by troublemakers. Or the frequency of the problem isn't significant enough to be worthy of attention.

Well, OK. Let's decide how to draw a line and where each student should stand. Which child is it OK to abuse? Whose child is the insignificant victim? How many children or students are we allowed to have abused before abuse is a big enough problem to bother with? When will we know that the OK-to-abuse group of children is enough and what will happen when we add one more to that? Do we save only the last victim who tipped the balance? Or do we face the dreaded task? Is it now time to expend resources and hold the bastion and each of its brotherhood members accountable for every child who has been neglected or abused?

Another whispered justification for allowing abuses in schools to go unstopped seems to be that no one can stop all abuse, so why try. This includes justifying statements such as "We're never going to be able to stop this completely" and turning a blind and disinterested eye. With the nature of being human as it is, it's highly probable that we can't stop all abuse. We can't stop all neglect. We can't stop all bullying between kids. So, let's pretend it doesn't help to keep trying. After all, nothing needs to be done further when we have put so many abuses behind us and are now a truly civilized society at last. Right?

The brotherhood of teachers in America who shelters abuse and neglect is a relatively new topic for the media. When some event finally involves law enforcement or is so heinous that social media propels it with much speed and the public has access to the information, there is little that the enormous bureaucracy of America's schools can do to halt the leak.

But the leaks are few and almost wholly the work of the media when the media is ready and able to do this work. It would be dangerous to assume that the leaks spotlight anything but ground-level reporting. As parents and as students, we know what we might see if we dig down from the surface to the underbelly.

The struggle to bring voice to the whispers is fearsome. As individuals, we are essentially powerless, and as a group of parents and students, our voices are not raised above a whisper. That struggle that moves fear to voice has been well-documented when we talk of other bastions and other brotherhoods. Our fears still move us to silence. Maybe we can push a little; maybe the conversation can now be a bit more open with some new brave heroes taking the lead.

There is no help for this other than beginning a conversation. Martin Luther King Jr. echoed other great minds. He was talking about all of us when he talked about how our lives end when we stay silent about things that matter. It's just no good to live a lifetime of impotence, of injury, and of injustice and die without speaking above a whisper or without being heard.

There is no getting over injustices and injury in our lifetimes. They remain forever in memory, and no magic can cause them to disappear from the weave of all our life experiences. Just as we can recall the smell of a fresh peach or the feel of a kitten's fur, memory lingers fairly or unfairly. You hear people deaf to abuse and neglect say, without thinking and carelessly, such things as "Get over it," "What does it matter now?" or "Get a thicker skin!"

But of course there is no cure for the childhood traumas meted out at the hands of our guardians and role models. Lest we forget, our nation's schools might very well be the only sanctuary available to many of our young, a place where they seek to be recognized, led, supported, and guided. When they come to the first desk they can call their own and share their learning and themselves with someone they know to be well educated and qualified enough to be put in charge, they do not heal when they find that they might be abused and neglected. Instead of sanctuary, they have acquired a well-rounded distrust and a permanent experience of themselves as an unacceptable loss and failure in an important part of their lives. If nowhere else in life can change our princes and princesses to see themselves as frogs, it can be left to our nation's schools.

We can all see that we haven't yet found our voices as a larger group, but we can have the hope of setting the goal as others have done before us. Because we haven't found the voice to call out to the American education system, it doesn't mean that we never will. Others before us have confronted the abuses of other brotherhoods and their overreaching bastions. We have become familiar with the heroes who have ferreted out the truth from whispers, singly making loud noises, fighting to demand accountability, and frequently failing. But here we are, shyly and only occasionally saying what we really know about the last bastion of cloaked abuse, the brotherhood of child abuse and child neglect in America's schools.

# Works Cited

"4-Year-Old Student Handcuffed, Rutherford and Greene Sheriff React." NBC29 WVIR. 18 Dec. 2014. http://www.nbc29.com/story/27665553/4-year-old-student-handcuffed-rutherford-and-greene-sheriff-react.

Ablow, Keith. "'Scream Rooms' in Schools Are Psychological Sadism." Fox News. 25 Feb. 2014. http://www.foxnews.com/health/2014/02/25/scream-rooms-in-schools-are-psychological-sadism.html.

Adams, John. *Treason Unmask'd; Or, The Queen's Title, the Revolution, and the Hanover Succession Vindicated*. Booksellers of London and Westminster, 1713.

Addams, Jane. "The Subjective Necessity for Social Settlements." *Philanthropy and Social Progress*, edited by Henry C. Adams, 1893, pp. 1–26.

Anderson, Meg, and Kavitha, Cardoza. "Mental Health in Schools: A Hidden Crisis Affecting Millions of Students." NPR. 31 Aug. 2016. http://www.npr.org/sections/ed/2016/08/31/464727159/mental-health-in-schools-a-hidden-crisis-affecting-millions-of-students.

Arak, Joel. "Panty-Check Principal Demoted." CBS News. 18 Jun. 2002. http://www.cbsnews.com/news/panty-check-principal-demoted/.

Baddour, Dylan. "Northeast Texas Middle School Teacher Gives 'ghetto Awards' to Special Needs Students." Houston Chronicle. June 08, 2015. http://www.chron.com/news/houston-texas/texas/article/Northeast-Texas-middle-school-teacher-gives-6313768.php.

Baldas, Tresa and Ann Zaniewski. "Judge Locks Up 4 More Detroit Principals." *Governing the States and Localities.* 09 Sept. 2016. http://www.governing.com/topics/education/tns-detroit-school-prison-principals.html

Balko, Radley. "Georgia Deputies Conduct Warrantless Search of High School, Pat Down 900 Students." *Washington Post.* 27 Apr. 2017. https://www.washingtonpost.com/news/the-watch/wp/2017/04/27/report-georgia-deputies-conduct-warrantless-search-of-high-school-pat-down-900-students/?utm_term=.a21f80b7bb6b.

Barajas, Michael. "UPDATED HISD History Teacher Accused of Choking Student." Houston Press. May 22, 2016. http://www.houstonpress.com/news/updated-hisd-history-teacher-accused-of-choking-student-6715687.

Beyer, Monica. "Cafeteria Beating Lands Middle Schooler with Autism in the Hospital for 5 Days." She Knows. 5 Feb. 2015. http://www.sheknows.com/parenting/articles/1076509/12-year-old-with-autism-severely-beaten-at-school.

Binggeli, Nelson J., Stuart N. Hart, and Marla R. Brassard. *Psychological Maltreatment of Children.* New York Sage Publications, 2001.

Bond, Allison. "Yelling, Threatening Parents Harm Teens' Mental Health." Reuters. 10 Dec. 2013. http://www.reuters.com/article/2013/12/10/us-yelling-parents-teens-idUSBRE9B914020131210.

Bouvier, John. A Law Dictionary, Adapted to the Constitution and Laws of the United States. 1856. <a href=»http://legal-dictionary.thefreedictionary.com/in+loco+parentis»>in loco parentis</a>

"Bully." *Cambridge Dictionary*. http://dictionary.cambridge.org/dictionary/english/bully.

"Bully." Dictionary.com. http://www.dictionary.com/browse/bullying?s=t.

"Bullying." *Collins English Dictionary*, Complete and Unabridged, 12th Edition, HarperCollins, 2014.

"Bullying Suicide Statistics." No Bullying—Bullying & Cyberbullying Resources. NOBullying.com. 13 Oct. 2016. https://nobullying.com/bullying-suicide-statistics/

Butler, Jennifer. "How Safe Is the Schoolhouse." AUTCOM—The Autism National Committee. 13 Dec. 2016. http://www.autcom.org/.

"California B." CA—Various Statutes. Bully Police USA. http://www.bullypolice.org/ca_law.html.

California, Department of Education, "2016-17 Budget Act Letter." *2016-17 Budget Act Letter - Education Budget* www.cde.ca.gov/fg/fr/eb/budletter16-17.asp.

―――――"Schools Chief Torlakson Reports Across-the-Board Progress Toward Career and College Readiness in CAASPP Results." *Statewide Student Test Results Released - Year 2016* (California State Department of Education. 24 Aug. 2016. Web. www.cde.ca.gov/nr/ne/yr16/yr16rel57.asp.

―――――, EdSource, and the Fiscal Crisis & Management Assistance Team. Ed-Data. Education Data Partnership. 2015. http://www.ed-data.k12.ca.us/App_Resx/EdDataClassic/fsTwoPanel.aspx#!bottom=/_layouts/EdDataClassic/Accountability/PerformanceReports.asp?tab=3&reportNumber=1&level=04&fyr=1213#StateTests.

―――――"Enrollment/Number of Schools by Grade Span & Type". CalEdFacts. July 13, 2017. http://www.cde.ca.gov/ds/sd/cb/cefenrollgradetype.asp.

California Education Code 2005, Sections 35294.20-35294.25 Article 10.41.

Ceasar, Stephen. "State May Be Forced to Intervene in Jefferson High Scheduling Issues." *Los Angeles Times.* 2 Oct. 2014. http://www.latimes.com/local/education/la-me-jefferson-lawsuit-20141003-story.html.

Chandler, Raymond. *The Long Goodbye.* New York Houghton Mifflin, 1953.

Chasmar, Jessica. "Middle School Teacher Charged with Giving Student Lap Dance in Class." *Washington Times.* 27 Apr. 2014. http://www.washingtontimes.com/news/2014/apr/27/middle-school-teacher-charged-giving-student-lap-d/#ixzz307l517Ze.

―――――"Texas School District Sorry after Administrator Blames Boys' Bad Grades on Girls' 'Tight Clothing.'" *Washington Times*, 07 Sept. 2016. http://www.washingtontimes.com/news/2016/sep/7/texas-school-district-sorry-after-administrator-bl/.

Chesterton, Gilbert Keith. "Christmas Thoughts on Vivisection." *London Illustrated News*. 4 Jan. 1908.

———*Twelve Types*. Arthur R. Humphreys, 1902.

Child Welfare Information Gateway. (2013). *What is child abuse and neglect? Recognizing the signs and symptoms*. Washington, DC: U.S. Department of Health and Human Services, Children's Bureau.

———— (2016). *Mandatory reporters of child abuse and neglect*. Washington, DC: U.S. Department of Health and Human Services, Children's Bureau.

———— (2017). *About CAPTA: A legislative history*. Washington, DC: U.S. Department of Health and Human Services, Children's Bureau.

"Compulsory Education Laws: Background." Findlaw. http://education.findlaw.com/education-options/compulsory-education-laws-background.html.

Crain, Esther. "Mom Arrested for Punishing Son for Missing Curfew." *Yahoo! News*, Yahoo!, 2 June 2015, www.yahoo.com/news/mom-arrested-for-punishing-son-for-missing-curfew-120557020952.html.

Crime Sider Staff. "NYC Teacher Charged in Sex Crimes against 6 Students." CBS News. CBS Interactive. 01 Oct. 2014. https://www.cbsnews.com/news/sean-shaynak-new-york-city-teacher-charged-in-sex-crimes-against-6-students/.

Crum, Maddie. "The US Illiteracy Rate Hasn't Changed in 10 Years." The Huffington Post. 06 Sept. 2013. http://www.huffingtonpost.com/2013/09/06/illiteracy-rate_n_3880355.html.

Davis, Lisa. "Can *Vergara v. California* Fix Our Schools?" California Lawyer. 30 Jul. 2015. http://www.callawyer.com/2015/08/can-vergara-v-california-fix-our-schools/.

Dostoyevsky, Fyodor. *Brothers Karamazov*. New York Simon and Schuster, 2013.

Dungca, Nicole. "Oregon Senate Passes Bill Banning Locking Students in 'Seclusion Cells." OregonLive.com. 01 Apr. 2013. http://www.oregonlive.com/portland/index.ssf/2013/04/oregon_senate_passes_bill_bann.html.

Edelman, Susan. "No Pay, No Play! Poor Kids Banned from School Carnival." *New York Post*. 14 Jun. 2015. http://nypost.com/2015/05/24/no-pay-no-play-kids-who-cant-pay-10-fee-banned-from-school-carnival/.

Education GPS. *OCED*. 06 Sep. 2017. http://gpseducation.oecd.org/Home.

Erwin, Elizabeth. "Valley Schools Put Students in Padded 'Scream Rooms.'" Azfamily.com 3TV CBS 5. Meredith Corporation. 23 Feb. 2012. http://www.azfamily.com/story/17007347/so-called-scream-rooms-used-in-valley-schools.

Fang, Xiangming, et al. "The Economic Burden of Child Maltreatment in the United States and Implications for Prevention." *Child Abuse and Neglect* 36, no. 2 (2012): 156–65.

Fessler, Pam. "Child Abuse and Neglect Laws Aren't Being Enforced, Report Finds." NPR. 27 Jan. 2015. http://www.npr.org/sections/health-shots/2015/01/27/381636056/child-abuse-and-neglect-laws-arent-being-enforced-report-finds.

Fitzgerald, Corey. "Adult and Family Literacy in the US; Limitations to Our Nation's Success." Scientific Learning. 17 Jul. 2014. http://www.scilearn.com/blog/low-literacy-united-states.

"Florida Teacher Suspended after Filming Kindergartner Beating Other Students." Fox News. FOX News Network. 15 Feb. 2015. http://www.foxnews.com/us/2015/02/15/florida-teacher-given-suspension-for-videotaping-kindergartner-beating-other.html.

"Former US House Speaker Dennis Hastert Accused of Child Molestation." Yahoo! News. 09 Apr. 2016. https://in.news.yahoo.com/former-us-house-speaker-dennis-hastert-accused-child-095321543.html.

Frankl, Viktor E. *Man's Search for Meaning*. Boston, Beacon, 2006.

Frohlich, Thomas C., and Alexander, Kent. "States with the Best (and Worst) Schools." 247wallst.com. 21 Jan. 2015. http://247wallst.com/special-report/2015/01/09/americas-best-and-worst-school-systems/#ixzz3ZlyiWbh0.

Garcia, Bernice. "Special-Ed Kid Turned Camera on Bully Teacher." *NY Daily News*. 18 Nov. 2011. http://www.nydailynews.com/news/national/teacher-bullied-special-needs-student-secretly-caught-shocking-verbal-abuse-cell-phone-video-article-1.979568.

Golgowski, Nina. "SEE IT: Ky. Teacher Seen Dragging Boy Facing Assault Charge." *NY Daily News*. 1 Jan. 2015. http://www.nydailynews.com/news/national/ky-teacher-dragging-boy-facing-assault-charge-article-1.2087242.

Gonzalez, Jonathan. "Timeline: Miramonte School Scandal." NBC Southern California. 02 Sep. 2015. http://www.nbclosangeles.com/news/local/Timeline-Miramonte-School-Scandal-138970604.html.

Goodwin, Jennifer. "Mental Abuse of Kids Leaves Lifelong Scars." Consumer HealthDay. 30 Jul. 2012. https://consumer.healthday.com/mental-health-information-25/behavior-health-news-56/mental-abuse-of-kids-leaves-lifelong-scars-667059.html.

Gordon, William. The History of the Rise, Progress, and Establishment of the Independence of the United States of America: Including an Account of the Late War, and of the Thirteen Colonies, from Their Origin to that Period. No. 581. Samuel Campbell, 1801.

Hart, Stuart N., and Maria R. Brassard. "A Major Threat to Children's Mental Health: Psychological Maltreatment." *American Psychologist* 42, no. 2 (1987): 160–5. http://dx.doi.org/10.1037/0003–066X.2.2.

Havel, Vaclav, and Karel Hvizdala. *Disturbing the Peace: A Conversation with Karel* Hvizdala. New York, Vintage, 1990.

Hawkins, Beth. "Many Minnesota Students Are Subjected to Lunch Refusals, Including 'Tray Pulls.'" MinnPost. 02 Nov. 2014. http://www.minnpost.com/learning-curve/2014/02/many-minnesota-students-are-subjected-lunch-refusals-including-tray-pulls.

Hibbard, Roberta, et al. "Clinical Report: Psychological Maltreatment." *Pediatrics* 130, no. 2 (2012): 372–8.

High, Brenda. "State Anti-Bullying Laws." Bully Police USA. 2010. http://www.bullypolice.com/StateLaws.pdf.

Hill, Angela, and Matthew Mosk. "Senators Demand Schools End 'Scream Rooms' for Troubled Kids." ABC News. 12 Feb. 2014. http://abcnews.go.com/Blotter/senators-demand-schools-end-scream-rooms-troubled-kids/story?id=22478317.

Himes, Thomas. "LAUSD Admits Purging Files on Miramonte Child Predator Mark Berndt." *LA Daily News*. LA Daily News. 02 May 2014. http://www.dailynews.com/general-news/20140502/lausd-admits-purging-files-on-miramonte-child-predator-mark-berndt.

Holmes, Lindsay, and Anna Almendrala. "There's Been a Startling Rise in Suicide Rates in the US." The Huffington Post. 22 Apr. 2016. http://www.huffingtonpost.com/entry/suicide-rates-rising-us_us_5714f800e4b0060ccda3b5d8.

"In Loco Parentis." *Education Law*. http://usedulaw.com/345-in-loco-parentis.html.

"In Loco Parentis." *Merriam-Webster*. http://www.merriam-webster.com/dictionary/in%20loco%20parentis.

Jackson, Shirley. *The Lottery*. New York Avon, 1971.

Jung, Carl Gustav, and Edward Hoffman. *The Wisdom of Carl Jung*. New York, Citadel, 2003.

Kairys, Steven W., et al. "The Psychological Maltreatment of Children—Technical Report." *Pediatrics* 109, no. 4 (2002): e68.

Kalthoff, Ken. "Strong Reaction to Mansfield ISD Discipline Room." NBC 5 Dallas-Fort Worth. 12 May 2015. http://www.nbcdfw.com/news/

local/Strong-Reaction-to-Reports-of-Mansfield-School-Discipline-Room-255422271.html.

"Kids Sent Home Without Coats for Violating Dress Code." Mommyish. 04 Feb. 2015. http://www.mommyish.com/2015/02/04/kids-sent-home-without-coats-violating-dress-code-brings-new-meaning-term-passive-aggressive/.

Klein, Rebecca. "Student Reportedly Ordered to Lick His Desk Clean After Doodling on It." The Huffington Post. 05 Aug. 2013. http://wwwhuffingtonpost.com/2013/05/08/student-lick-desk_n_3238479.html.

Korn, Loren. "Flagler County Teacher Makes 4-Year-Old Unclog Dirty Toilet with Hands, Mom Says." WKMG. 03 Dec. 2015. http://www.clickorlando.com/news/flagler-county-teacher-makes-4-year-old-unclog-dirty-toilet-with-hands-mom-says.

Landau, Joel. "5th Grader Forced to Eat Lunch out of Trash Can." *NY Daily News*. 23 Feb. 2014. http://www.nydailynews.com/news/national/5th-grader-forced-eat-lunch-trash-article-1.1698729.

"Lawmakers Push to End 'Scream Rooms' for Punishing Students." Fox News. 08 Apr. 2017. http://www.foxnews.com/politics/2014/02/25/lawmakers-push-to-end-scream-rooms-to-punish-students/.

Lee, Henry K. "Family: Fremont Teacher Slapped Boy over Math Test." SFGate Blog. 08 May 2014. http://blog.sfgate.com/stew/2014/05/08/family-fremont-teacher-slapped-boy-over-math-test/.

Lerner, Will. "Parent Not Thrilled with Teacher Who Forced Student to Eat Food out of Garbage." Yahoo! News. 07 Mar. 2014. http://news.yahoo.com/blogs/oddnews/parent-not-thrilled-with-teacher-who-forced-student-to-eat-food-out-of-garbage-223700148.html?soc_src=copy.

LeRoy, Michelle, et al. "Parents Who Hit and Scream: Interactive Effects of Verbal and Severe Physical Aggression on Clinic-Referred Adolescents' Adjustment." *Child Abuse and Neglect* 38, no. 5 (2014): 893–901.

MacMillan, Harriet L., et al. "Interventions to prevent child maltreatment and associated impairment." *The Lancet* 373, no. 9659 (2009): 250–66.

Mathews, Jay. "How Do We Help Our Least Motivated, Most Disruptive Students?" *The Washington Post*. 31 May 2015. https://www.washingtonpost.com/local/education/how-do-we-help-our-least-motivated-most-disruptive-students/2015/05/31/fdfc9588-04bf-11e5-bc72-f3e16bf50bb6_story.html.

May, Rollo. *Love and Will*. New York, Norton. 1969.

Milgram, Stanley. Obedience to Authority: An Experimental View. New York, Harper Perennial, 1983.

Mill, John Stuart. "Inaugural Address: Delivered to the University of Saint Andrews, Feb. 1st 1867: Mill, John Stuart, 1806–1873:" *Internet Archive*. London: Longmans, Green, Reader, and Dyer, 1867. https://archive.org/details/inauguraladdress00milluoft.

Miva, R. "Stuart Chaifetz: Father Send Autistic Son Aiken to School Wired." *Fan Daily*, 10 Nov. 2012. http://fandaily.info/news/stuart-chaifetz-father-send-autistic-son-aiken-to-school-wired/.

Moran, Lee. "Teacher Forces Boy, 8, to Unclog Toilet with Bare Hands." *NY Daily News*. 04 Dec. 2014. http://www.nydailynews.com/news/national/teacher-forces-boy-8-unclog-toilet-bare-hands-article-1.2033132.

Murphy, Bill Jr. "Want to Raise Wildly Successful Kids? Science Says Do This for Them (but Their Schools Probably Won't)." *Inc.*, 09 Sept. 2016.

https://www.inc.com/bill-murphy-jr/want-to-raise-wildly-successful-kids-science-says-do-this-for-them-but-their-sch.html.

Nishioka, V., M. Coe, A. Burke, M. Hanita, and J. Sprague (2011). "Student-reported overt and relational aggression and victimization in grades 3–8." (Issues & Answers Report, REL 2011-No. 114). Washington, DC: US. Department of Education, Institute of Education Sciences, National Center for Education Evaluation and Regional Assistance, Regional Educational Laboratory Northwest. http://ies.ed.gov/ncee/edlabs.

"Los Angeles Schools Have Spent Over $300 Million on Sex Abuse Settlements in Just Four Years." *The Stream*, 28 May 2016. https://stream.org/los-angeles-schools-spent-300-million-sex-abuse-settlements-just-four-years/.

Nolan, Caitlin, and Corky Siemaszko. "Family Sues City for $10M after Queens Teacher Hits Student." *NY Daily News*. 10 Feb. 2015. http://www.nydailynews.com/new-york/education/family-sues-city-queens-teacher-punching-student-article-1.2109715.

Oppenheim, Richard. "Another School Bullying Case—This Time the Teacher Is Accused." California Business Litigation Blog, 15 Jun. 2012. https://www.californiabusinesslitigation.com/2012/06/another_school_bullying_case_t.html.

"Oregon Archives." Police State USA. 06 Sept. 2013. http://www.policestateusa.com/tag/oregon/.

Peart, Tanvier. "An Elementary Student's Hot Lunch Is Thrown Away in Front of Classmates." SheKnows. *Parenting*. 01 June 2015. http://www.sheknows.com/parenting/articles/1085250/10-year-old-shamed-by-school-for-past-due-account-lunch-thrown-away.

Petty, Lauren. "Parents Protest." NBC Connecticut. 11 Jun. 2017. http://www.nbcconnecticut.com/news/Parents-Protest-Scream-Rooms-In-Schools-137068823.html.

Phillips, Kristine. "Upset Teacher Wrote 'Focus' on a Student's Forehead. Now, He's Charged with Assault." *Washington Post*. 09 Oct. 2016. https://www.washingtonpost.com/news/education/wp/2016/10/09/upset-teacher-wrote-focus-on-a-students-forehead-now-hes-charged-with-assault/?utm_term=.fcd348c97fc5.

Plante, Thomas G. "Another Aftershock." *America Magazine*. 17 Jun. 2015. https://www.americamagazine.org/issue/478/article/another-aftershock.

"Police: Georgia Woman Locked Son out for Missing Curfew." OregonLive.com. The Associated Press. 03 June 2015. http://www.oregonlive.com/kiddo/index.ssf/2015/06/police_georgia_woman_locked_so.ht

Price, Chris. "School Officer and Principal Caught Threatening, Beating 14-year-old Student." Atlanta, GA News, Weather, Events, Photos. 04 May 2017. http://www.cbs46.com/story/35343016/school-officer-principal-caught-on-camera-beating-14-year-old-student.

Reilly, Steve. "Teachers Who Sexually Abuse Students Still Find Classroom Jobs." *USA Today*. Gannett Satellite Information Network. 22 Dec. 2016. https://www.usatoday.com/story/news/2016/12/22/teachers-who-sexually-abuse-students-still-find-classroom-jobs/95346790/.

Pugh, Greg. "Alaska School Stomps on Third Grader's Free Exercise Rights, ID's Her as a 'Bully.'" Restoring Liberty. 23 Apr. 2012. http://joemiller.us/2012/04/alaska-school-stomps-on-third-graders-free-exercise-rights-ids-her-as-a-bully/.

Ross, Chuck. "Nebraska Democratic Party Official Fired After Saying He Wished Steve Scalise Had Died [AUDIO]." *The Daily Caller*. 23 Jun. 2017. http://dailycaller.com/2017/06/23/nebraska-democratic-party-official-fired-after-saying-he-wished-steve-scalise-had-died-audio/.

Russell, Karl, and Mary Williams Walsh. "The State of State Teachers' Pension Plans by KARL RUSSELL and MARY WILLIAMS WALSH." *Matt Crowe 's Blog*. N.p., 06 Mar. 2017. <https://mattcroweahhha.wordpress.com/2017/03/06/the-state-of-state-teachers-pension-plans-by-karl-russell-and-mary-williams-walsh/>.

*Safford Unified School Dist. #1 v. Redding*, 557 US 364. 2009.

Samuels, Christina. "What's Really Happening with Special Education Enrollment?" *Education Week*. 27 Apr. 2016. http://blogs.edweek.org/edweek/speced/2016/04/special_education_enrollment_increases.html#.

"School Puts Troubled Kids in 'Scream Room.'" *NBC News*. 11 Jan. 2012. http://usnews.nbcnews.com/_news/2012/01/11/10113042-school-puts-troubled-kids-in-scream-room.

Singer, Isaac Bashevis. "Isaac Bashevis Singer Talks...about Everything." *New York Times Magazine*. 26 Nov. 1978. http://www.nytimes.com/1978/11/26/archives/isaac-bashevis-singer-talks-about-everything-the-first-of-a-twopart.html.

Speciale, Samuel. "W.Va. Students Caught Screening 'Fifty Shades of Grey' During Class." *Charleston Gazette-Mail*. 4 May 2015. http://www.wvgazettemail.com/article/20150514/DM01/150519550/1282.

*Safford Unified School District #1, et al. v. April Redding* 557 US____(2009). 1–22. Supreme Court of the United States. 2009. Print. https://www.supremecourt.gov/opinions/08pdf/08-479.pdf.

Stampler, Laura. "School Punishes Blind 8-Year-Old by Replacing Cane with Pool Noodle." *Time*. 18 Dec. 2014. http://time.com/3639778/blind-boy-cane-noodle-dakota-nafzinger/.

State of California, California Department of Education. "CA State Board of Education Policy." California Education Code Section 35294. Mar. 2001. http://www.cde.ca.gov/be/ms/po/documents/policy01-02-mar2001.pdf.

————"California Laws & Codes." Laws & Regulations. http://www.cde.ca.gov/re/lr/cl/.

————California Legislature. "AB-2180 Tolerance in Public Schools." California Legislative Information. 2004.

————"SB-719 School Safety." California Legislative Information. 2003.

Stokes, Kyle. "Taxpayers Stuck with Bill for LAUSD Sex Abuse Settlements." Southern California Public Radio. May 26, 2016. http://www.scpr.org/news/2016/05/26/61048/as-lausd-battles-insurers-taxpayers-left-with-bill/.

StopBullying.gov. Department of Health and Human Services. 2012. https://www.stopbullying.gov/.

Strauss, Eric M., et al. "Five Most Shocking Teacher Meltdowns Caught on Tape." ABC News. 20 Mar. 2012. http://abcnews.go.com/US/shocking-teacher-meltdowns-caught-tape/story?id=15919999.

Taguchi, Emily, and Nadine Shubailat. "'Passing the Trash': 2 Women Say the Teachers Who Sexually Abused Them Were Allowed to Continue Teaching." ABC News. 26 Apr. 2017. http://abcnews.go.com/US/passing-trash-women-teachers-sexually-abused-allowed-continue/story?id=46626326.

Thomas, Shawndrea. "Caught on Camera: McKinley Junior Attacked by Nearly 20 Students." FOX2now.com. February 03, 2015. http://fox2now.com/2015/02/03/caught-on-camera-mckinley-junior-attacked-by-nearly-20-students/.

Tolstoy, Leo. *Master and Man: The Kreutzer Sonata Dramas*. The Complete Works of Lyof N. Tolstoi. Vol. 11. T. Crowell, 1899.

Tolstoy, Leo, and Nathan Haskell Dole. *The Novels and Other Works of Lyof N. Tolstoï*. Vol. 23. New York, C. Scribner's Sons, 1902.

"Top Educators Say Teacher Quality Isn't the Key to Student Achievement." Yahoo! News. 22 May 2015. http://news.yahoo.com/top-educators-teacher-quality-isn-t-key-student-202213791.html.

Tucker, Allyson M. Applying the Fourth Amendment to Schools, *New Jersey v. TLO*, 105 S. Ct. 733 (1985), 31 *Wash. U. J. Urb. & Contemp. L.* 439 (1987).

United States, Centers for Disease Control and Prevention. "Children's Mental Health." Division of Human Development and Disabilities, National *Center* on Birth Defects and Developmental Disabilities, Centers for Disease Control and Prevention. 23 Mar. 2017. https://www.cdc.gov/childrensmentalhealth/basics.html.

————"Youth Risk Behavior Surveillance System (YRBSS)." Adolescent and School Health. 11 Aug. 2016. https://www.cdc.gov/healthyyouth/data/yrbs/index.htm.

————"Playground Injuries: Fact Sheet." Centers for Disease Control and Prevention. 29 Mar. 2012. http://www.cdc.gov/HomeandRecreationalSafety/Playground-Injuries/playgroundinjuries-factsheet.htm.

United States, Department of Education. "Fast Facts-Teacher Trends." Nation Center for Education Statistics. 2016. http://nces.ed.gov/fastfacts/display.asp?id=28.

————"Characteristics of Public and Private Elementary and Secondary School Teachers in the United States: Results from the 2011–12 Schools and Staffing Survey. First Look. NCES 2013–314" National Center for Education Statistics, by Goldring, Rebecca, et al. 2013.

————"Digest of Educational Statistics 51st Edition." National Center for Educational Statistics. NCES 2016–014. Institute of Education Sciences. Table 226.10 2016 https://nces.ed.gov/pubs2016/2016014.pdf.

————"IDEA: Building the Legacy of IDEA 2004." Individuals with Disabilities Education Act (IDEA), 2004. . http://idea-b.ed.gov/explore/view/p/, root, dynamic, TopicalArea, 1, html.

————"Key Policy Letters Signed by the Education Secretary or Deputy Secretary." Laws & Guidance. 31 May 2009. https://www2.ed.gov/policy/elsec/guid/secletter/090731.html.

————"National Assessment of Adult Literacy (NAAL)—What Is NAAL?" National Assessment of Adult Literacy. 2015 https://nces.ed.gov/naal/index.asp.

————"Restraint and Seclusion: Resource Document," Washington, DC, 2012. www.ed.gov/policy/restraintseclusion.

————"Summary of Seclusion and Restraint Statutes, Regulations, Policies and Guidance, by State and Territories." Laws & Guidance. 17 Oct. 2013. https://www2.ed.gov/policy/seclusion/seclusion-state-summary.html.

————"The Nation's Report Card." The National Assessment of Educational Progress. 2016. https://www.nationsreportcard.gov/.

————"The NCES Fast Facts Tool Provides Quick Answers to Many Education Questions. NCES 2016" National Center for Education Statistics, Home Page, a Part of the US Department of Education. https://nces.ed.gov/fastfacts/dailyarchive.asp.

————"What Is Bullying." StopBullying.gov. 29 Feb. 2012. https://www.stopbullying.gov/what-is-bullying/index.html.

————Administration for Children and Families, Children's Bureau. "Definitions of Child Abuse and Neglect." Child Welfare Information Gateway. https://www.childwelfare.gov/pubPDFs/define.pdf.

————"Links to State and Tribal Child Welfare Law and Policy." Child Welfare Information Gateway, Mar. 2015. https://www.childwelfare.gov/pubPDFs/resources.pdf.

————"State Statutes Search." Child Welfare Information Gateway. https://www.childwelfare.gov/topics/systemwide/laws-policies/state/.

United States, Department of Health and Human Services, "Child Maltreatment 2014." Administration for Children and Families. 25 Jan. 2016. https://www.acf.hhs.gov/.

————StopBullying.gov. 2012. https://www.stopbullying.gov/.

United States, Government Accountability Office, "Seclusions and Restraints." Testimony Before the Committee on Education and Labor, House of Representatives. 19 May 2009. http://www.gao.gov/new.items/d09719t.pdf.

United States, Government Printing Office. "Title 34: Education." Electronic Code of Federal Regulations (e-CFR). 26 May 2017. https://www.ecfr.gov/cgi-bin/searchECFR?ob=r&idno=&q1=child%2Bfind&r=&SID=c96a5096e19932e5fb1be43e37faef58&mc=true.

*United States v. Wunderlich*, 342 US 98, 103. 1951.

"Valley Schools Put Students in Padded 'Scream Rooms.'" *CBS 5 AZ KPHO*. 23 Feb. 2012. http://www.kpho.com/story/17007347/so-called-scream-rooms-used-in-valley-schools.

Waldman, Annie. "Los Angeles and New York Pin Down School Kids and Then Say It Never Happened." ProPublica. 08 Dec. 2014. https://www.propublica.org/article/los-angeles-and-new-york-pin-down-school-kids-and-then-say-it-never-happened.

Walker, Tim. "Long-Term Impact of School Bullying May Be Worse Than You Think." NEA Today. 19 Oct. 2016. http://neatoday.org/2016/10/06/long-term-impact-of-school-bullying/.

Wallace, Ben. "West Feliciana Teacher Accused of Slapping, Taking Food from First-grader Arrested Monday, Posts Bail." *The Advocate*. 21 Mar. 2017. http://www.theadvocate.com/baton_rouge/news/communities/west_feliciana/article_78359688-9a86-50e5-93a0-5d1da738d0fc.html.

Walsh, Mary Williams. "New York Is Investigating Advisers to Pension Funds." *New York Times*. 05 Nov. 2013. https://dealbook.nytimes.com/2013/11/05/new-york-is-investigating-advisers-to-pension-funds/.

"Want Kids to Do Better in School? Get Serious about Mental Health." Yahoo! News. 29 May 2015. http://news.yahoo.com/want-kids-better-school-serious-mental-health-212624342.html.

Dailymail.com, Lydia Warren for. "Outrage as Six-year-old Boy Is Forced to Eat Lunch Alone behind a Screen after His Parents Dropped Him off Late to School." *Daily Mail Online*. Associated Newspapers, 27 Feb. 2015. http://www.dailymail.co.uk/news/article-2972459/Outrage-six-year-old-boy-forced-eat-lunch-screen-parents-dropped-late-school.html.

Warren, Lydia. "Horrifying Surveillance Footage Shows School Security Guard Beating Wheelchair-bound Student and Dumping Him on to the Floor." *Daily Mail Online*. Associated Newspapers, 30 May 2014. http://www.dailymail.co.uk/news/article-2643968/Horrifying-surveillance-footage-shows-school-security-guard-beating-wheelchair-bound-student-attack.html.

Washington, George. *Letter to Bushrod Washington*. MS. Mount Vernon, 1783.

West, Tara. "Autistic Boy's Hand Crushed as Teachers Slam Door to 'Scream Room.' Turned on Fan to Drown Out Screams." *The Inquisitr*. 16 Feb. 2015. http://www.inquisitr.com/1844645/autistic-boys-hand-crushed-as-teachers-slam-door-to-scream-room-turned-on-fan-to-drown-out-screams/.

Wheeler, Jason. "Students Forced to Expose Underwear for Inspection." USA Today. 28 Jan. 2015. https://www.usatoday.com/story/news/nation/2015/01/28/students-drop-pants/22463461/.

Whyte, William H., Jr. *The Organization Man*. New York. Simon and Schuster 1956.

Winton, Richard, and Howard Blume. "L.A. School District Reaches $88-million Settlement in Sex Misconduct Cases at Two Campuses." Los Angeles Times. May 16, 2016. http://www.latimes.com/local/lanow/la-me-ln-l.a.-school-abuse-settlements-20160516-snap-story.html.

Wipond, Rob. "Many School Districts Still Not Reporting Use of Restraints." Mad in America, 14 Dec. 2014. http://www.madinamerica.com/2014/12/many-school-districts-still-reporting-use-restraints/.

Yevtushenko, Yevgeny. "Excerpts from Yevtushenko Statement." *New York Times*. 18 Feb 1974. http://www.nytimes.com/1974/02/18/archives/excerpts-from-yevtushenko-statement.html.

"Youth Suicide Facts & Stats." The Jason Foundation. 2015. http://jasonfoundation.com/youth-suicide/facts-stats/.

Zachariah, Holly. "Former Kindergarten Teacher Accused of Secretly Taping 25 Students in Bathroom." *The Columbus Dispatch*. 08 Mar. 2015. http://www.dispatch.com/content/stories/local/2015/03/07/ashland-teacher.html.

Zadrozny, Brandy. "The Schools That Starve Students to Punish Deadbeat Parents." The Daily Beast.com. 30 Jan. 2014. http://www.thedailybeast.com/articles/2014/01/30/the-schools-that-starve-students-to-punish-deadbeat-parents.html.Zadrozny, Brandy.

Zander, Megan. "Kids Sent Home Without Coats For Violating Dress Code." *Mommyish*. 04 Feb. 2015. <http://www.mommyish.com/kids-sent-home-without-coats-violating-dress-code-brings-new-meaning-term-passive-aggressive/>.

Zhao, Emmeline. "'Isolation Booth' At Mint Valley Elementary School Has Parents Outraged." The Huffington Post. 29 Nov. 2012. http://www.huffingtonpost.com/2012/11/29/isolation-booth-mint-valley-elementary_n_2213506.html,

Zimmerman, Neetzan. "Kindergarten Teacher in Trouble for Ordering Students to Hit Classmate Accused of Bullying." Gawker.com. 20 Aug. 2017. http://gawker.com/5919316/kindergarten-teacher-in-trouble-for-ordering-students-to-hit-classmate-accused-of-bullying.

Made in the USA
San Bernardino, CA
23 November 2017